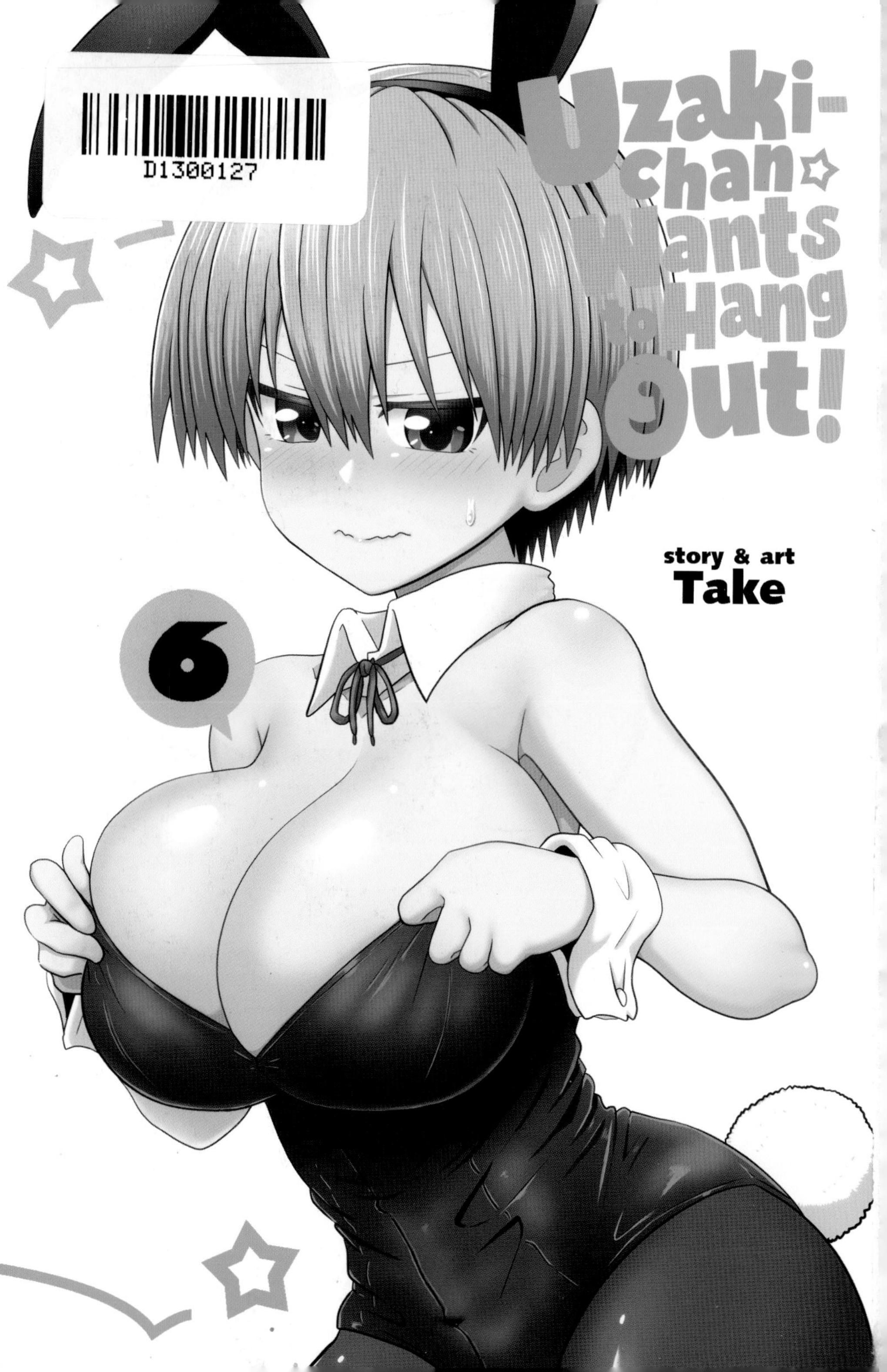
Uzaki-chan Wants to Hang Out!
6
story & art
Take

C O N T E N T S

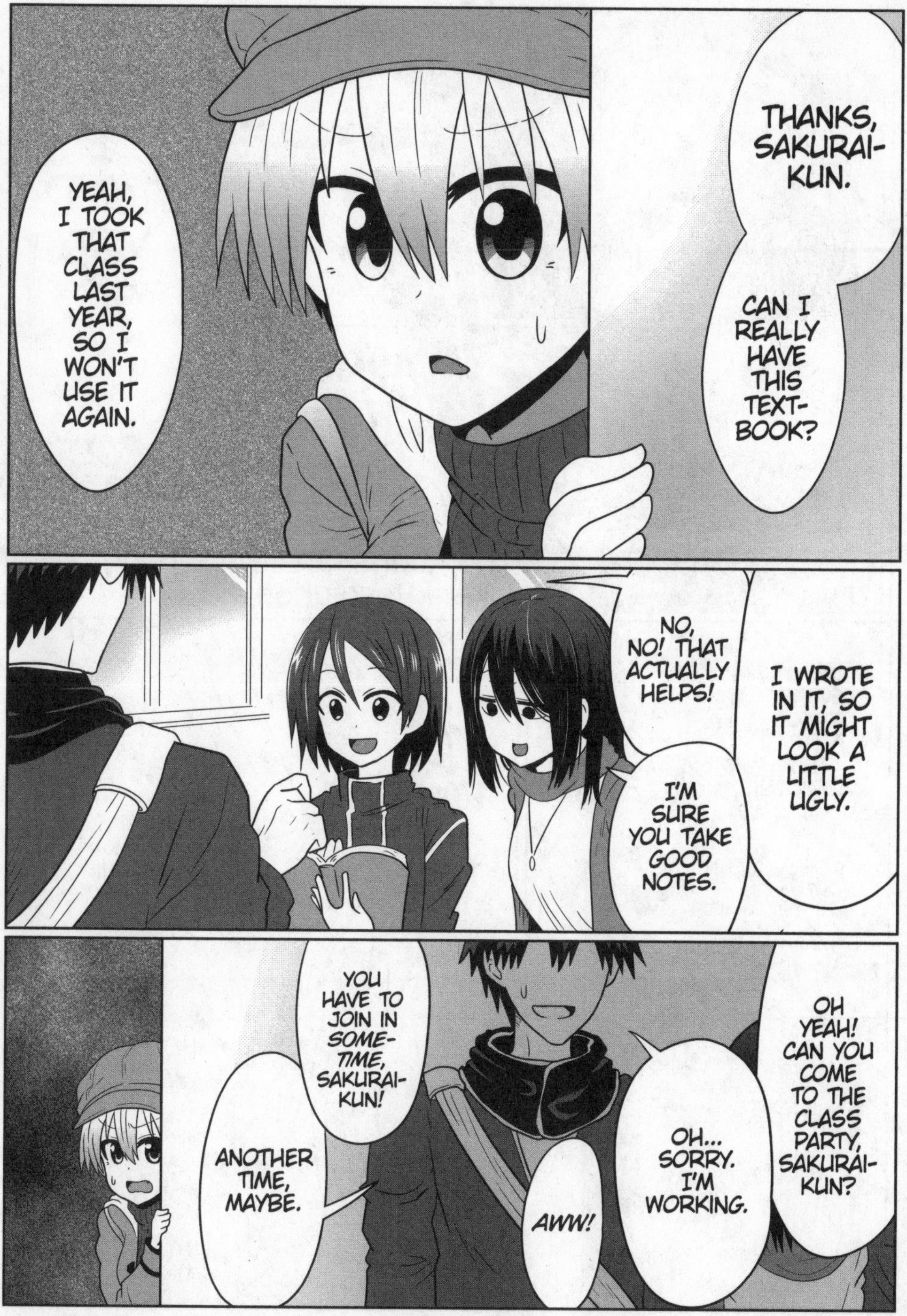
THANKS, SAKURAI-KUN.
CAN I REALLY HAVE THIS TEXTBOOK?
YEAH, I TOOK THAT CLASS LAST YEAR, SO I WON'T USE IT AGAIN.
I WROTE IN IT, SO IT MIGHT LOOK A LITTLE UGLY.
NO, NO! THAT ACTUALLY HELPS!
I'M SURE YOU TAKE GOOD NOTES.
OH YEAH! CAN YOU COME TO THE CLASS PARTY, SAKURAI-KUN?
OH... SORRY. I'M WORKING.
AWW!
YOU HAVE TO JOIN IN SOMETIME, SAKURAI-KUN!
ANOTHER TIME, MAYBE.

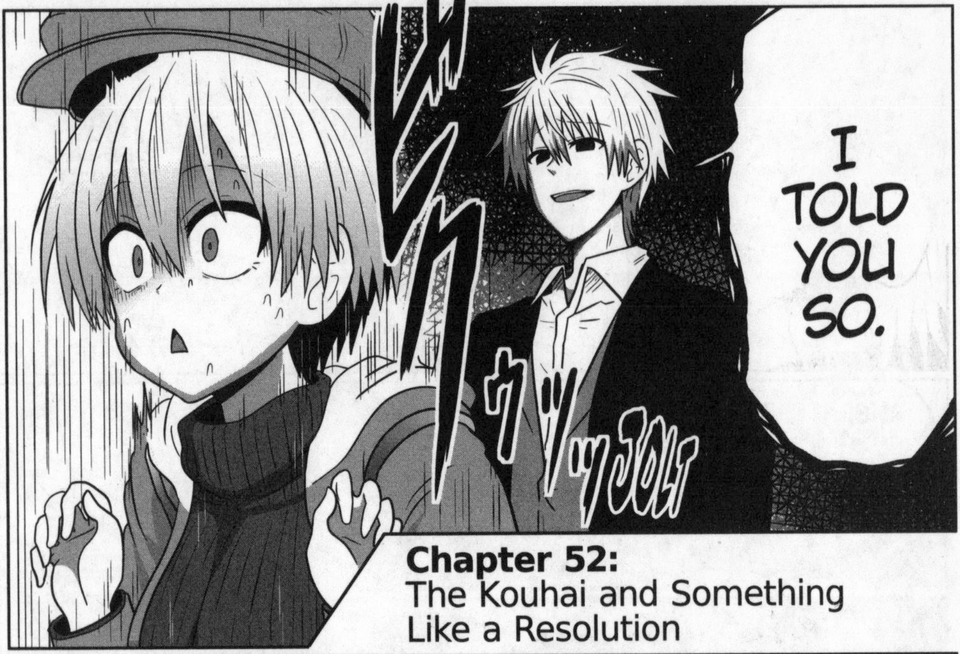
JOLT
I TOLD YOU SO.

Chapter 52:
The Kouhai and Something Like a Resolution

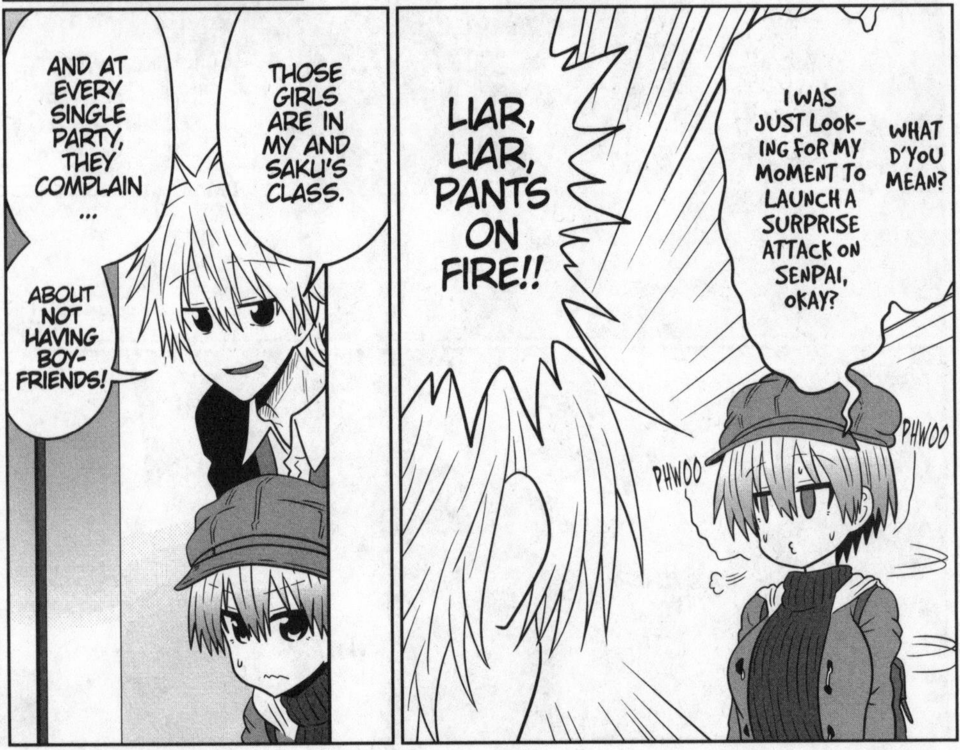
WHAT D'YOU MEAN?
I WAS JUST LOOKING FOR MY MOMENT TO LAUNCH A SURPRISE ATTACK ON SENPAI, OKAY?
LIAR, LIAR, PANTS ON FIRE!!
PHWOO
PHWOO
THOSE GIRLS ARE IN MY AND SAKU'S CLASS.
AND AT EVERY SINGLE PARTY, THEY COMPLAIN ...
ABOUT NOT HAVING BOY-FRIENDS!

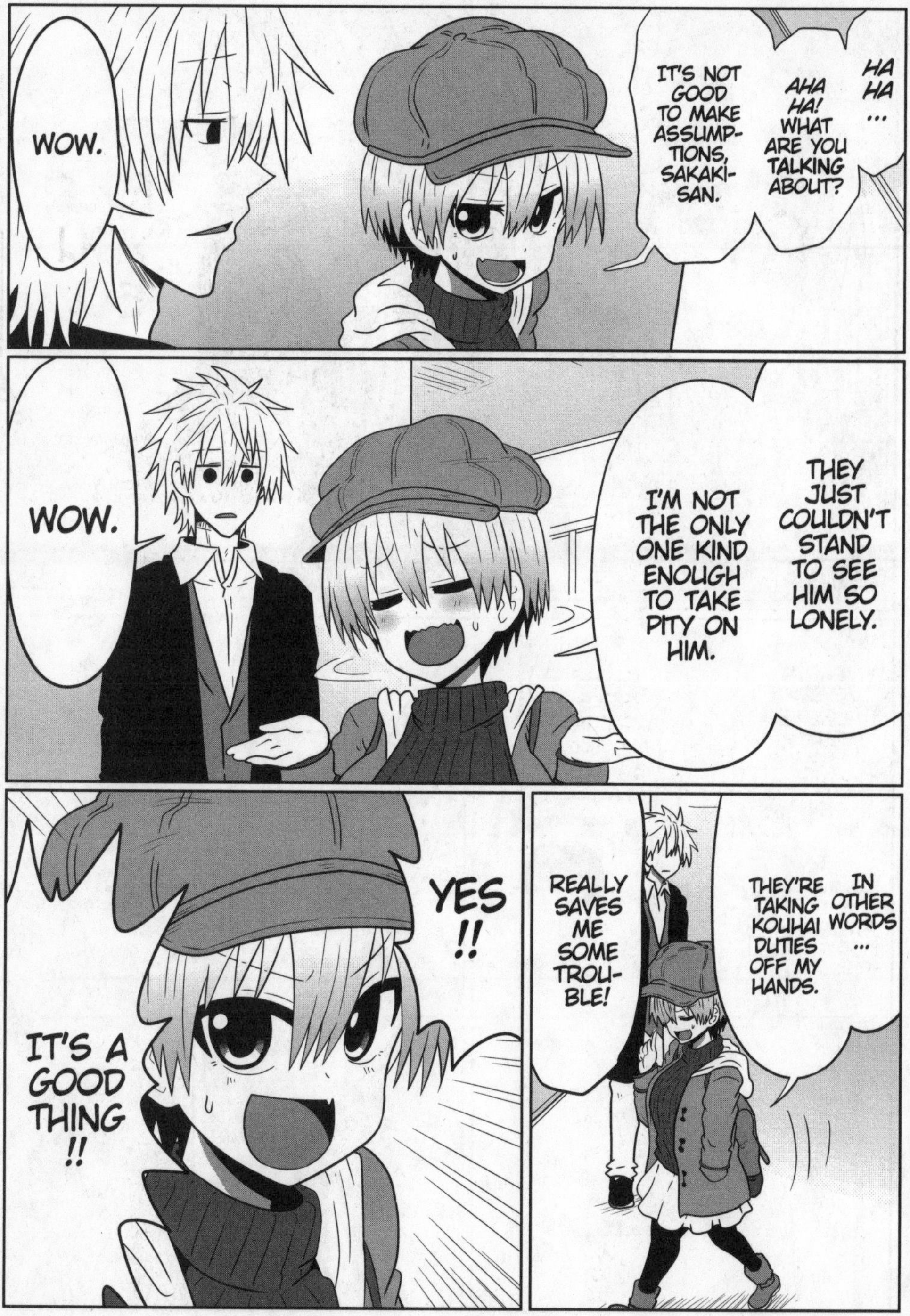
HA HA ...
AHA HA! WHAT ARE YOU TALKING ABOUT?
IT'S NOT GOOD TO MAKE ASSUMPTIONS, SAKAKI-SAN.
WOW.
THEY JUST COULDN'T STAND TO SEE HIM SO LONELY.
I'M NOT THE ONLY ONE KIND ENOUGH TO TAKE PITY ON HIM.
WOW.
IN OTHER WORDS ...
THEY'RE TAKING KOUHAI DUTIES OFF MY HANDS.
REALLY SAVES ME SOME TROUBLE!
YES !!
IT'S A GOOD THING !!

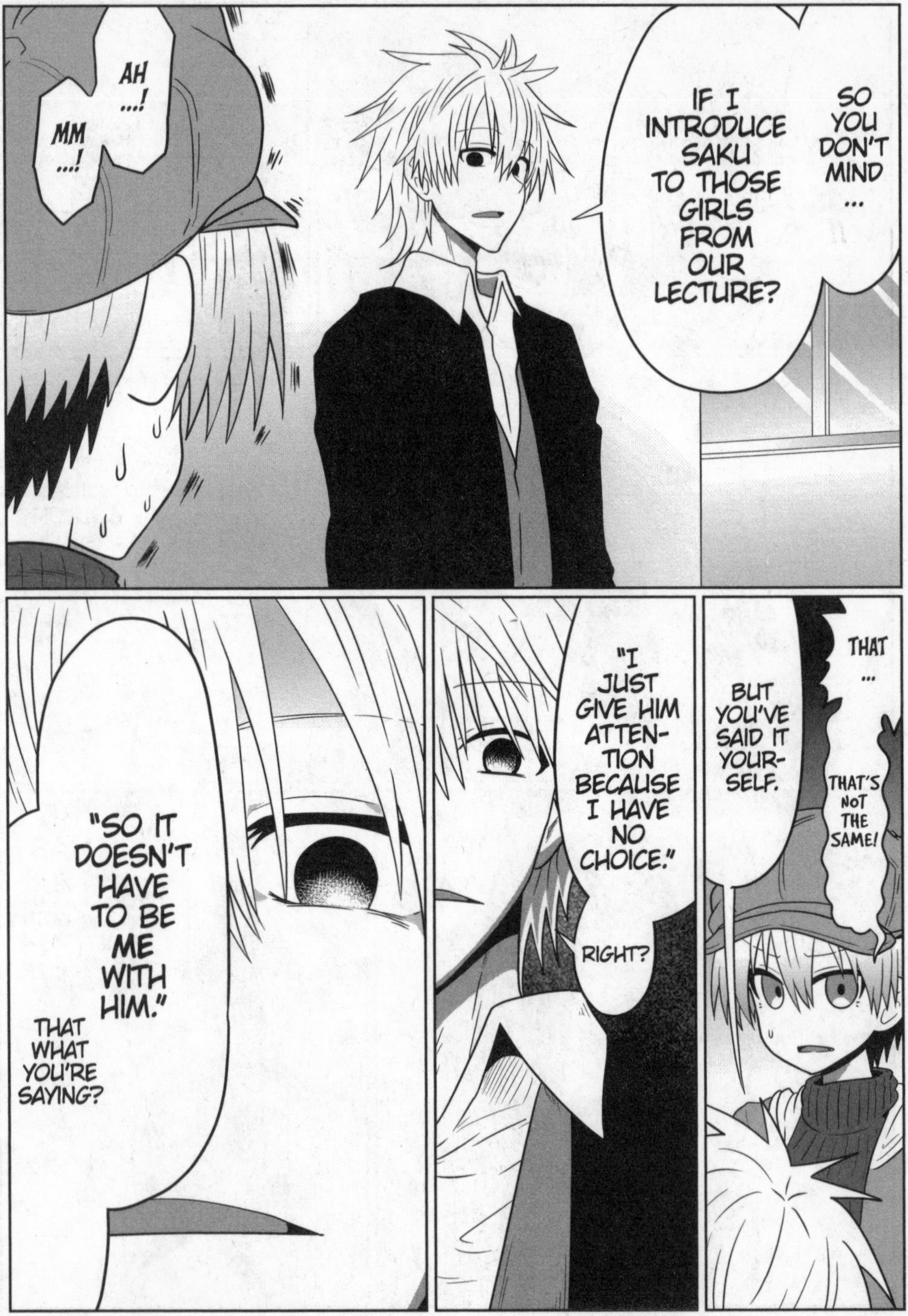
SO YOU DON'T MIND ...
IF I INTRODUCE SAKU TO THOSE GIRLS FROM OUR LECTURE?
AH ...! MM ...!
THAT ...
THAT'S NOT THE SAME!
BUT YOU'VE SAID IT YOURSELF.
"I JUST GIVE HIM ATTENTION BECAUSE I HAVE NO CHOICE."
RIGHT?
"SO IT DOESN'T HAVE TO BE ME WITH HIM."
THAT WHAT YOU'RE SAYING?

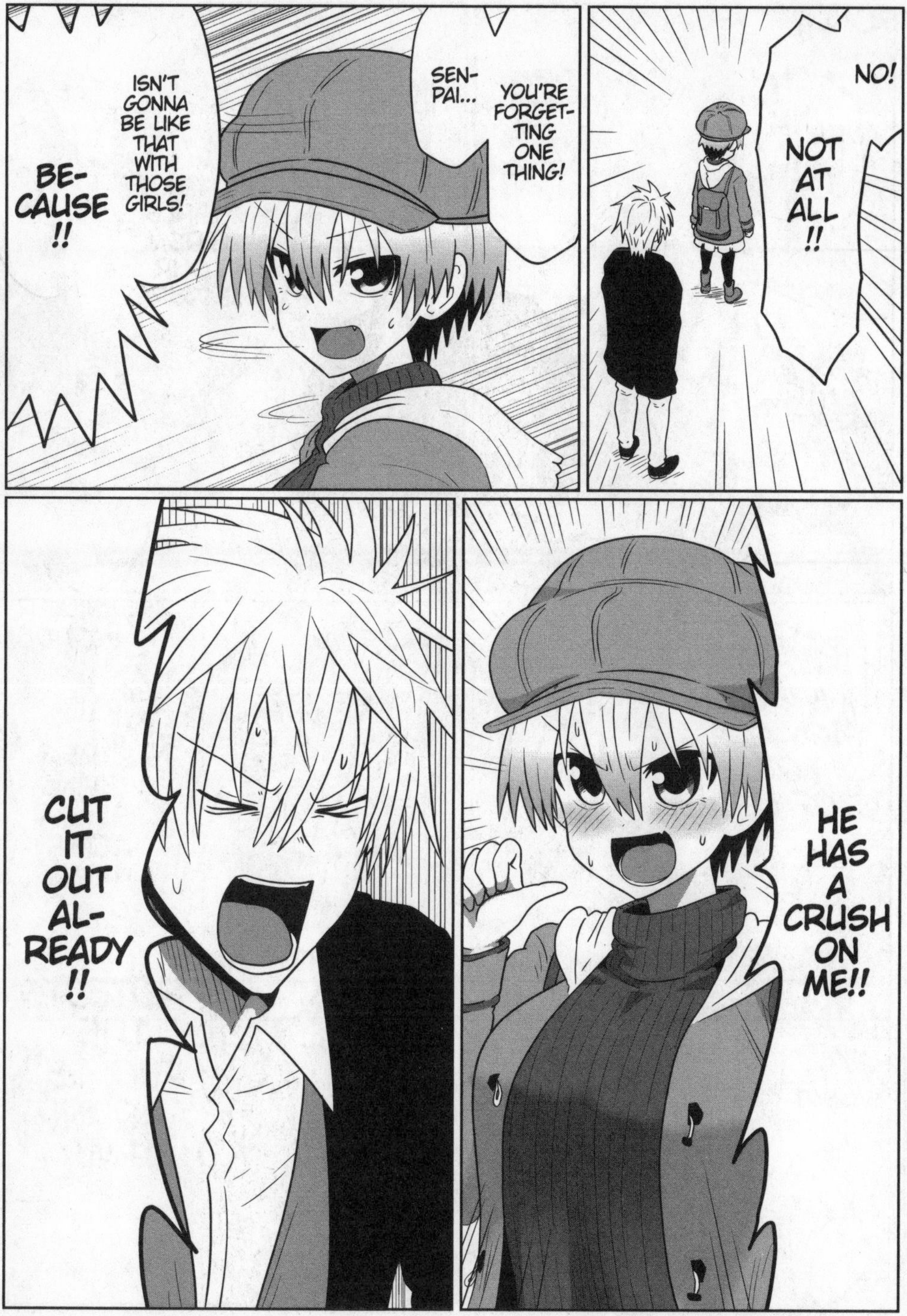
NO!
NOT AT ALL!!
SEN-PAI...
YOU'RE FORGET-TING ONE THING!
ISN'T GONNA BE LIKE THAT WITH THOSE GIRLS!
BE-CAUSE!!
HE HAS A CRUSH ON ME!!
CUT IT OUT AL-READY!!

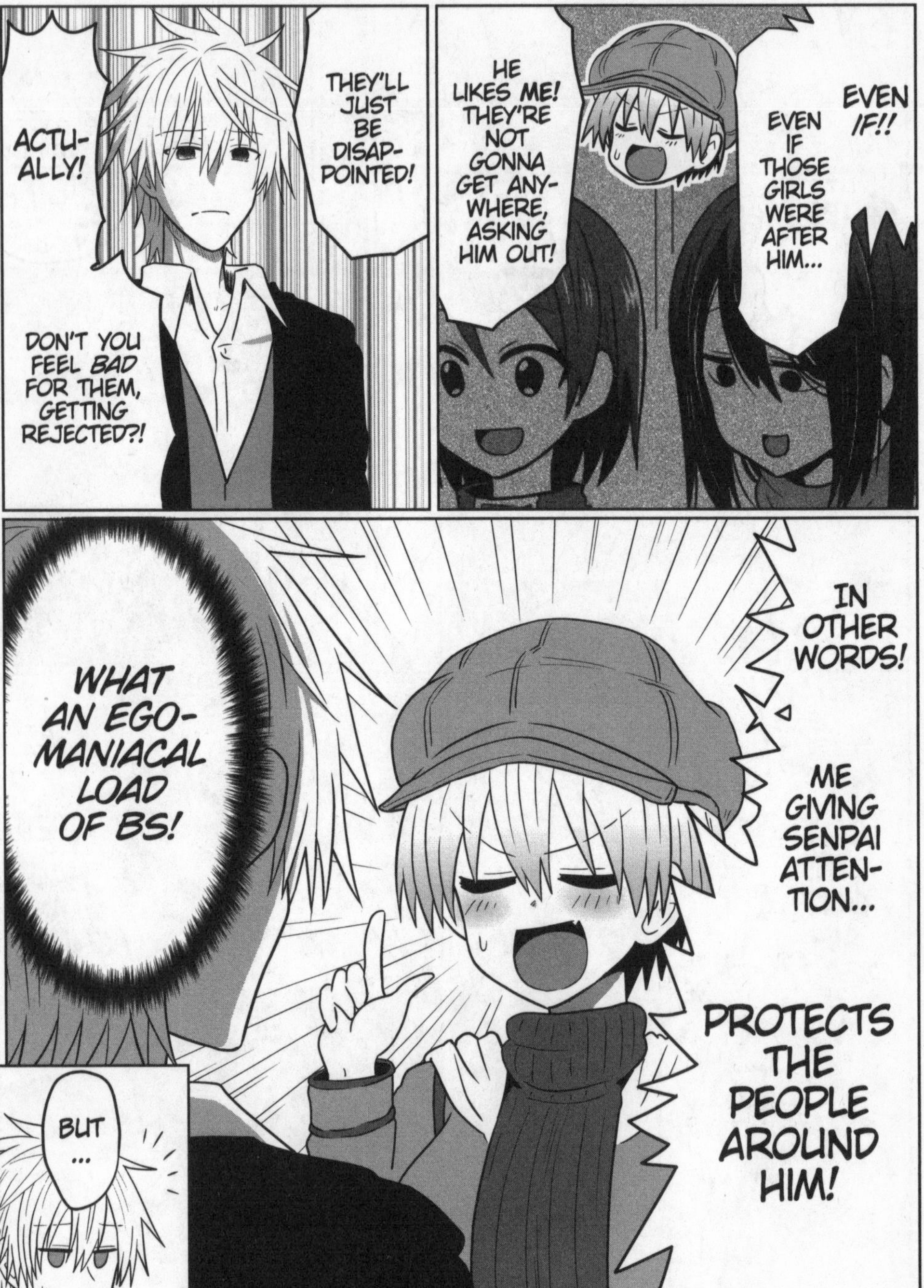
EVEN IF!!
EVEN IF THOSE GIRLS WERE AFTER HIM...
HE LIKES ME! THEY'RE NOT GONNA GET ANYWHERE, ASKING HIM OUT!
THEY'LL JUST BE DISAPPOINTED!
ACTUALLY!
DON'T YOU FEEL *BAD* FOR THEM, GETTING REJECTED?!
IN OTHER WORDS!
ME GIVING SENPAI ATTENTION...
PROTECTS THE PEOPLE AROUND HIM!
WHAT AN EGOMANIACAL LOAD OF BS!
BUT...

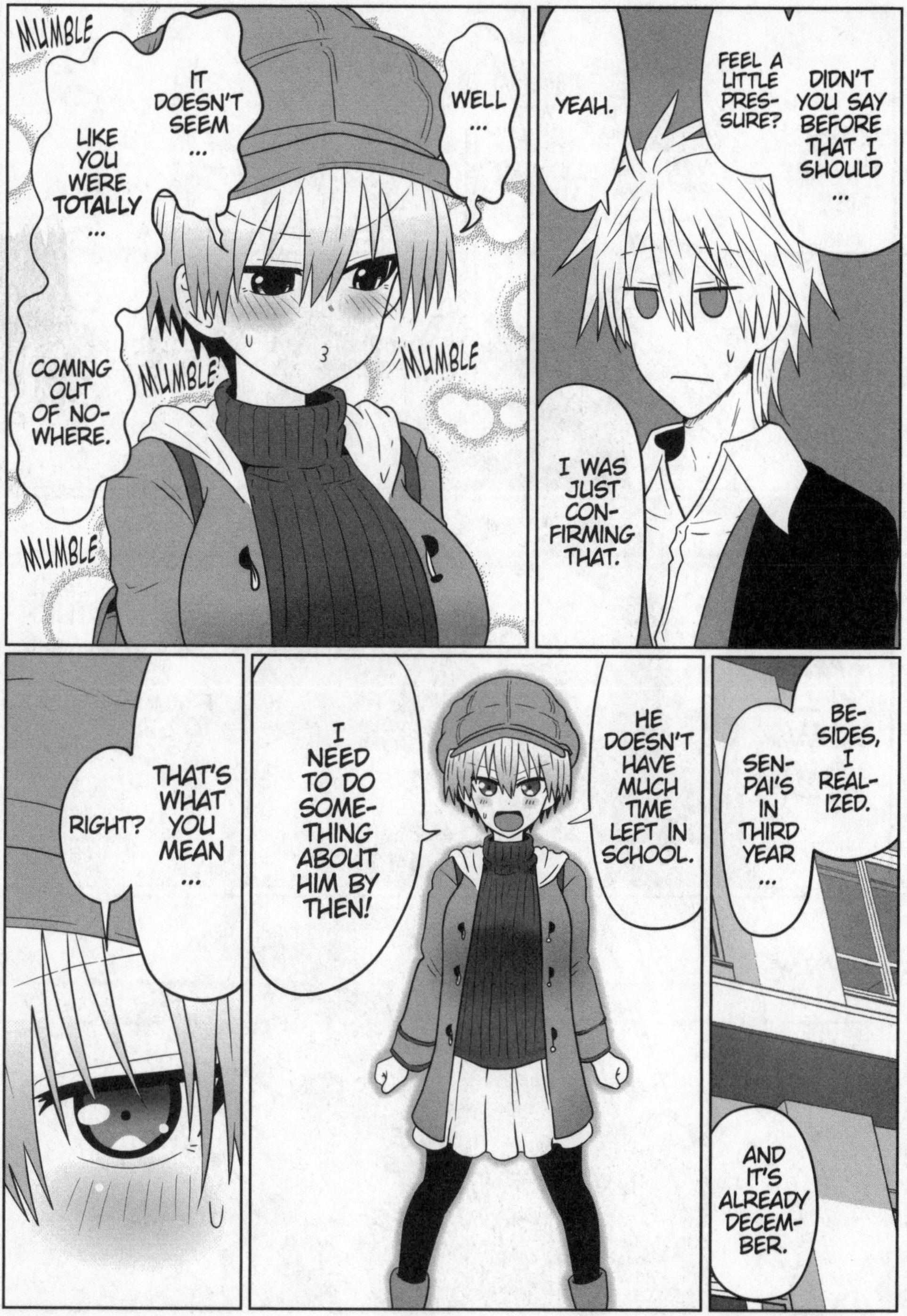
DIDN'T YOU SAY BEFORE THAT I SHOULD ...
FEEL A LITTLE PRES-SURE?
YEAH.
I WAS JUST CON-FIRMING THAT.
WELL ...
IT DOESN'T SEEM ...
LIKE YOU WERE TOTALLY ...
MUMBLE
MUMBLE
MUMBLE
COMING OUT OF NO-WHERE.
MUMBLE
BE-SIDES, I REAL-IZED.
SEN-PAI'S IN THIRD YEAR ...
AND IT'S ALREADY DECEM-BER.
HE DOESN'T HAVE MUCH TIME LEFT IN SCHOOL.
I NEED TO DO SOME-THING ABOUT HIM BY THEN!
THAT'S WHAT YOU MEAN ...
RIGHT?

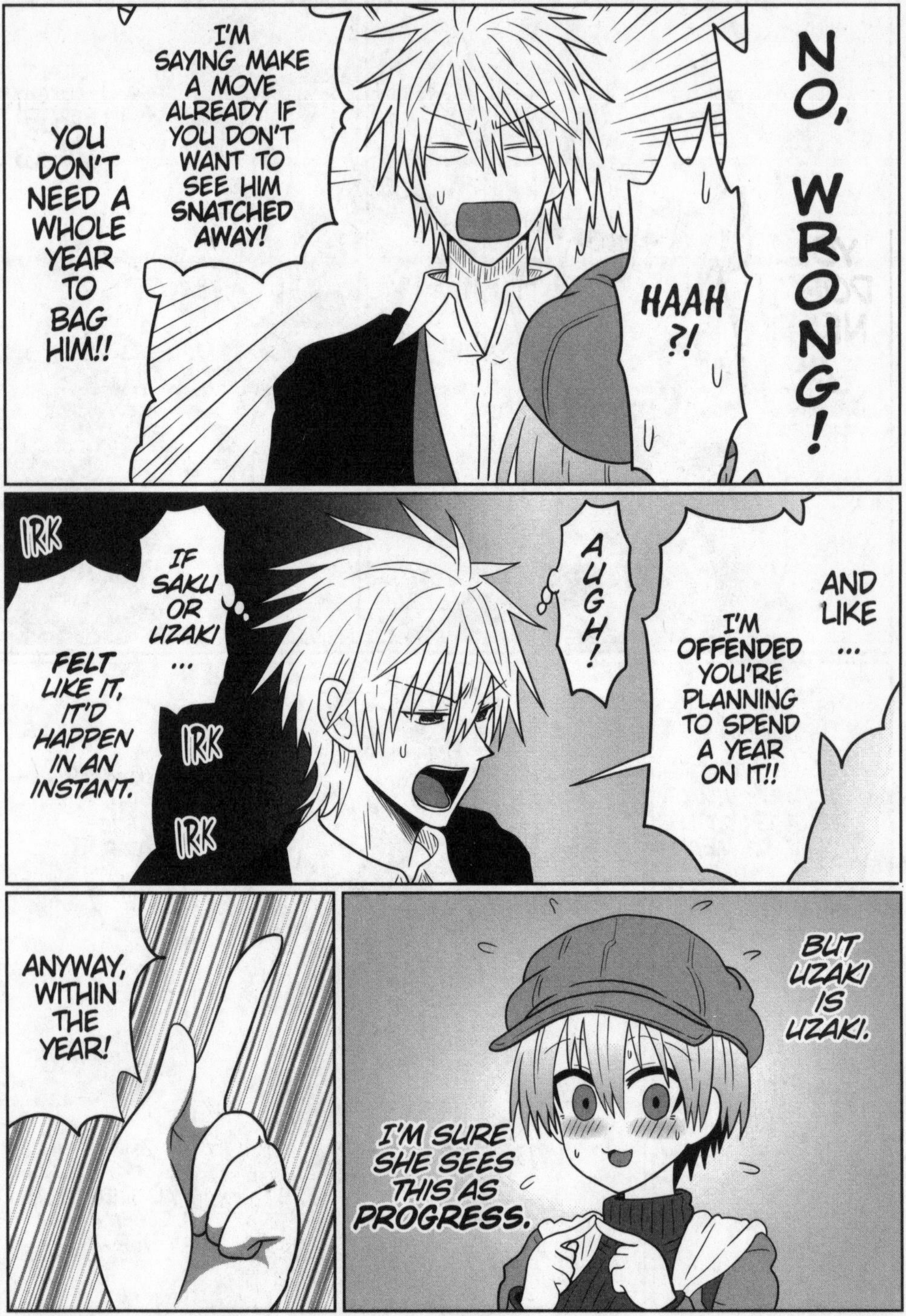
NO, WRONG!
HAAH ?!
I'M SAYING MAKE A MOVE ALREADY IF YOU DON'T WANT TO SEE HIM SNATCHED AWAY!
YOU DON'T NEED A WHOLE YEAR TO BAG HIM!!
AND LIKE ...
I'M OFFENDED YOU'RE PLANNING TO SPEND A YEAR ON IT!!
AUGH!
IF SAKU OR UZAKI ...
FELT LIKE IT, IT'D HAPPEN IN AN INSTANT.
IRK
IRK
IRK
BUT UZAKI IS UZAKI.
I'M SURE SHE SEES THIS AS PROGRESS.
ANYWAY, WITHIN THE YEAR!

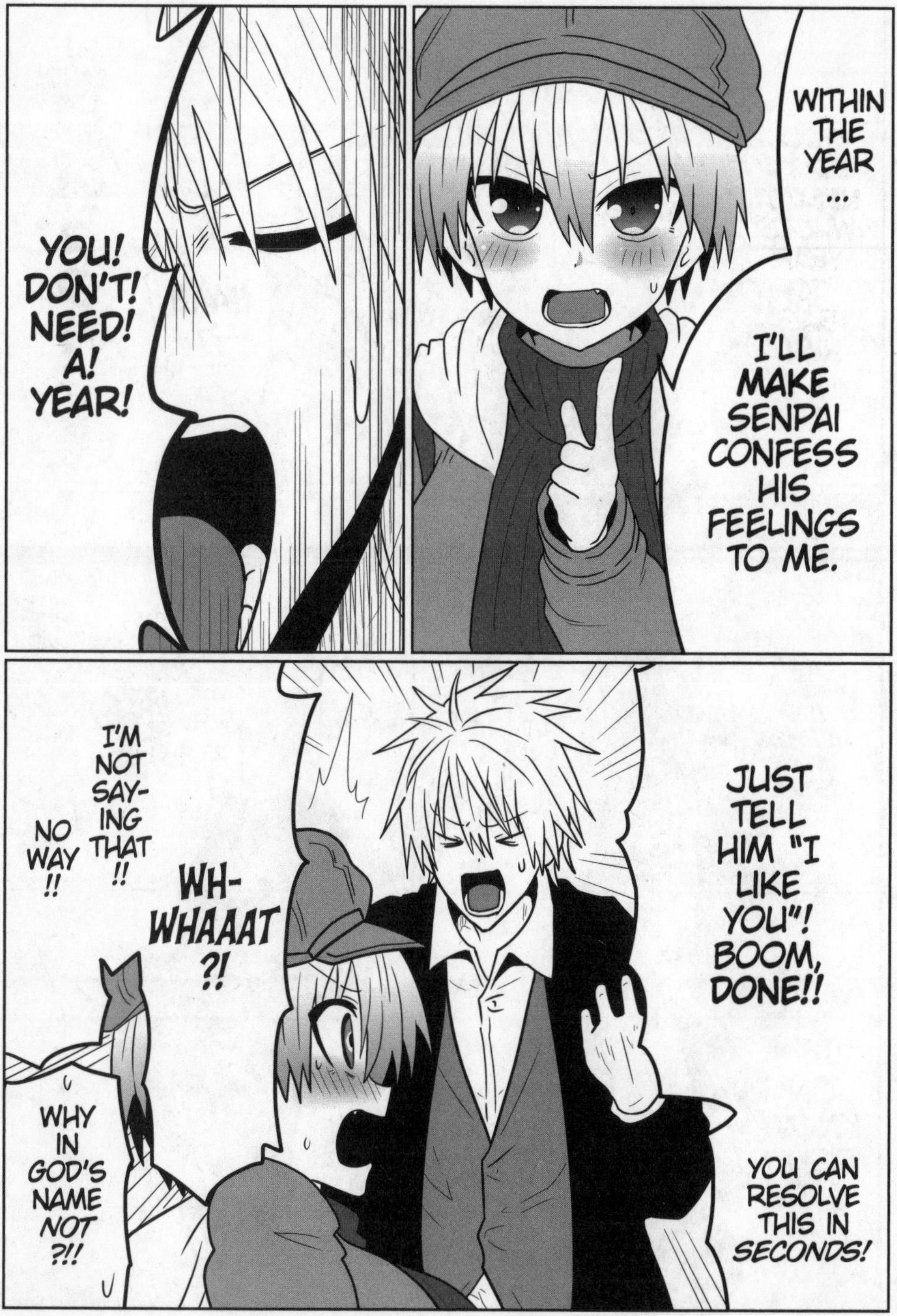
WITHIN THE YEAR ...
I'LL MAKE SENPAI CONFESS HIS FEELINGS TO ME.
YOU! DON'T! NEED! A! YEAR!
JUST TELL HIM "I LIKE YOU"! BOOM, DONE!!
YOU CAN RESOLVE THIS IN *SECONDS!*
WH-WHAAAT ?!
I'M NOT SAYING THAT !!
NO WAY !!
WHY IN GOD'S NAME *NOT* ?!!

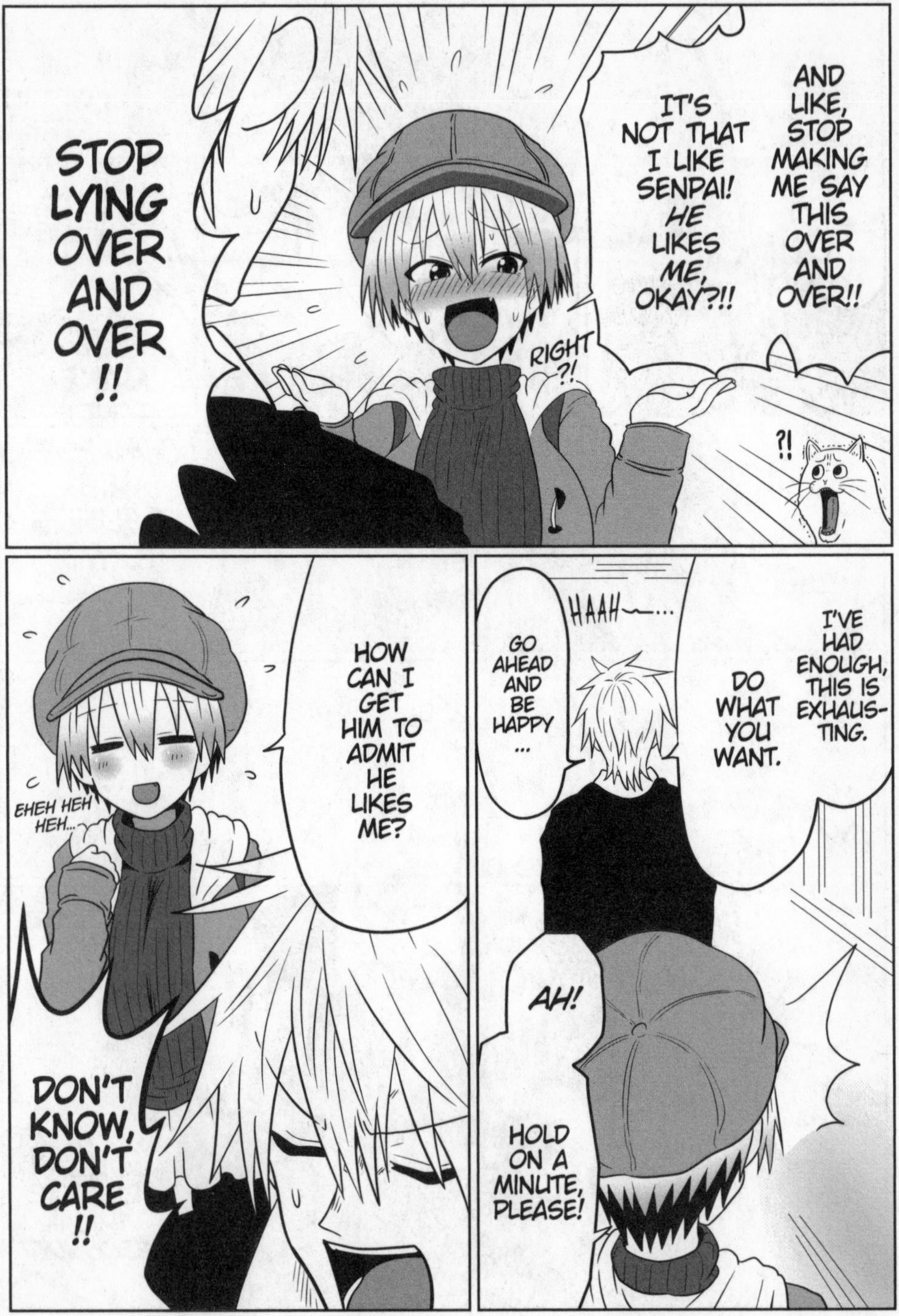
AND LIKE, STOP MAKING ME SAY THIS OVER AND OVER!!
IT'S NOT THAT I LIKE SENPAI! HE LIKES ME, OKAY?!!
RIGHT?!
?!
STOP LYING OVER AND OVER!!
I'VE HAD ENOUGH, THIS IS EXHAUS-TING.
DO WHAT YOU WANT.
HAAH~...
GO AHEAD AND BE HAPPY...
AH!
HOLD ON A MINUTE, PLEASE!
HOW CAN I GET HIM TO ADMIT HE LIKES ME?
EHEH HEH HEH...
DON'T KNOW, DON'T CARE!!

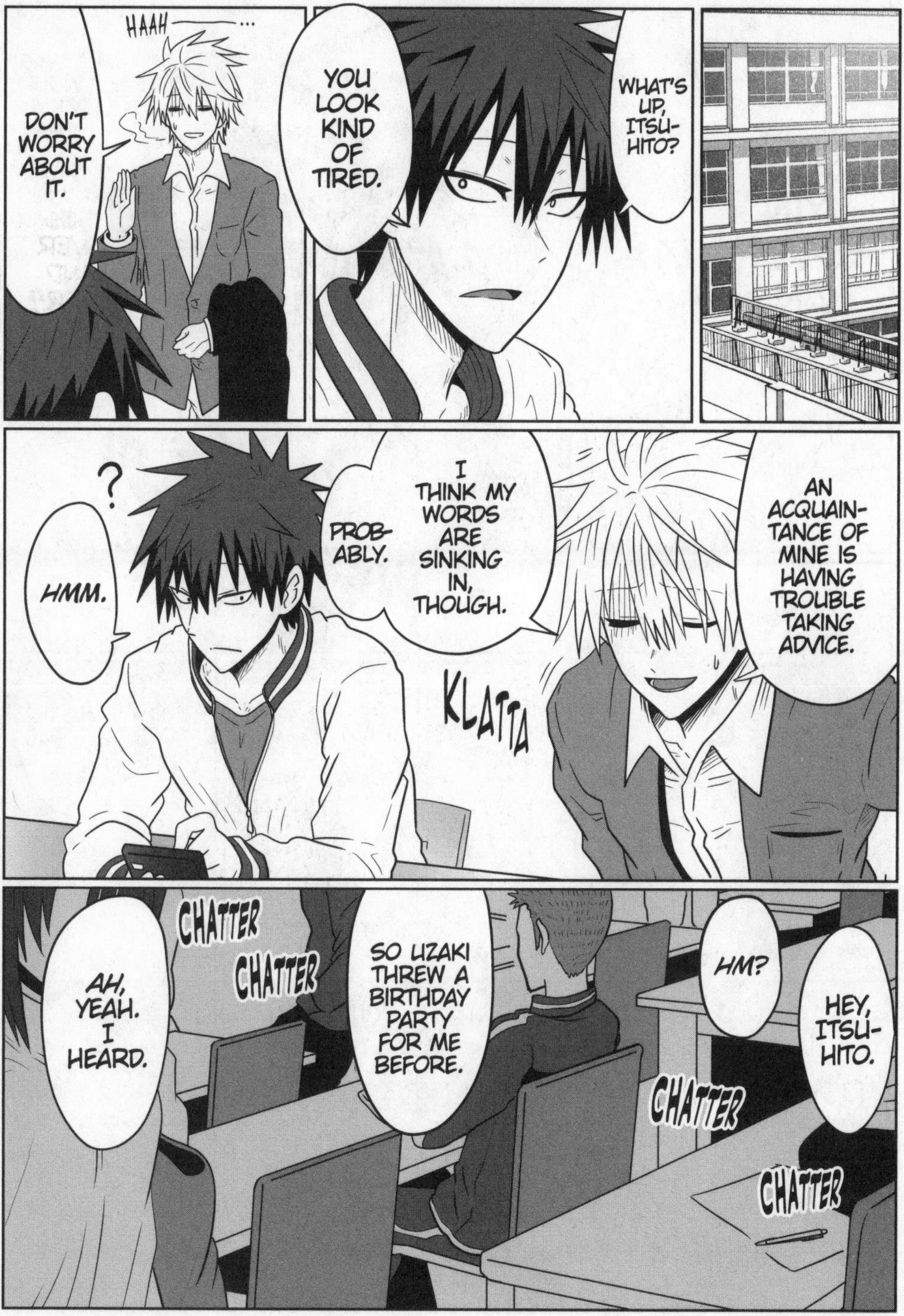
WHAT'S UP, ITSUHITO?
YOU LOOK KIND OF TIRED.
HAAH———...
DON'T WORRY ABOUT IT.
AN ACQUAINTANCE OF MINE IS HAVING TROUBLE TAKING ADVICE.
I THINK MY WORDS ARE SINKING IN, THOUGH.
KLATTA
PROBABLY.
HMM.
?
HEY, ITSUHITO.
HM?
SO UZAKI THREW A BIRTHDAY PARTY FOR ME BEFORE.
CHATTER
CHATTER
CHATTER
CHATTER
AH, YEAH. I HEARD.

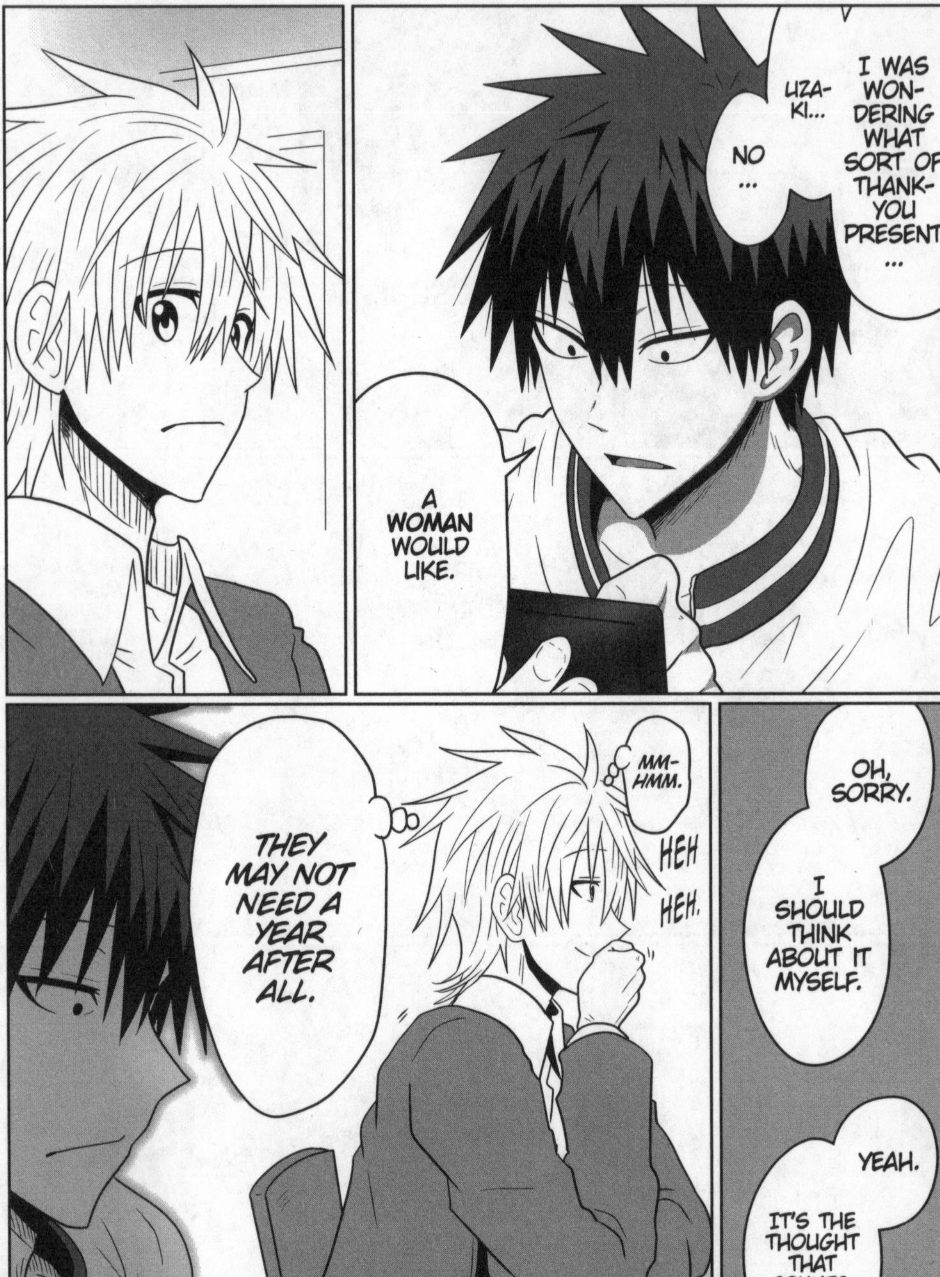
UZA-KI...
NO ...
I WAS WON-DERING WHAT SORT OF THANK-YOU PRESENT ...
A WOMAN WOULD LIKE.
OH, SORRY.
I SHOULD THINK ABOUT IT MYSELF.
YEAH.
IT'S THE THOUGHT THAT COUNTS.
MM-HMM.
HEH HEH.
THEY MAY NOT NEED A YEAR AFTER ALL.

The usual.

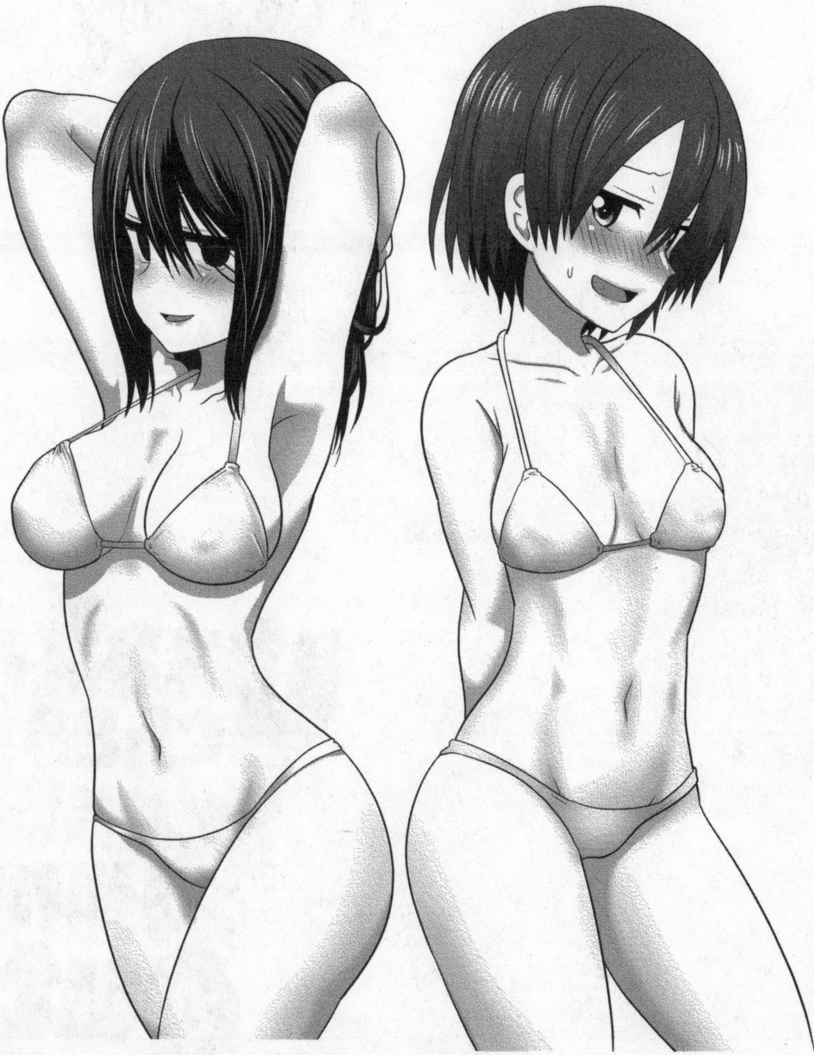

Uzaki-chan Wants to Hang Out!

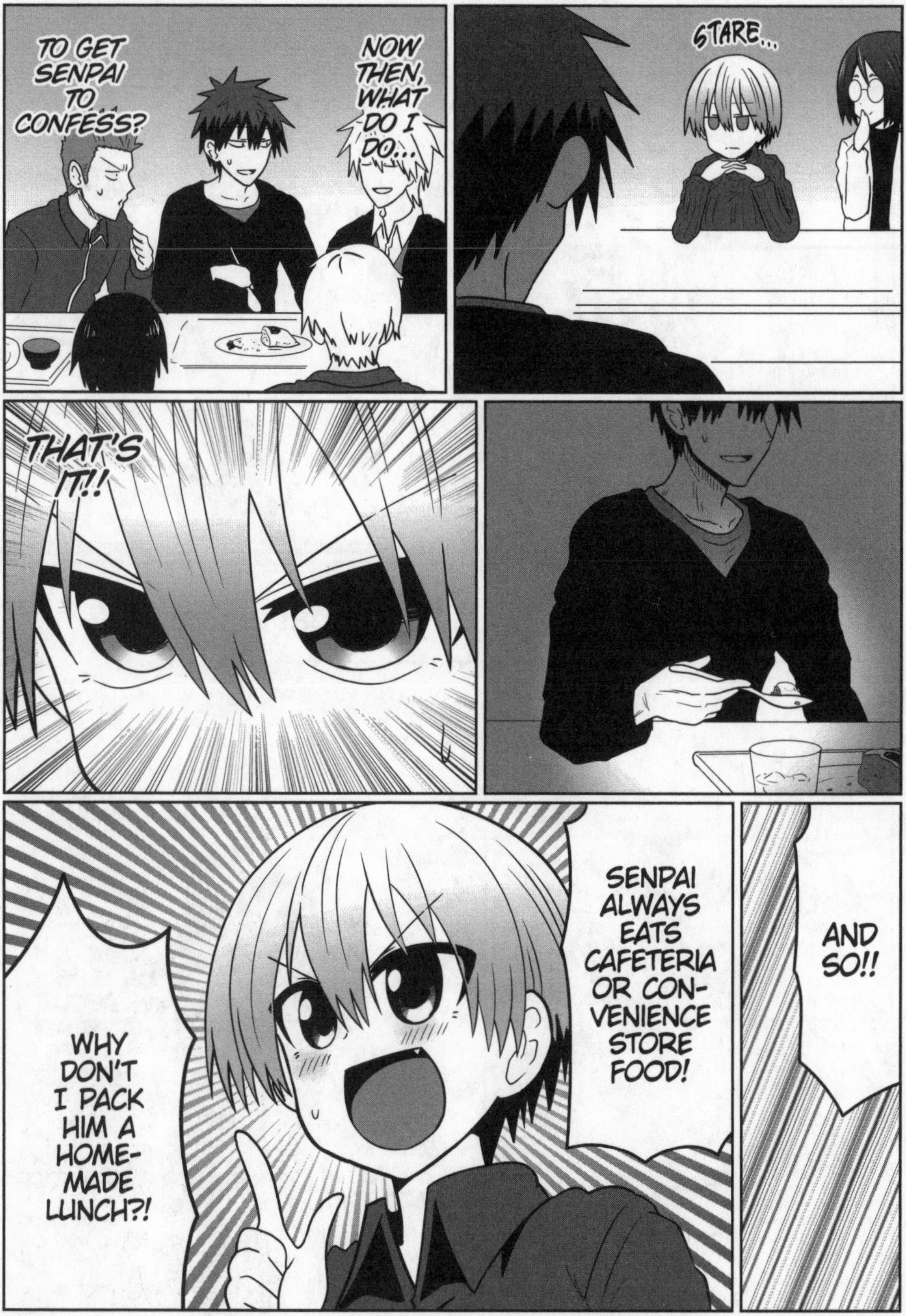
STARE...
NOW THEN, WHAT DO I DO...
TO GET SENPAI TO CONFESS?
THAT'S IT!!
AND SO!!
SENPAI ALWAYS EATS CAFETERIA OR CON-VENIENCE STORE FOOD!
WHY DON'T I PACK HIM A HOME-MADE LUNCH?!

Chapter 53: The Kouhai and the Cliché

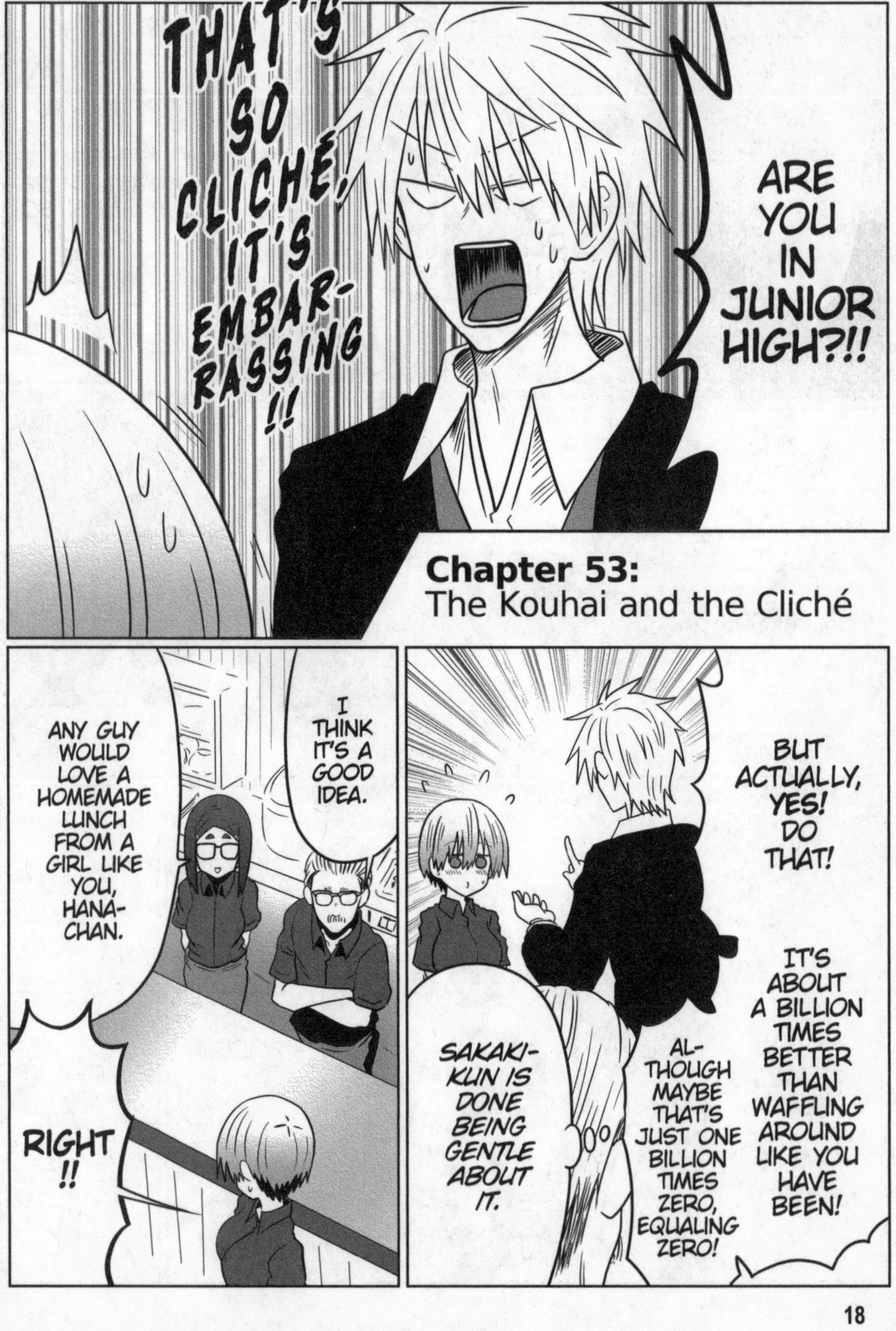
ARE YOU IN JUNIOR HIGH?!!
THAT'S SO CLICHE, IT'S EMBARRASSING!!
Chapter 53:
The Kouhai and the Cliché
BUT ACTUALLY, YES! DO THAT!
IT'S ABOUT A BILLION TIMES BETTER THAN WAFFLING AROUND LIKE YOU HAVE BEEN!
ALTHOUGH MAYBE THAT'S JUST ONE BILLION TIMES ZERO, EQUALING ZERO!
SAKAKI-KUN IS DONE BEING GENTLE ABOUT IT.
I THINK IT'S A GOOD IDEA.
ANY GUY WOULD LOVE A HOMEMADE LUNCH FROM A GIRL LIKE YOU, HANA-CHAN.
RIGHT!!

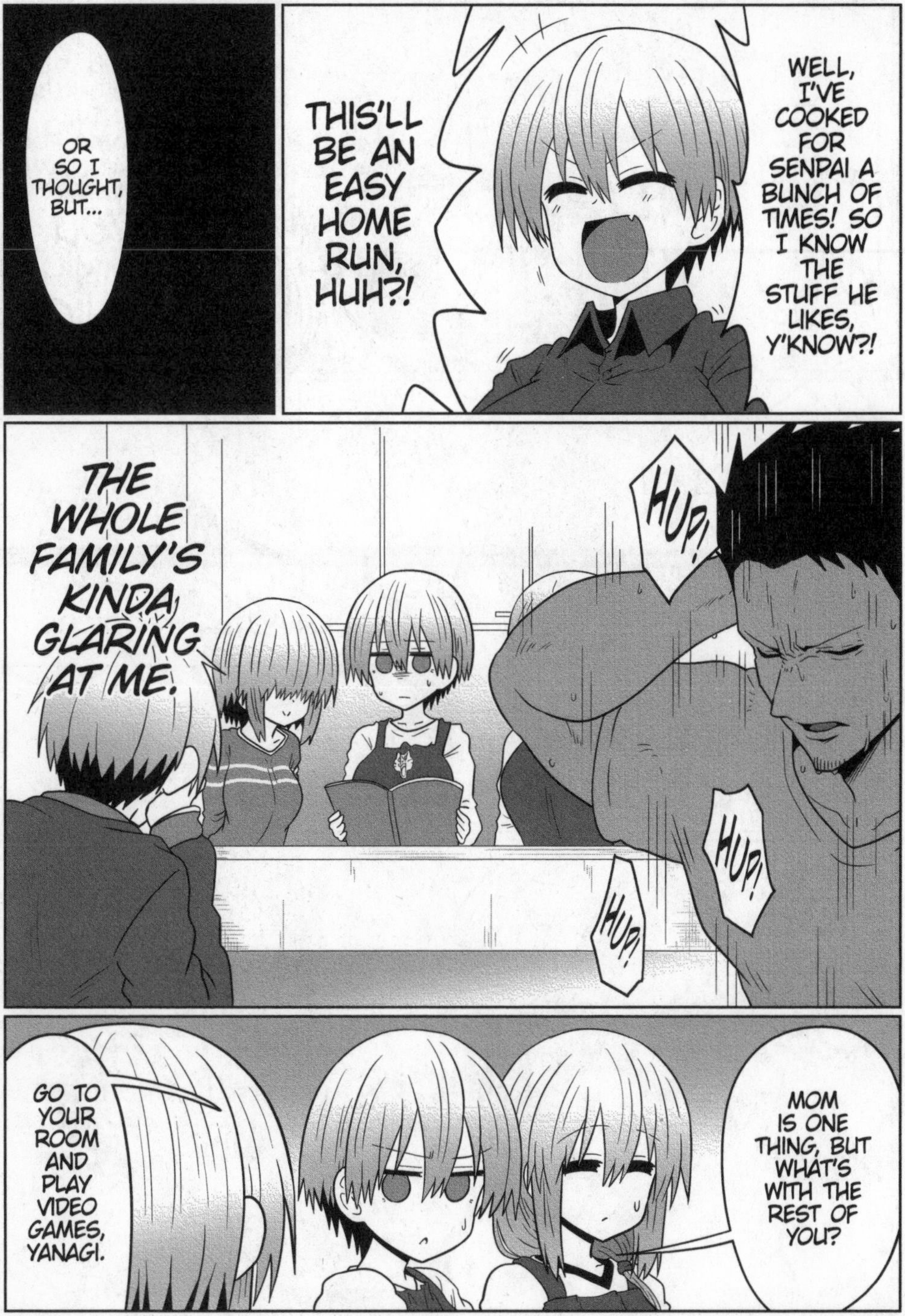
WELL, I'VE COOKED FOR SENPAI A BUNCH OF TIMES! SO I KNOW THE STUFF HE LIKES, Y'KNOW?!
THIS'LL BE AN EASY HOME RUN, HUH?!
OR SO I THOUGHT, BUT...
HUP!
THE WHOLE FAMILY'S KINDA GLARING AT ME.
HUP!
HUP!
MOM IS ONE THING, BUT WHAT'S WITH THE REST OF YOU?
GO TO YOUR ROOM AND PLAY VIDEO GAMES, YANAGI.

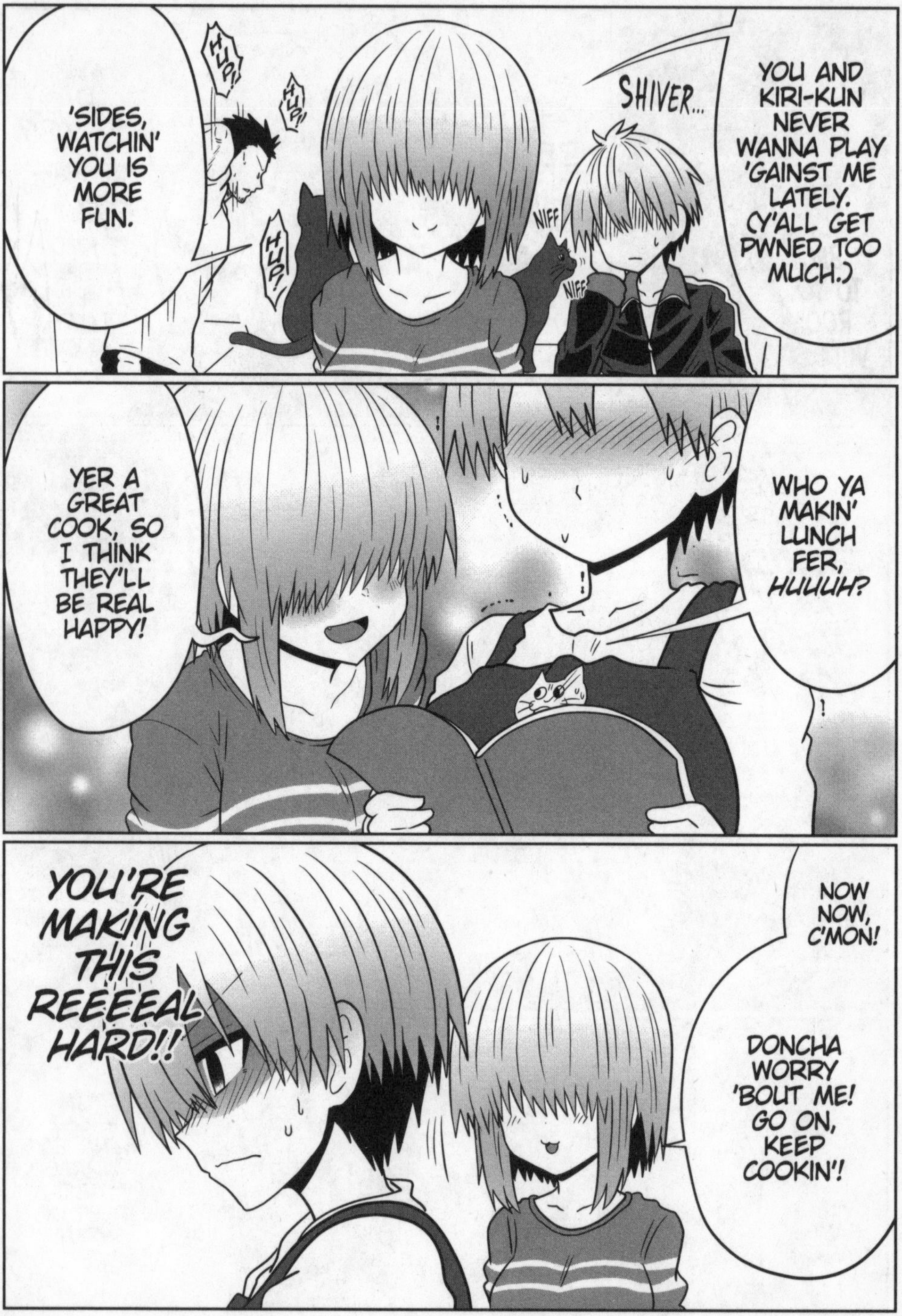
YOU AND KIRI-KUN NEVER WANNA PLAY 'GAINST ME LATELY. (Y'ALL GET PWNED TOO MUCH.)
SHIVER...
NIFF
NIFF
HUP!
HUP!
HUP!
'SIDES, WATCHIN' YOU IS MORE FUN.
WHO YA MAKIN' LUNCH FER, *HUUUH*?
YER A GREAT COOK, SO I THINK THEY'LL BE REAL HAPPY!
NOW NOW, C'MON!
DONCHA WORRY 'BOUT ME! GO ON, KEEP COOKIN'!
YOU'RE MAKING THIS REEEEAL HARD!!

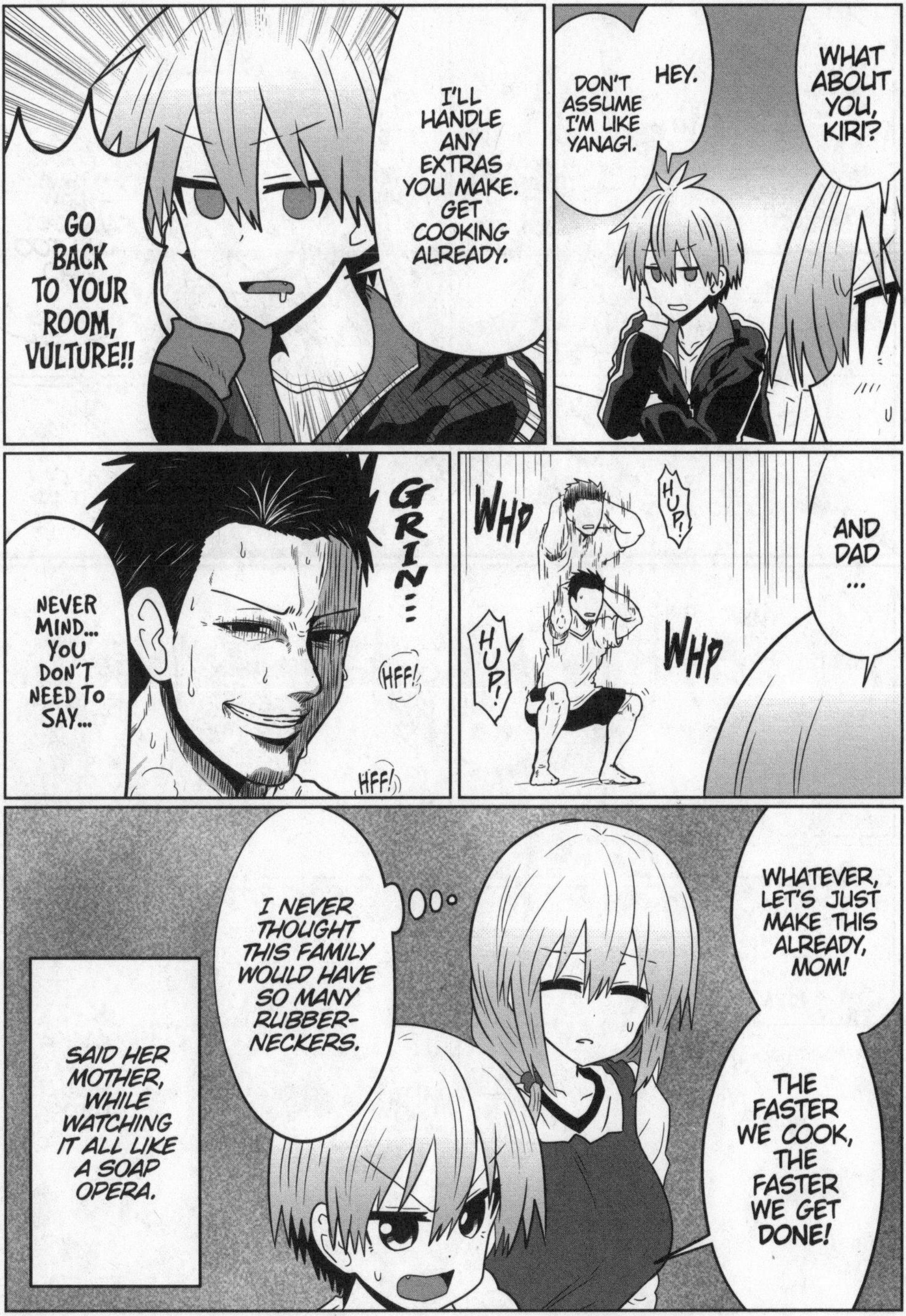
WHAT ABOUT YOU, KIRI?
HEY.
DON'T ASSUME I'M LIKE YANAGI.
I'LL HANDLE ANY EXTRAS YOU MAKE. GET COOKING ALREADY.
GO BACK TO YOUR ROOM, VULTURE!!
AND DAD ...
HUP!
WHP
WHP
HUP!
GRIN
HFF!
NEVER MIND... YOU DON'T NEED TO SAY...
HFF!
WHATEVER, LET'S JUST MAKE THIS ALREADY, MOM!
THE FASTER WE COOK, THE FASTER WE GET DONE!
I NEVER THOUGHT THIS FAMILY WOULD HAVE SO MANY RUBBER-NECKERS.
SAID HER MOTHER, WHILE WATCHING IT ALL LIKE A SOAP OPERA.

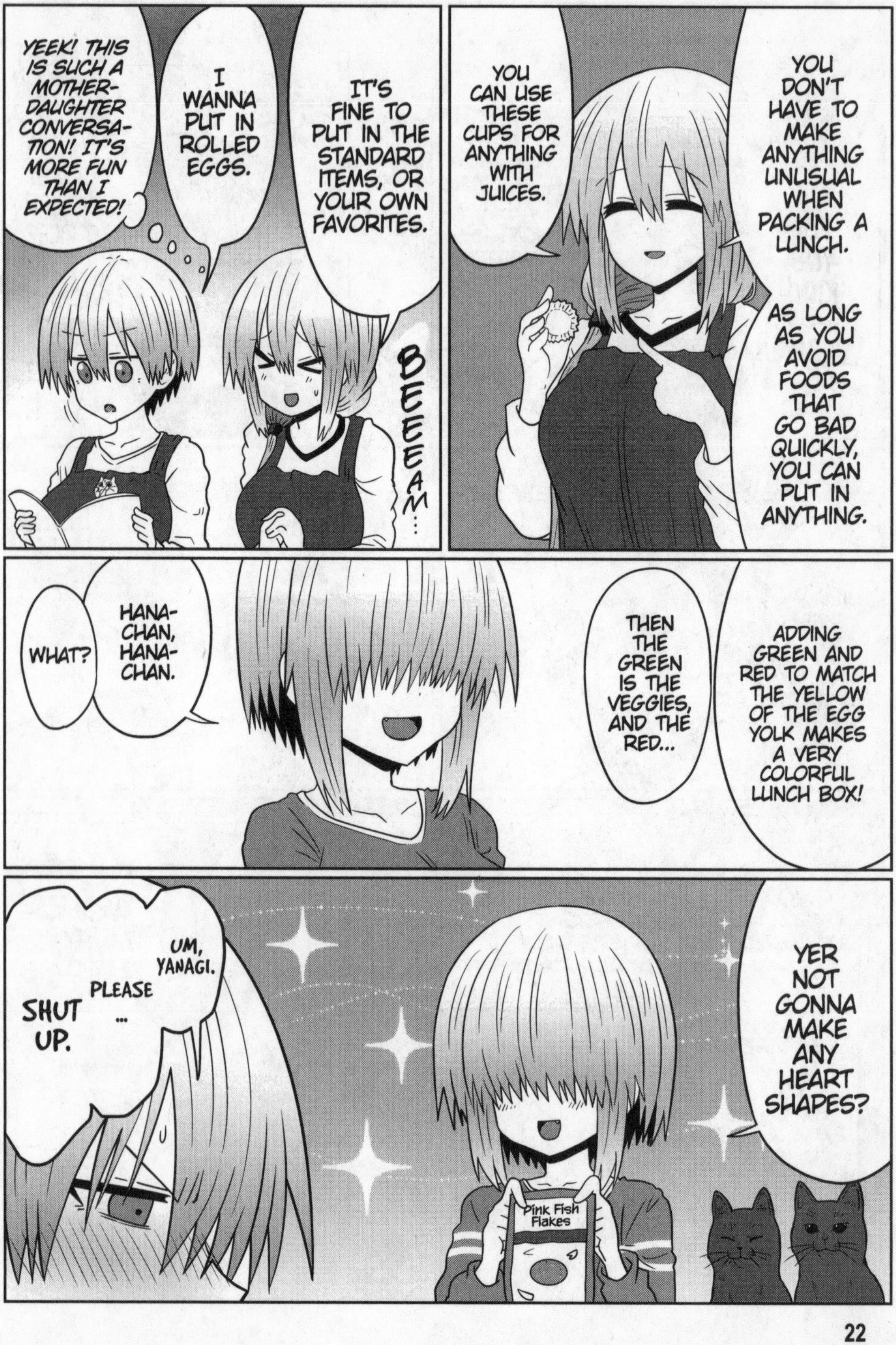
YOU DON'T HAVE TO MAKE ANYTHING UNUSUAL WHEN PACKING A LUNCH.
AS LONG AS YOU AVOID FOODS THAT GO BAD QUICKLY, YOU CAN PUT IN ANYTHING.
YOU CAN USE THESE CUPS FOR ANYTHING WITH JUICES.
IT'S FINE TO PUT IN THE STANDARD ITEMS, OR YOUR OWN FAVORITES.
I WANNA PUT IN ROLLED EGGS.
YEEK! THIS IS SUCH A MOTHER-DAUGHTER CONVERSATION! IT'S MORE FUN THAN I EXPECTED!
BEEEEAM...
ADDING GREEN AND RED TO MATCH THE YELLOW OF THE EGG YOLK MAKES A VERY COLORFUL LUNCH BOX!
THEN THE GREEN IS THE VEGGIES, AND THE RED...
HANA-CHAN, HANA-CHAN.
WHAT?
YER NOT GONNA MAKE ANY HEART SHAPES?
Pink Fish Flakes
UM, YANAGI.
PLEASE ...
SHUT UP.

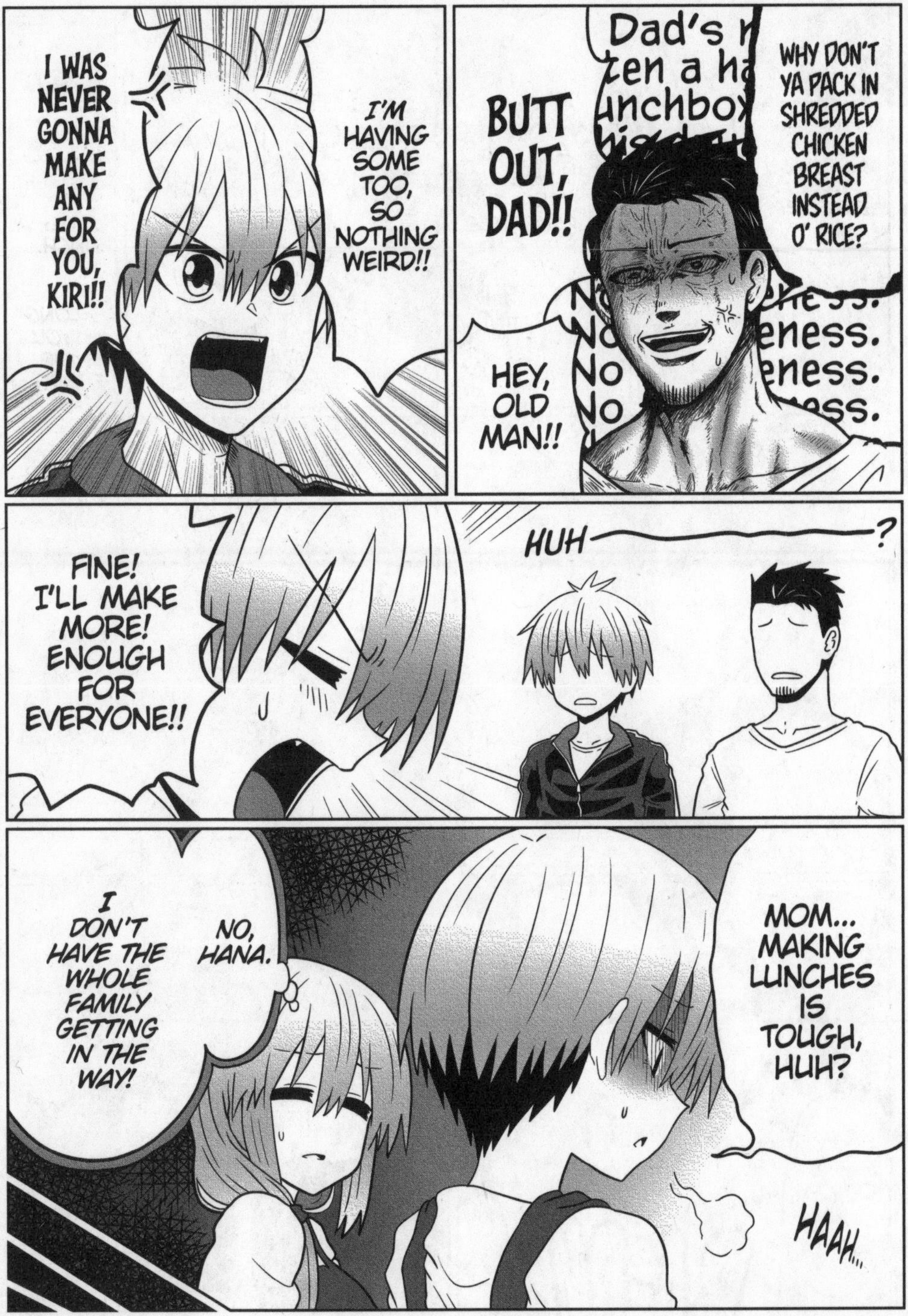
WHY DON'T YA PACK IN SHREDDED CHICKEN BREAST INSTEAD O' RICE?
BUTT OUT, DAD!!
HEY, OLD MAN!!
I'M HAVING SOME TOO, SO NOTHING WEIRD!!
I WAS NEVER GONNA MAKE ANY FOR YOU, KIRI!!
HUH———?
FINE! I'LL MAKE MORE! ENOUGH FOR EVERYONE!!
MOM... MAKING LUNCHES IS TOUGH, HUH?
HAAH...
NO, HANA.
I DON'T HAVE THE WHOLE FAMILY GETTING IN THE WAY!

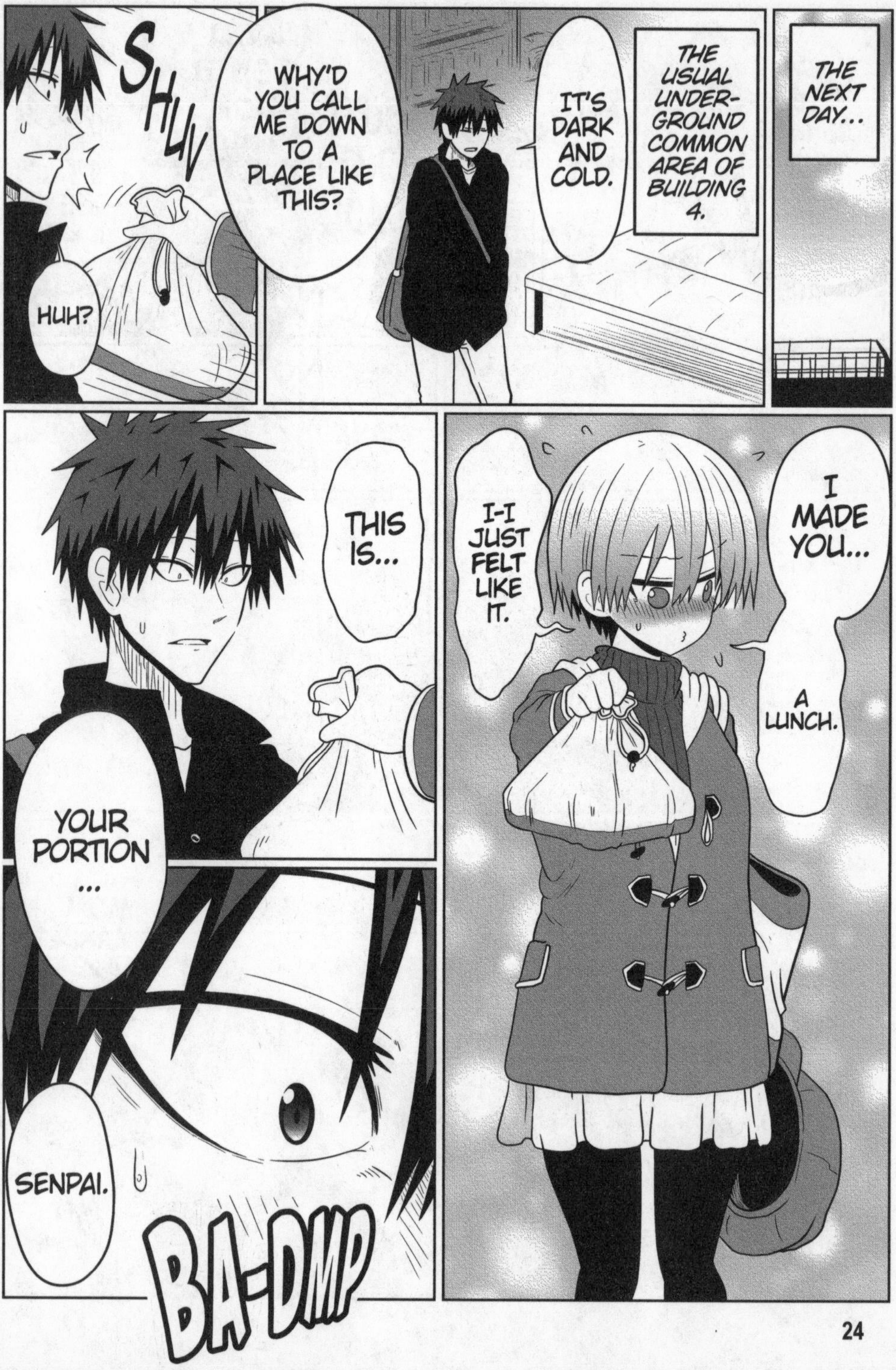
THE NEXT DAY...
THE USUAL UNDER-GROUND COMMON AREA OF BUILDING 4.
IT'S DARK AND COLD.
WHY'D YOU CALL ME DOWN TO A PLACE LIKE THIS?
SHUV
HUH?
I MADE YOU...
A LUNCH.
I-I JUST FELT LIKE IT.
THIS IS...
YOUR PORTION...
SENPAI.
BA-DMP

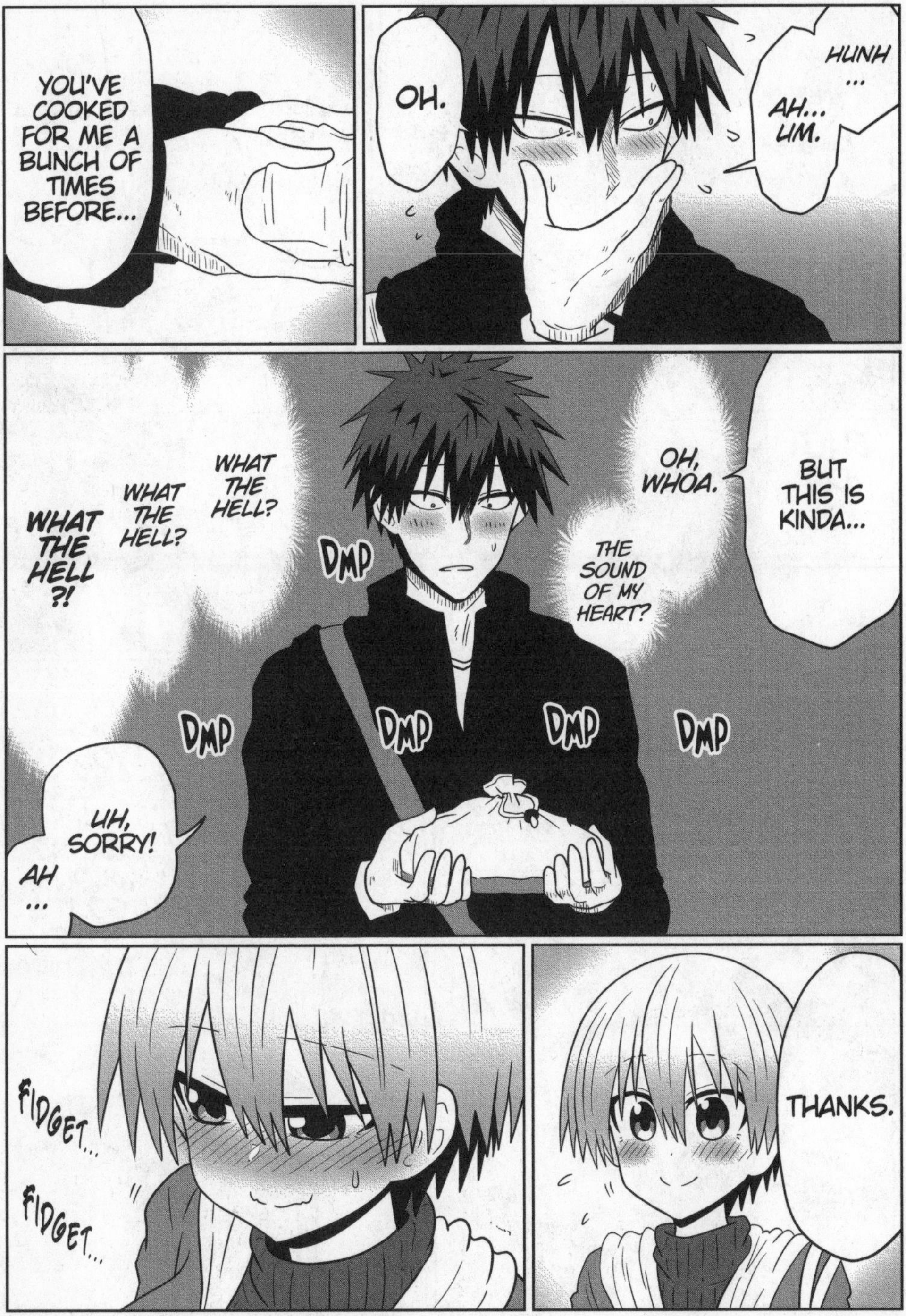
HUNH ... AH... UM.
OH.
YOU'VE COOKED FOR ME A BUNCH OF TIMES BEFORE...
BUT THIS IS KINDA...
OH, WHOA.
THE SOUND OF MY HEART?
WHAT THE HELL?
WHAT THE HELL?
WHAT THE HELL ?!
DMP
DMP
DMP
DMP
DMP
UH, SORRY!
AH ...
THANKS.
FIDGET...
FIDGET...

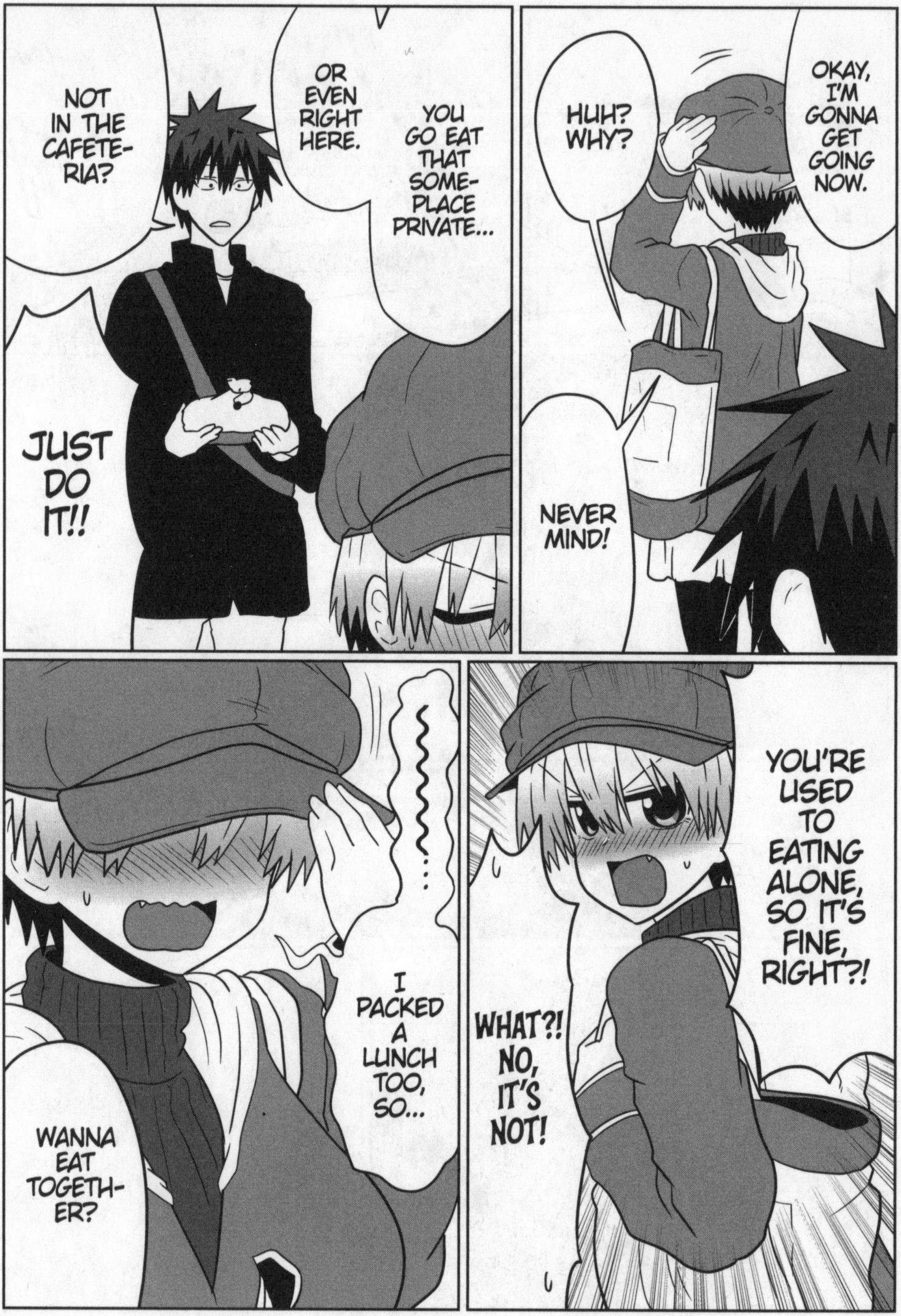
OKAY, I'M GONNA GET GOING NOW.
HUH? WHY?
NEVER MIND!
YOU GO EAT THAT SOME-PLACE PRIVATE...
OR EVEN RIGHT HERE.
NOT IN THE CAFETE-RIA?
JUST DO IT!!
YOU'RE USED TO EATING ALONE, SO IT'S FINE, RIGHT?!
WHAT?! NO, IT'S NOT!
~~~...
I PACKED A LUNCH TOO, SO...
WANNA EAT TOGETH-ER?
~~~

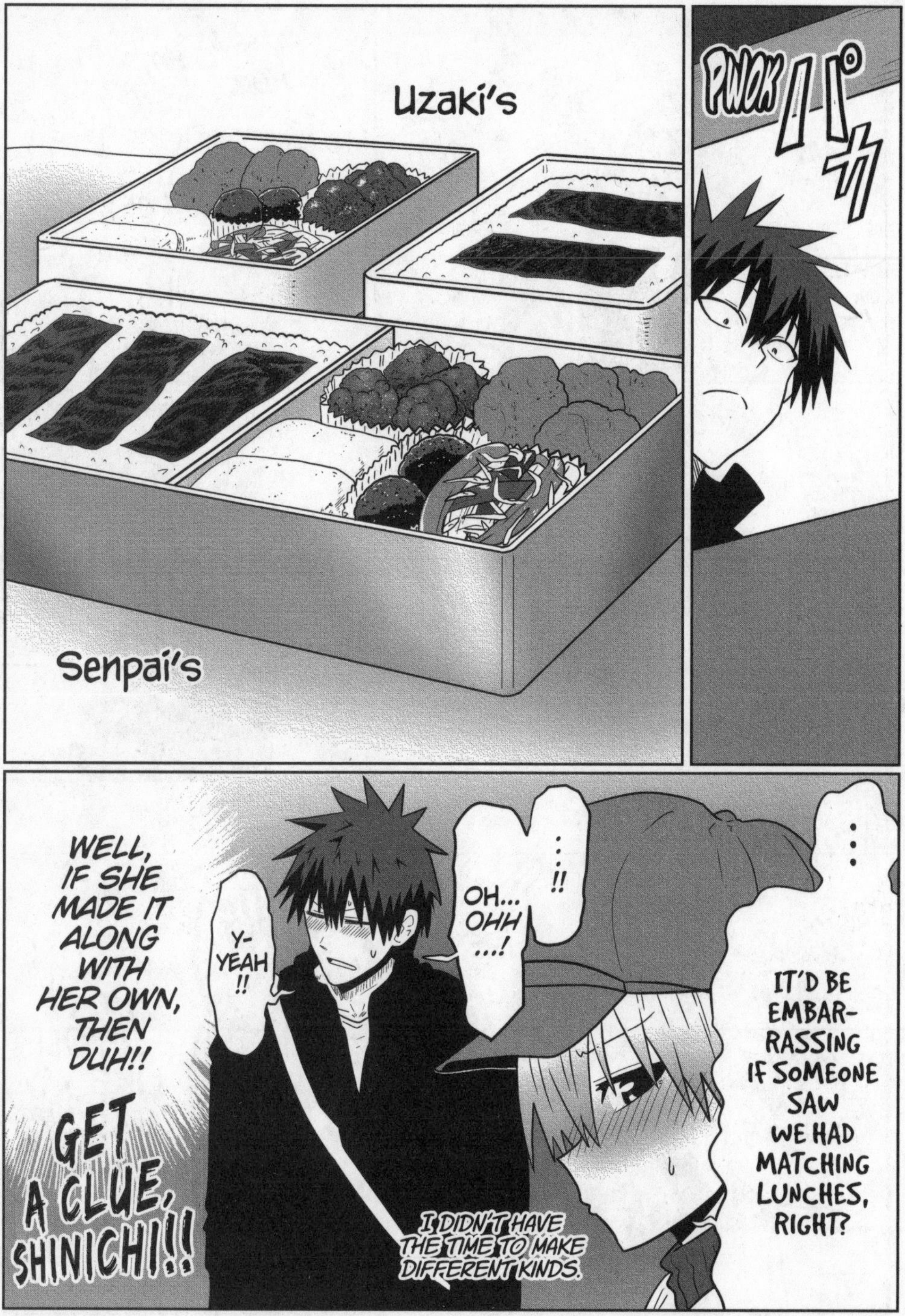
PWOK パカ
Uzaki's
Senpai's
...
IT'D BE EMBARRASSING IF SOMEONE SAW WE HAD MATCHING LUNCHES, RIGHT?
...!!
OH... OHH ...!
I DIDN'T HAVE THE TIME TO MAKE DIFFERENT KINDS.
Y-YEAH!!
WELL, IF SHE MADE IT ALONG WITH HER OWN, THEN DUH!!
GET A CLUE, SHINICHI!!

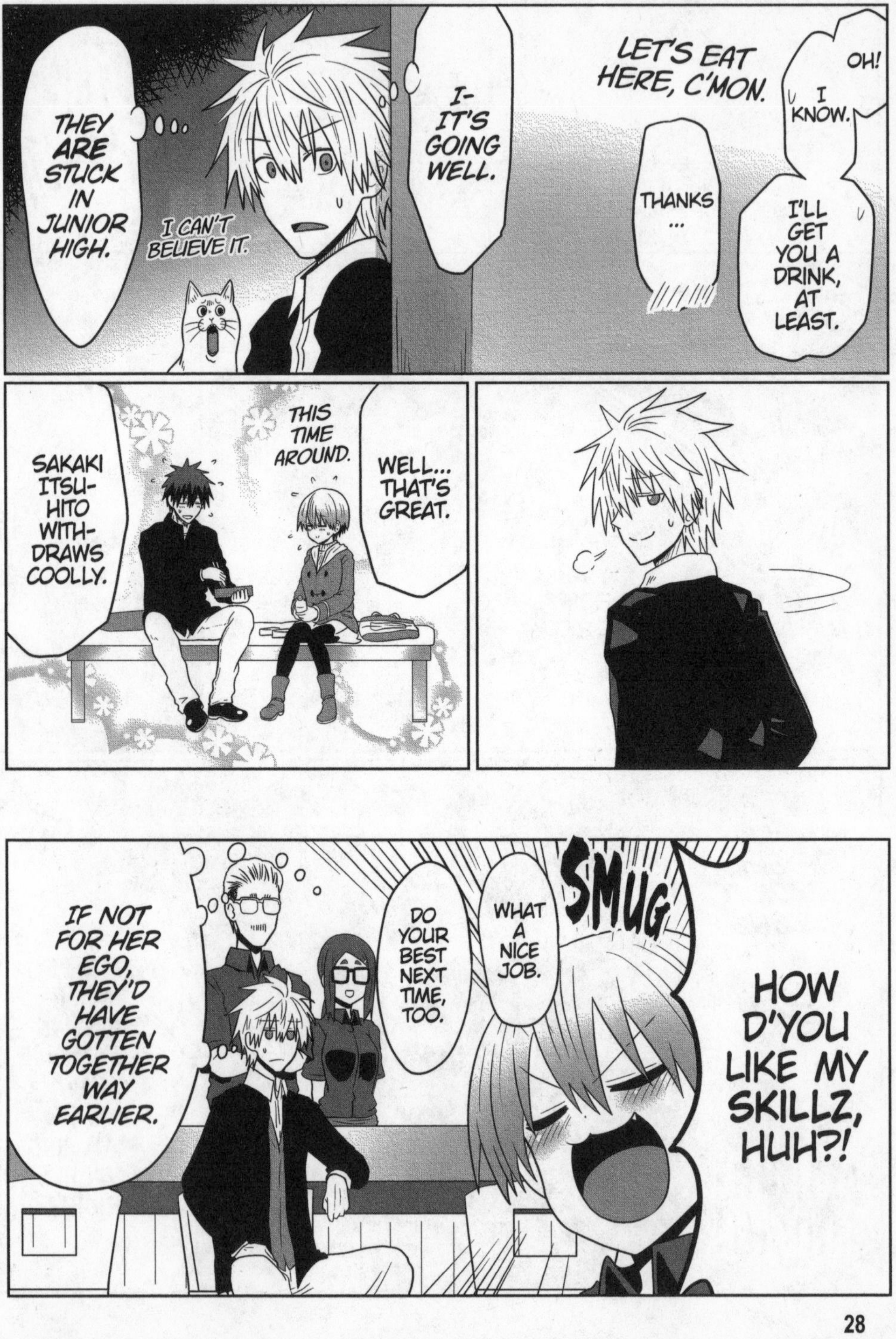
OH! I KNOW.
LET'S EAT HERE, C'MON.
I'LL GET YOU A DRINK, AT LEAST.
THANKS...
I- IT'S GOING WELL.
THEY ARE STUCK IN JUNIOR HIGH.
I CAN'T BELIEVE IT.
WELL... THAT'S GREAT.
THIS TIME AROUND.
SAKAKI ITSUHITO WITHDRAWS COOLLY.
HOW D'YOU LIKE MY SKILLZ, HUH?!
SMUG
WHAT A NICE JOB.
DO YOUR BEST NEXT TIME, TOO.
IF NOT FOR HER EGO, THEY'D HAVE GOTTEN TOGETHER WAY EARLIER.

LOOKIT THIS!!
MY DAUGHTER PACKED ME A HOMEMADE LUNCH!
COME LOOK, Y'ALL! AIN'T THIS GREAT?!
UZAKI FUJIO, AGE FORTY-SIX, MAKING HIS COWORKERS MAD AT HIM.
IT'S NOT LUNCH BREAK NOW, UZAKI-SAN.
PUT YOUR LUNCH AWAY.
DO YOUR WORK, COME ON.

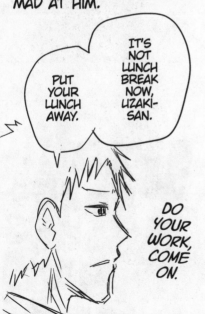

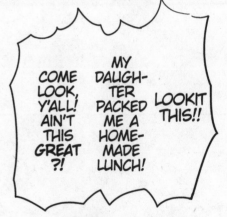

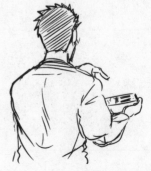

Uzaki-chan Wants to Hang Out!

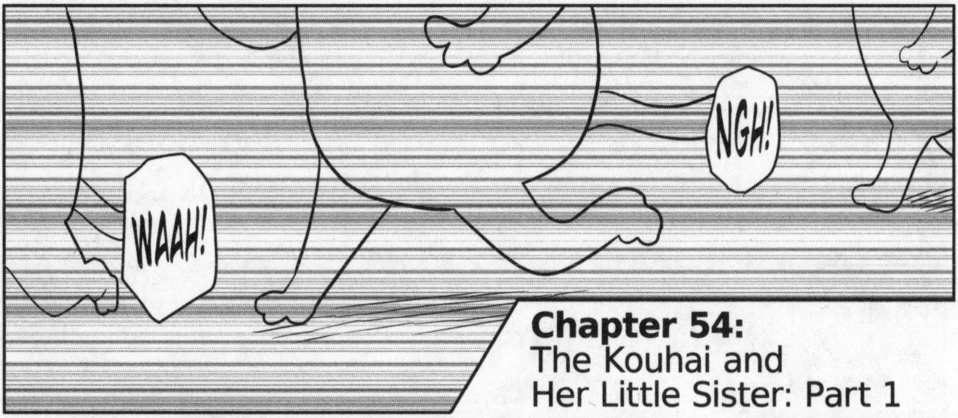
NGH!
WAAH!

Chapter 54:
The Kouhai and Her Little Sister: Part 1

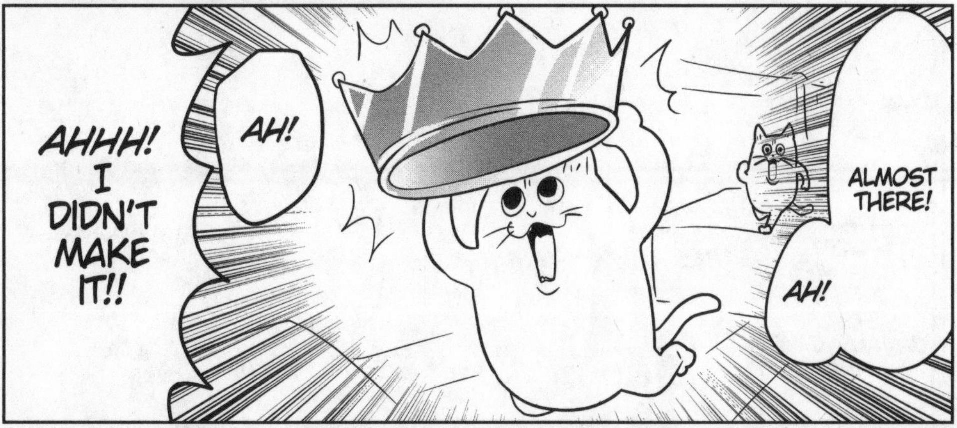
ALMOST THERE!
AH!
AH!
AHHH! I DIDN'T MAKE IT!!

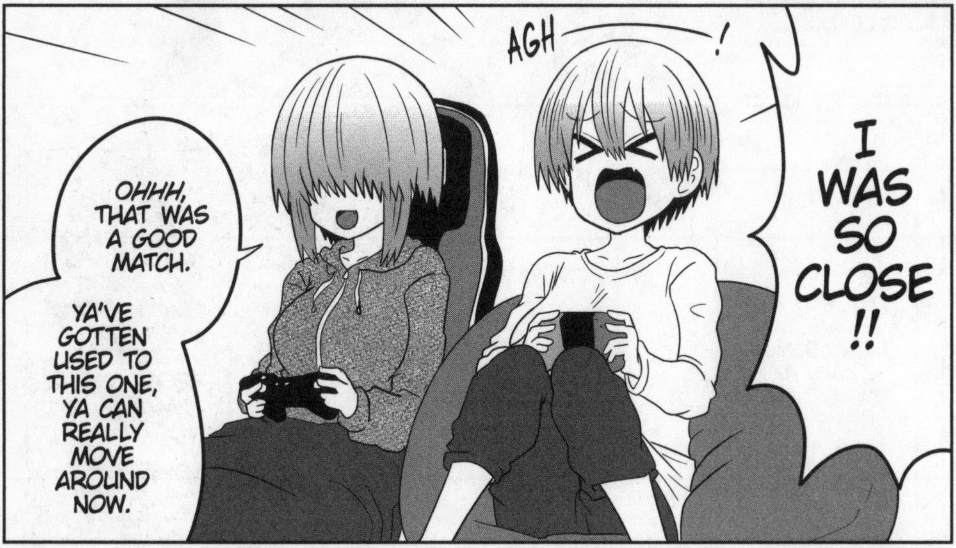
AGH—!
I WAS SO CLOSE!!
OHHH, THAT WAS A GOOD MATCH.
YA'VE GOTTEN USED TO THIS ONE, YA CAN REALLY MOVE AROUND NOW.

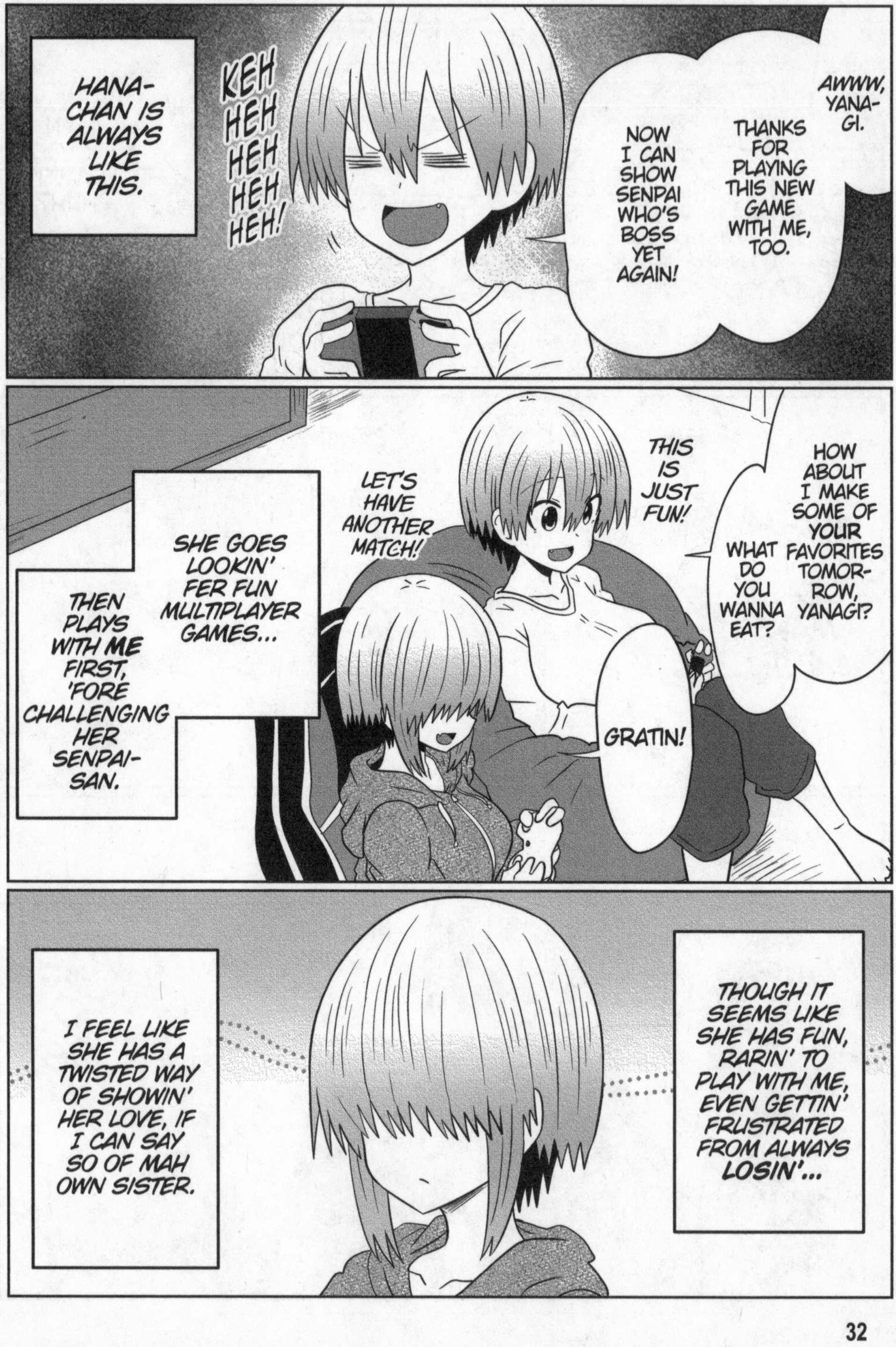
AWWW, YANAGI.
THANKS FOR PLAYING THIS NEW GAME WITH ME, TOO.
NOW I CAN SHOW SENPAI WHO'S BOSS YET AGAIN!
KEH HEH HEH HEH HEH!
HANA-CHAN IS ALWAYS LIKE THIS.
HOW ABOUT I MAKE SOME OF YOUR FAVORITES TOMORROW, YANAGI?
WHAT DO YOU WANNA EAT?
THIS IS JUST FUN!
LET'S HAVE ANOTHER MATCH!
GRATIN!
SHE GOES LOOKIN' FER FUN MULTIPLAYER GAMES...
THEN PLAYS WITH ME FIRST, 'FORE CHALLENGING HER SENPAI-SAN.
THOUGH IT SEEMS LIKE SHE HAS FUN, RARIN' TO PLAY WITH ME, EVEN GETTIN' FRUSTRATED FROM ALWAYS LOSIN'...
I FEEL LIKE SHE HAS A TWISTED WAY OF SHOWIN' HER LOVE, IF I CAN SAY SO OF MAH OWN SISTER.

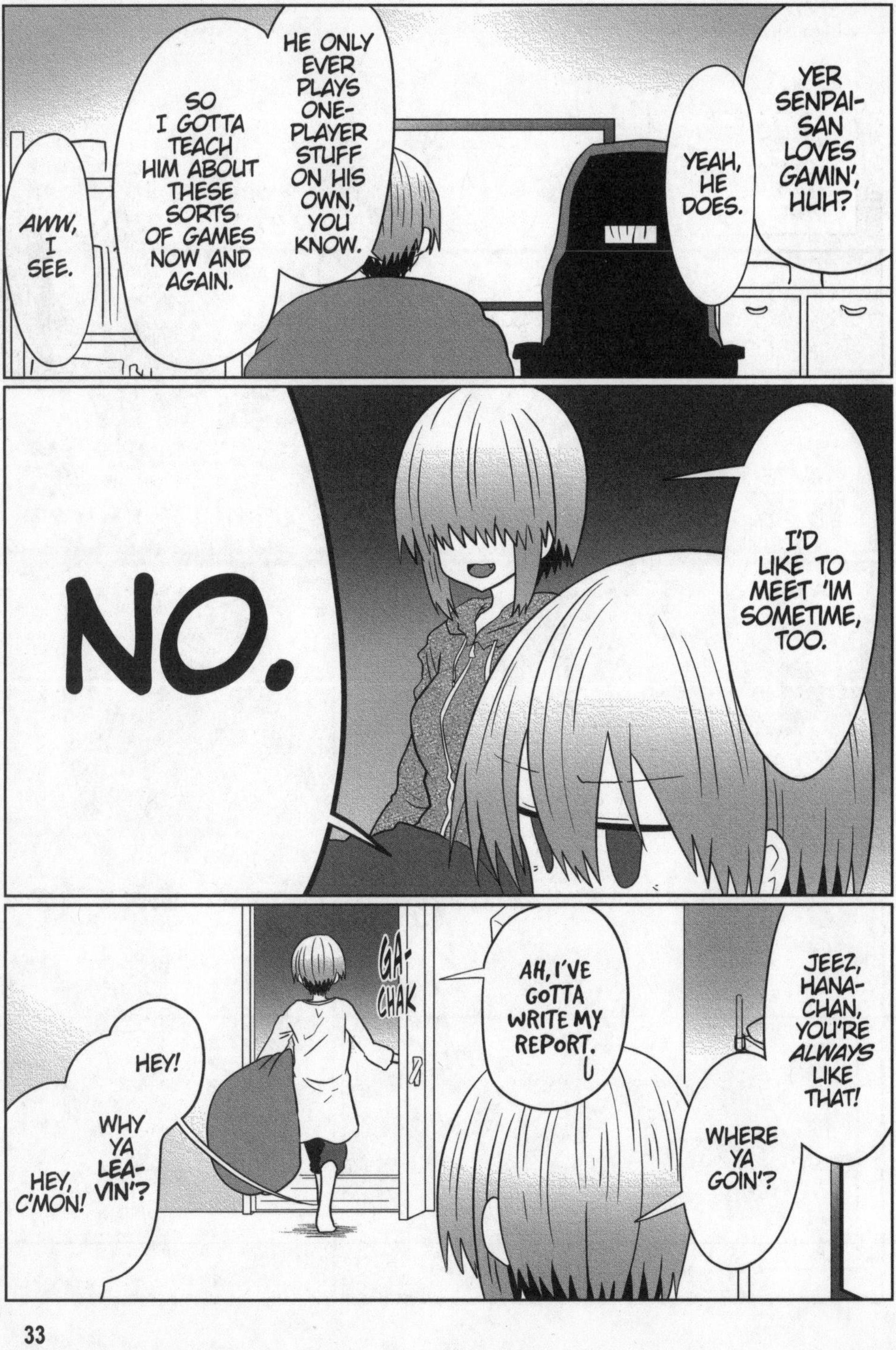
YER SENPAI-SAN LOVES GAMIN', HUH?
YEAH, HE DOES.
HE ONLY EVER PLAYS ONE-PLAYER STUFF ON HIS OWN, YOU KNOW.
SO I GOTTA TEACH HIM ABOUT THESE SORTS OF GAMES NOW AND AGAIN.
AWW, I SEE.
I'D LIKE TO MEET 'IM SOMETIME, TOO.
NO.
JEEZ, HANA-CHAN, YOU'RE ALWAYS LIKE THAT!
WHERE YA GOIN'?
AH, I'VE GOTTA WRITE MY REPORT.
GA-CHAK
HEY!
WHY YA LEA-VIN'?
HEY, C'MON!

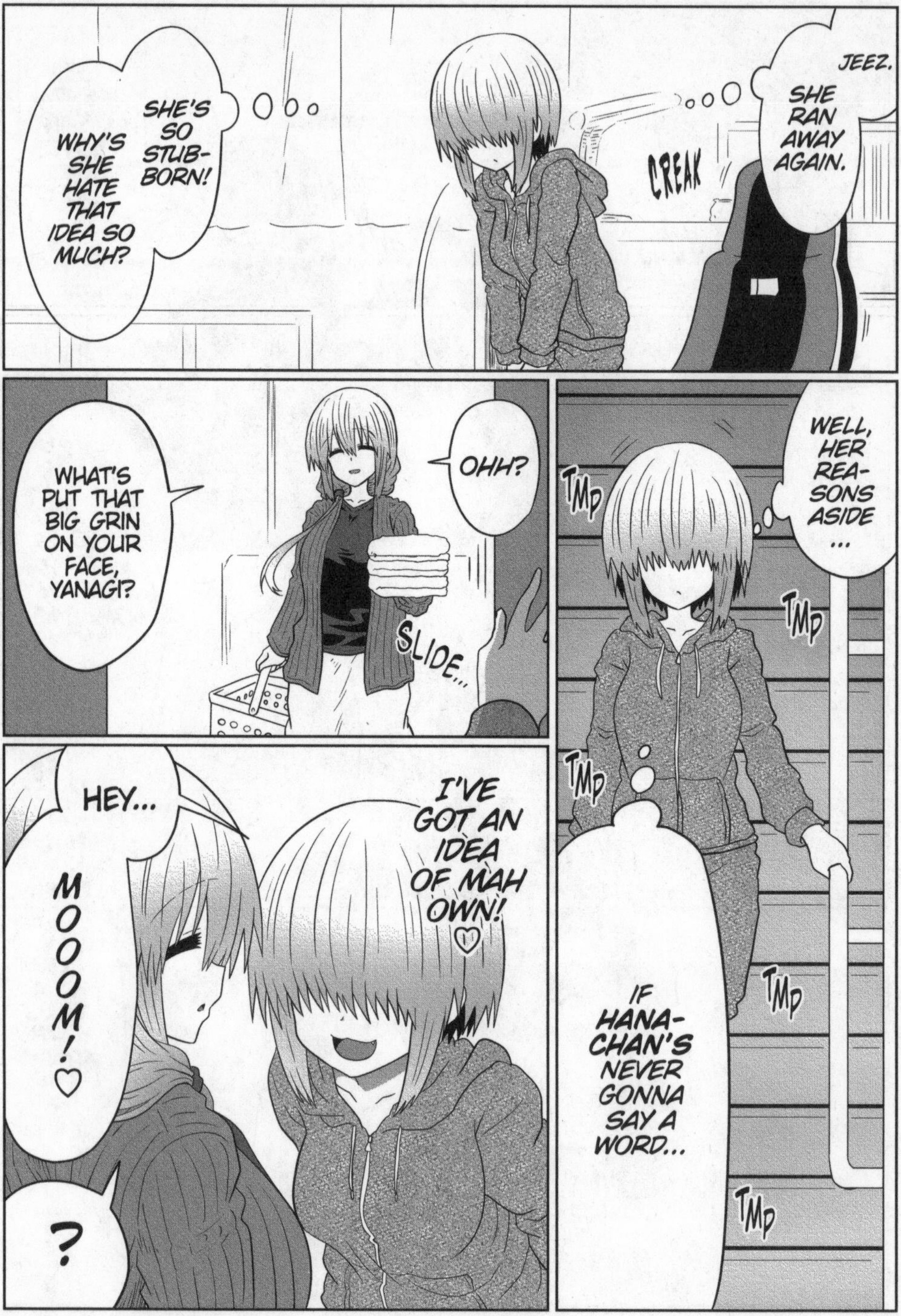
JEEZ. SHE RAN AWAY AGAIN.
CREAK
SHE'S SO STUB-BORN!
WHY'S SHE HATE THAT IDEA SO MUCH?
WELL, HER REA-SONS ASIDE ...
TMP
TMP
TMP
IF HANA-CHAN'S NEVER GONNA SAY A WORD...
TMP
TMP
OHH?
WHAT'S PUT THAT BIG GRIN ON YOUR FACE, YANAGI?
SLIDE...
I'VE GOT AN IDEA OF MAH OWN! ♡
HEY...
MOOOOM! ♡
?

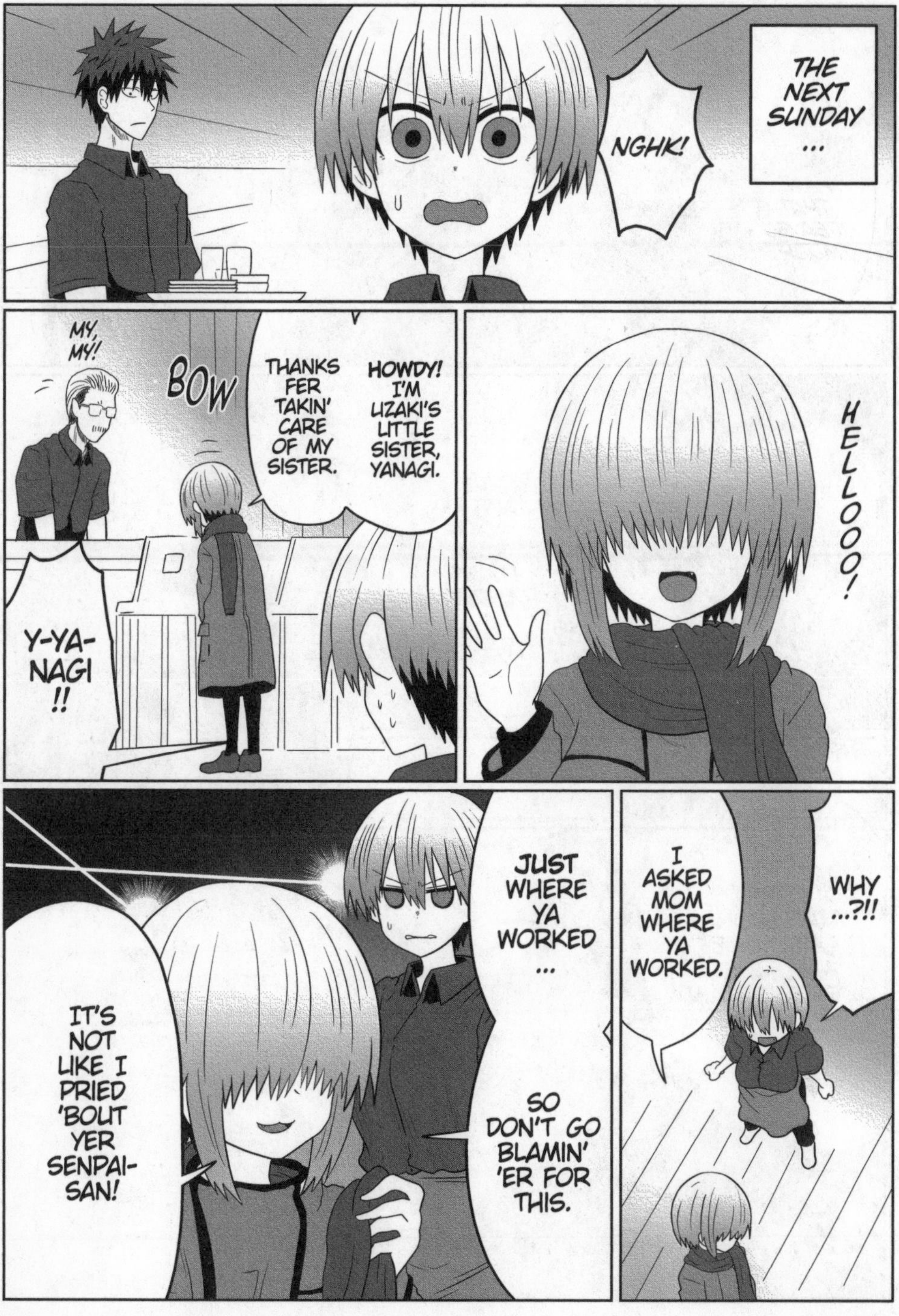
THE NEXT SUNDAY ...
NGHK!
HELLOOO!
HOWDY! I'M UZAKI'S LITTLE SISTER, YANAGI.
THANKS FER TAKIN' CARE OF MY SISTER.
BOW
MY, MY!
Y-YA-NAGI !!
WHY ...?!!
I ASKED MOM WHERE YA WORKED.
JUST WHERE YA WORKED ...
SO DON'T GO BLAMIN' 'ER FOR THIS.
IT'S NOT LIKE I PRIED 'BOUT YER SENPAI-SAN!

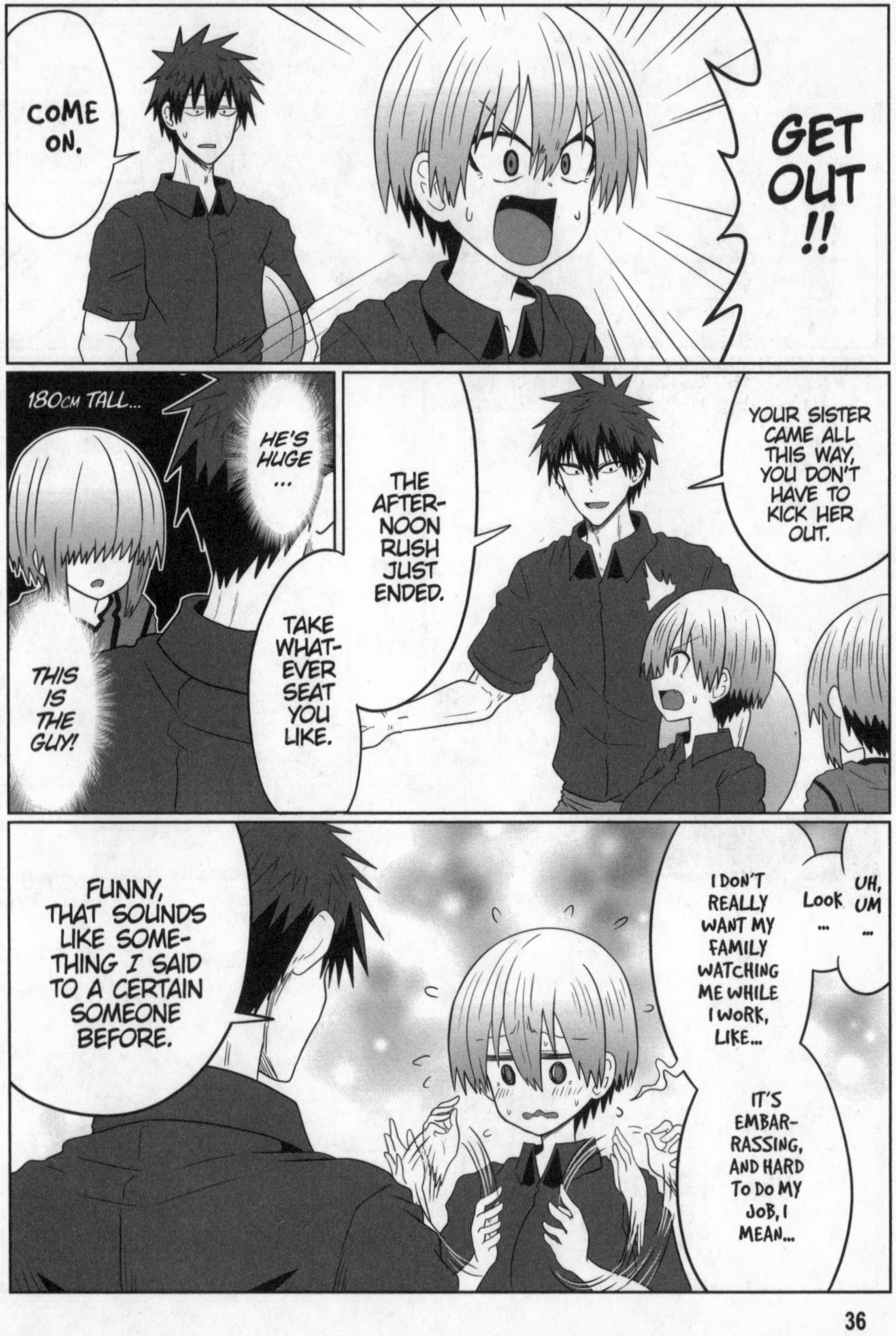
GET OUT!!
COME ON.
YOUR SISTER CAME ALL THIS WAY, YOU DON'T HAVE TO KICK HER OUT.
THE AFTER-NOON RUSH JUST ENDED.
TAKE WHAT-EVER SEAT YOU LIKE.
HE'S HUGE...
180CM TALL...
THIS IS THE GUY!
UH, UM...
Look...
I DON'T REALLY WANT MY FAMILY WATCHING ME WHILE I WORK, LIKE...
IT'S EMBAR-RASSING, AND HARD TO DO MY JOB, I MEAN...
FUNNY, THAT SOUNDS LIKE SOME-THING I SAID TO A CERTAIN SOMEONE BEFORE.

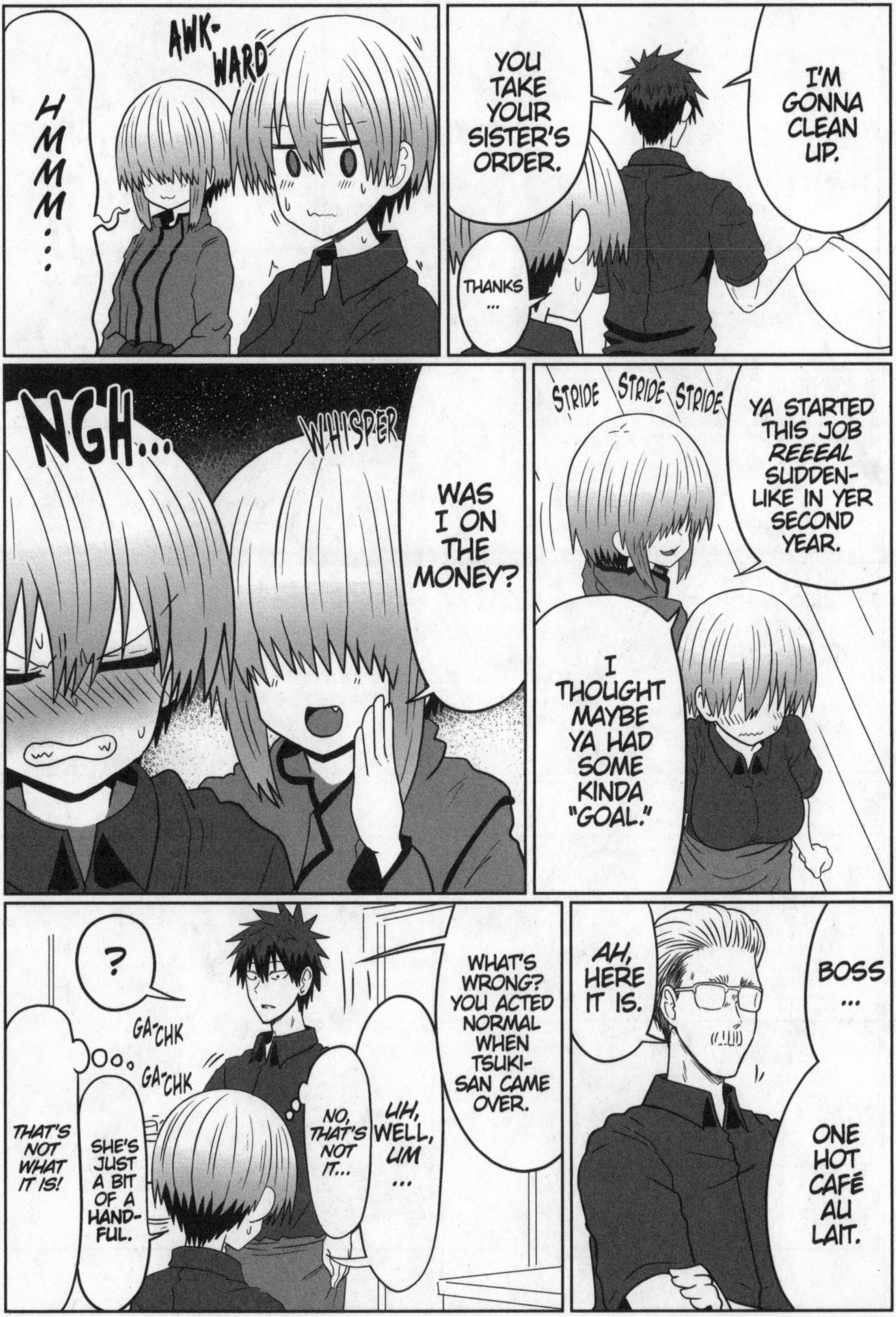
I'M GONNA CLEAN UP.
YOU TAKE YOUR SISTER'S ORDER.
THANKS ...
AWK-WARD
HMMM...
STRIDE STRIDE STRIDE
YA STARTED THIS JOB REEEAL SUDDEN-LIKE IN YER SECOND YEAR.
I THOUGHT MAYBE YA HAD SOME KINDA "GOAL."
WHISPER
WAS I ON THE MONEY?
NGH...
BOSS ...
AH, HERE IT IS.
ONE HOT CAFÉ AU LAIT.
WHAT'S WRONG? YOU ACTED NORMAL WHEN TSUKI-SAN CAME OVER.
UH, WELL, UM ...
NO, THAT'S NOT IT...
?
GA-CHK
GA-CHK
SHE'S JUST A BIT OF A HAND-FUL.
THAT'S NOT WHAT IT IS!

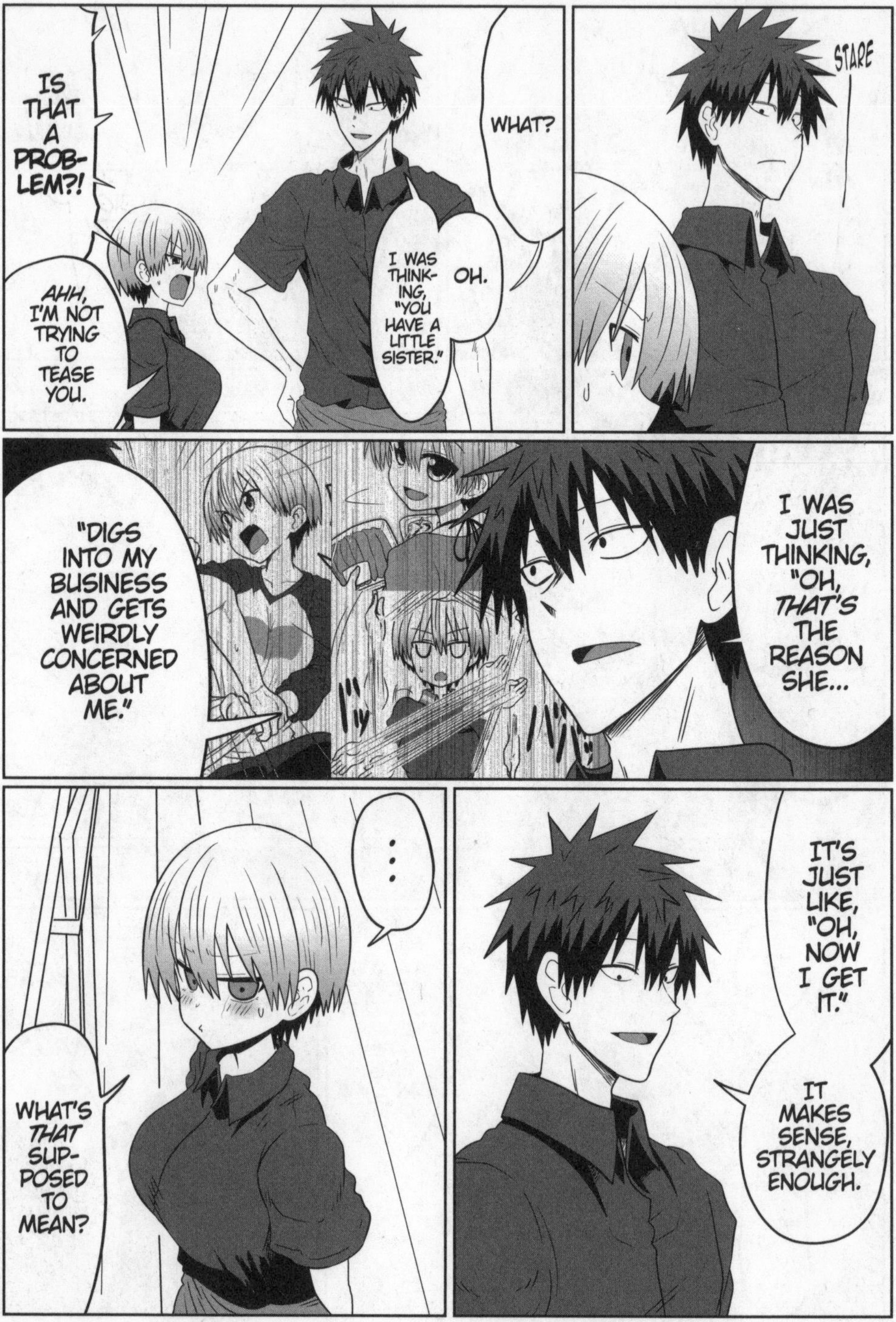
STARE
WHAT?
OH.
I WAS THINKING, "YOU HAVE A LITTLE SISTER."
IS THAT A PROBLEM?!
AHH, I'M NOT TRYING TO TEASE YOU.
I WAS JUST THINKING, "OH, THAT'S THE REASON SHE...
"DIGS INTO MY BUSINESS AND GETS WEIRDLY CONCERNED ABOUT ME."
IT'S JUST LIKE, "OH, NOW I GET IT."
IT MAKES SENSE, STRANGELY ENOUGH.
...
WHAT'S THAT SUPPOSED TO MEAN?

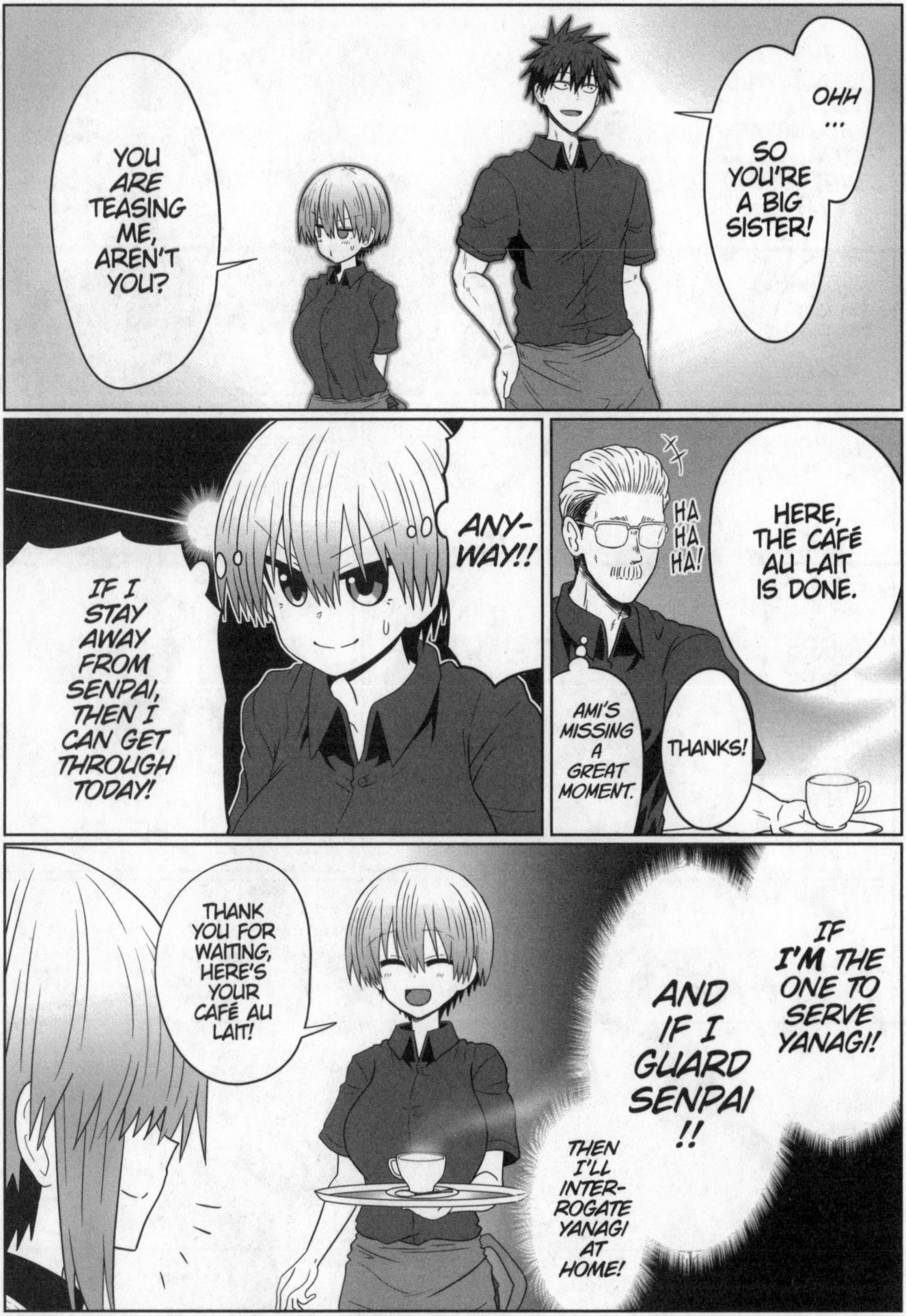
OHH ... SO YOU'RE A BIG SISTER!
YOU ARE TEASING ME, AREN'T YOU?
HERE, THE CAFÉ AU LAIT IS DONE.
HA HA HA!
THANKS!
AMI'S MISSING A GREAT MOMENT.
ANY-WAY!!
IF I STAY AWAY FROM SENPAI, THEN I CAN GET THROUGH TODAY!
IF I'M THE ONE TO SERVE YANAGI!
AND IF I GUARD SENPAI !!
THEN I'LL INTER-ROGATE YANAGI AT HOME!
THANK YOU FOR WAITING, HERE'S YOUR CAFÉ AU LAIT!

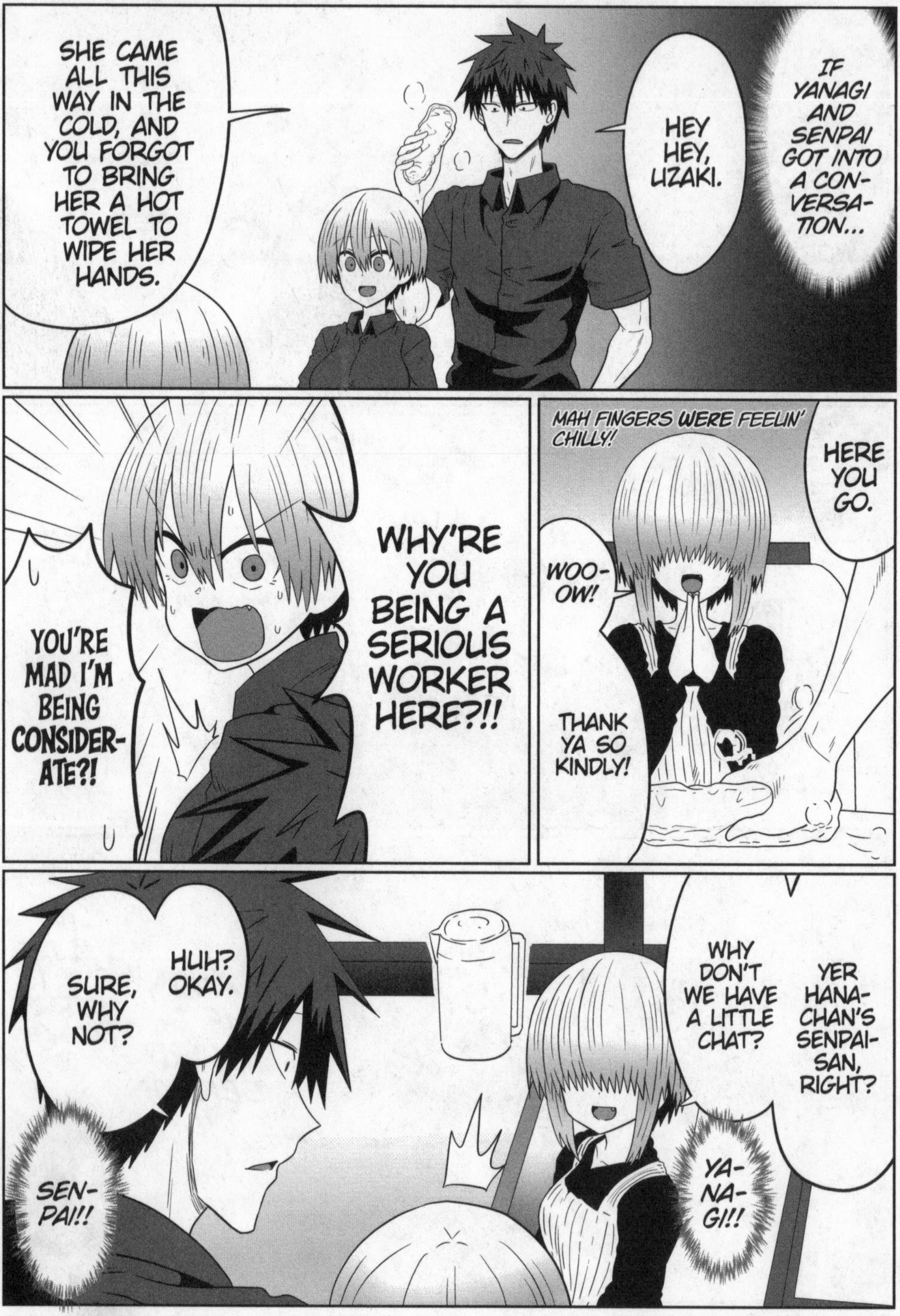
IF YANAGI AND SENPAI GOT INTO A CONVERSATION...
HEY HEY, UZAKI.
SHE CAME ALL THIS WAY IN THE COLD, AND YOU FORGOT TO BRING HER A HOT TOWEL TO WIPE HER HANDS.
HERE YOU GO.
MAH FINGERS WERE FEELIN' CHILLY!
WOOO-OW!
THANK YA SO KINDLY!
WHY'RE YOU BEING A SERIOUS WORKER HERE?!!
YOU'RE MAD I'M BEING CONSIDERATE?!
YER HANA-CHAN'S SENPAI-SAN, RIGHT?
WHY DON'T WE HAVE A LITTLE CHAT?
YA-NA-GI!!
HUH? OKAY.
SURE, WHY NOT?
SEN-PAI!!

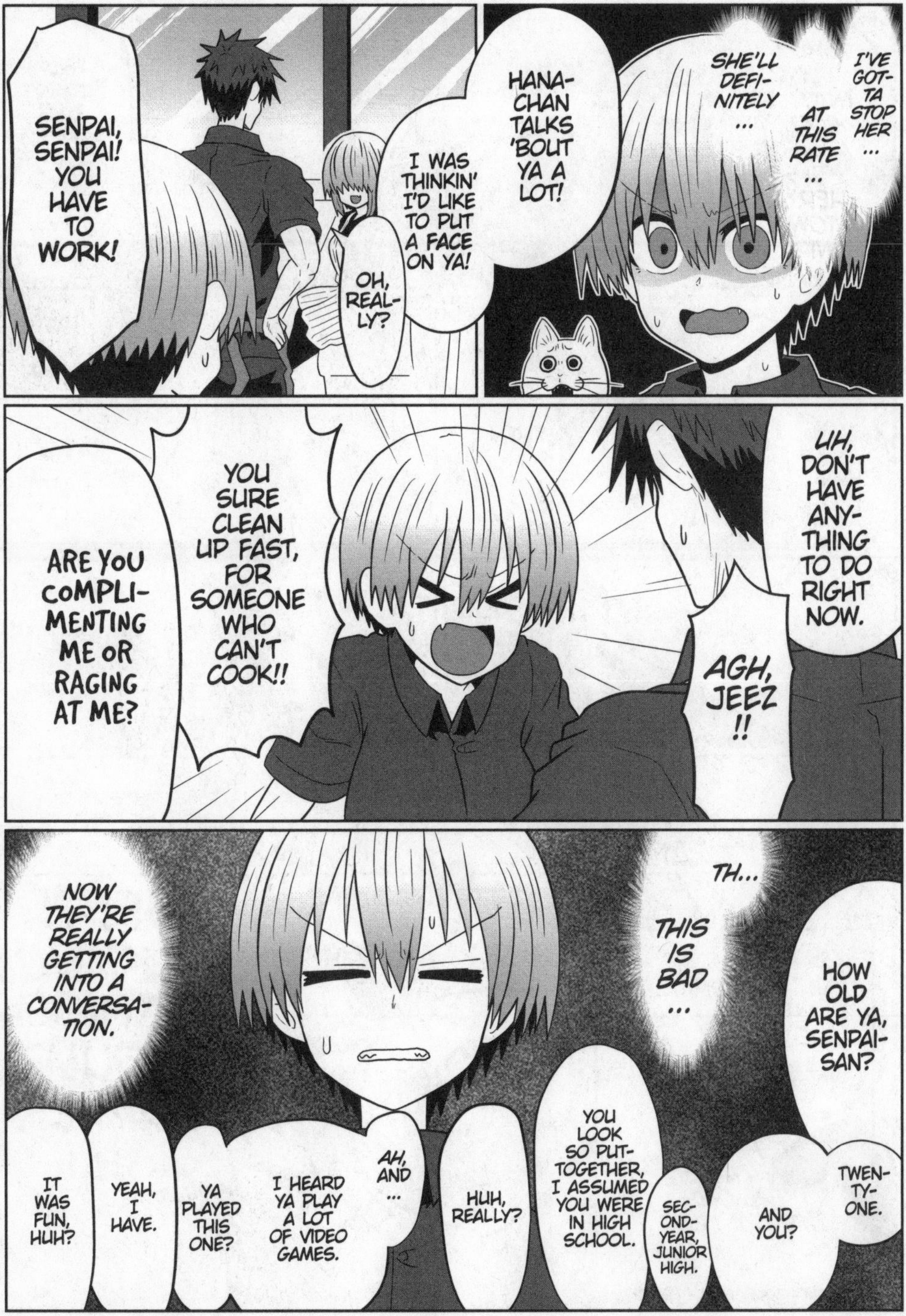
I'VE GOT-TA STOP HER ...
AT THIS RATE ...
SHE'LL DEFI-NITELY ...
HANA-CHAN TALKS 'BOUT YA A LOT!
I WAS THINKIN' I'D LIKE TO PUT A FACE ON YA!
OH, REAL-LY?
SENPAI, SENPAI! YOU HAVE TO WORK!
UH, DON'T HAVE ANY-THING TO DO RIGHT NOW.
AGH, JEEZ!!
YOU SURE CLEAN UP FAST, FOR SOMEONE WHO CAN'T COOK!!
ARE YOU COMPLI-MENTING ME OR RAGING AT ME?
TH...
THIS IS BAD ...
NOW THEY'RE REALLY GETTING INTO A CONVERSA-TION.
HOW OLD ARE YA, SENPAI-SAN?
TWEN-TY-ONE.
AND YOU?
SEC-OND-YEAR, JUNIOR HIGH.
YOU LOOK SO PUT-TOGETHER, I ASSUMED YOU WERE IN HIGH SCHOOL.
HUH, REALLY?
AH, AND ...
I HEARD YA PLAY A LOT OF VIDEO GAMES.
YA PLAYED THIS ONE?
YEAH, I HAVE.
IT WAS FUN, HUH?

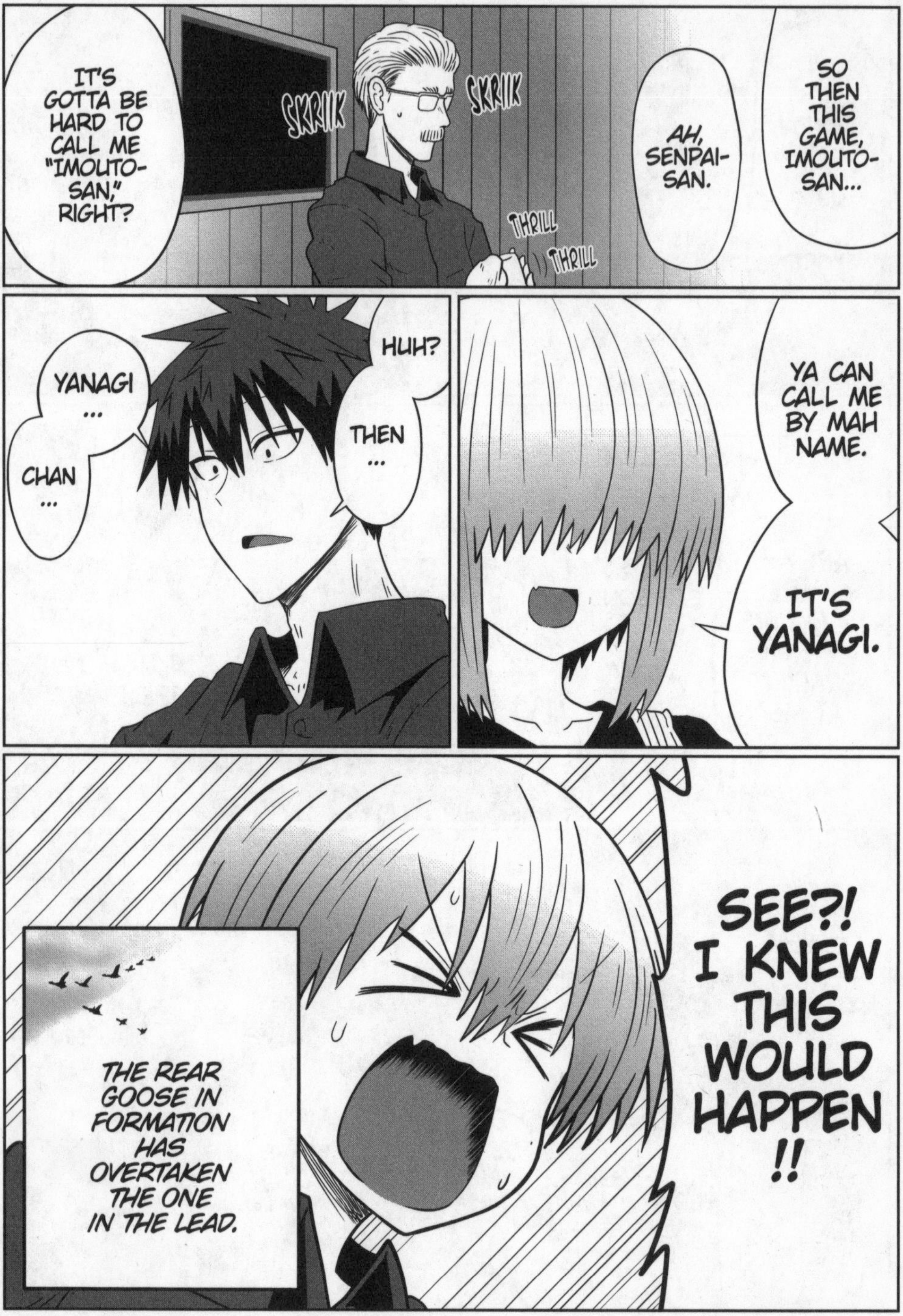
SO THEN THIS GAME, IMOUTO-SAN...
AH, SENPAI-SAN.
SKRIIK
SKRIIK
THRILL
THRILL
IT'S GOTTA BE HARD TO CALL ME "IMOUTO-SAN," RIGHT?
YA CAN CALL ME BY MAH NAME.
IT'S YANAGI.
HUH?
THEN ...
YANAGI ...
CHAN ...
SEE?! I KNEW THIS WOULD HAPPEN !!
THE REAR GOOSE IN FORMATION HAS OVERTAKEN THE ONE IN THE LEAD.

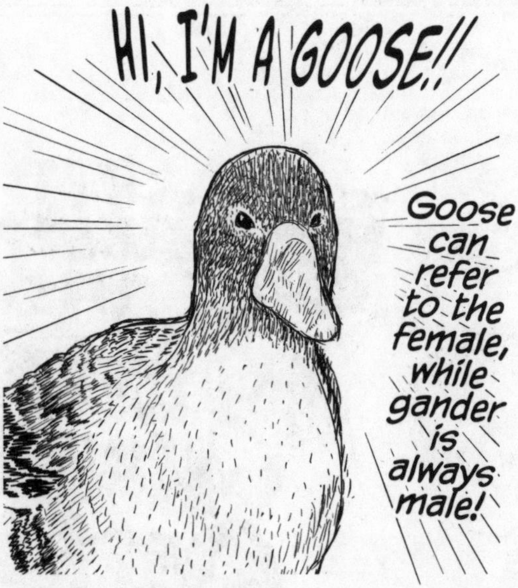
HI, I'M A GOOSE!!
Goose can refer to the female, while gander is always male!

Uzaki-chan Wants to Hang Out!

Chapter 55: The Kouhai and Her Little Sister: Part 2

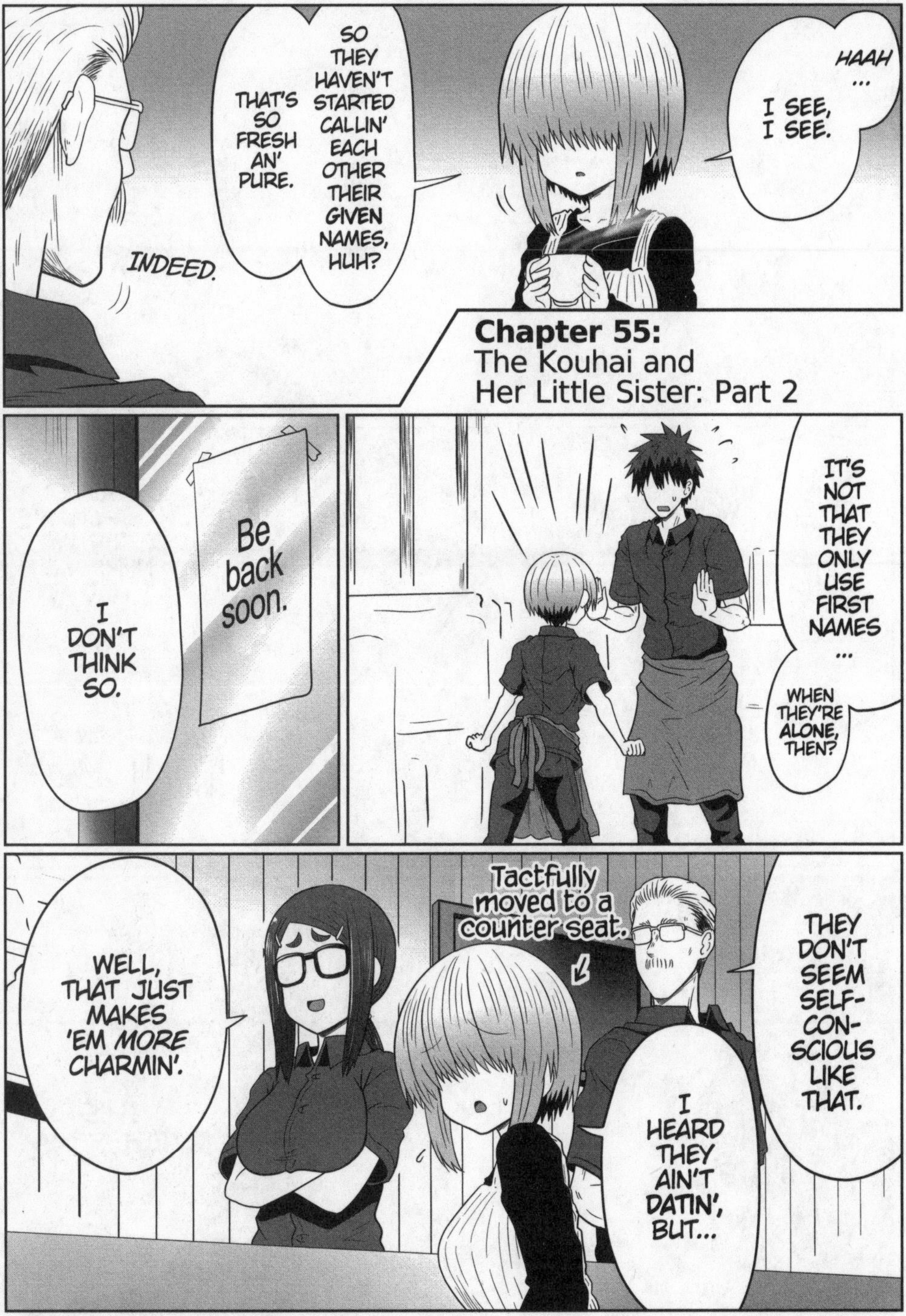
HAAH... I SEE, I SEE.
SO THEY HAVEN'T STARTED CALLIN' EACH OTHER THEIR GIVEN NAMES, HUH?
THAT'S SO FRESH AN' PURE.
INDEED.
IT'S NOT THAT THEY ONLY USE FIRST NAMES...
WHEN THEY'RE ALONE, THEN?
Be back soon.
I DON'T THINK SO.
THEY DON'T SEEM SELF-CONSCIOUS LIKE THAT.
Tactfully moved to a counter seat.
I HEARD THEY AIN'T DATIN', BUT...
WELL, THAT JUST MAKES 'EM *MORE* CHARMIN'.

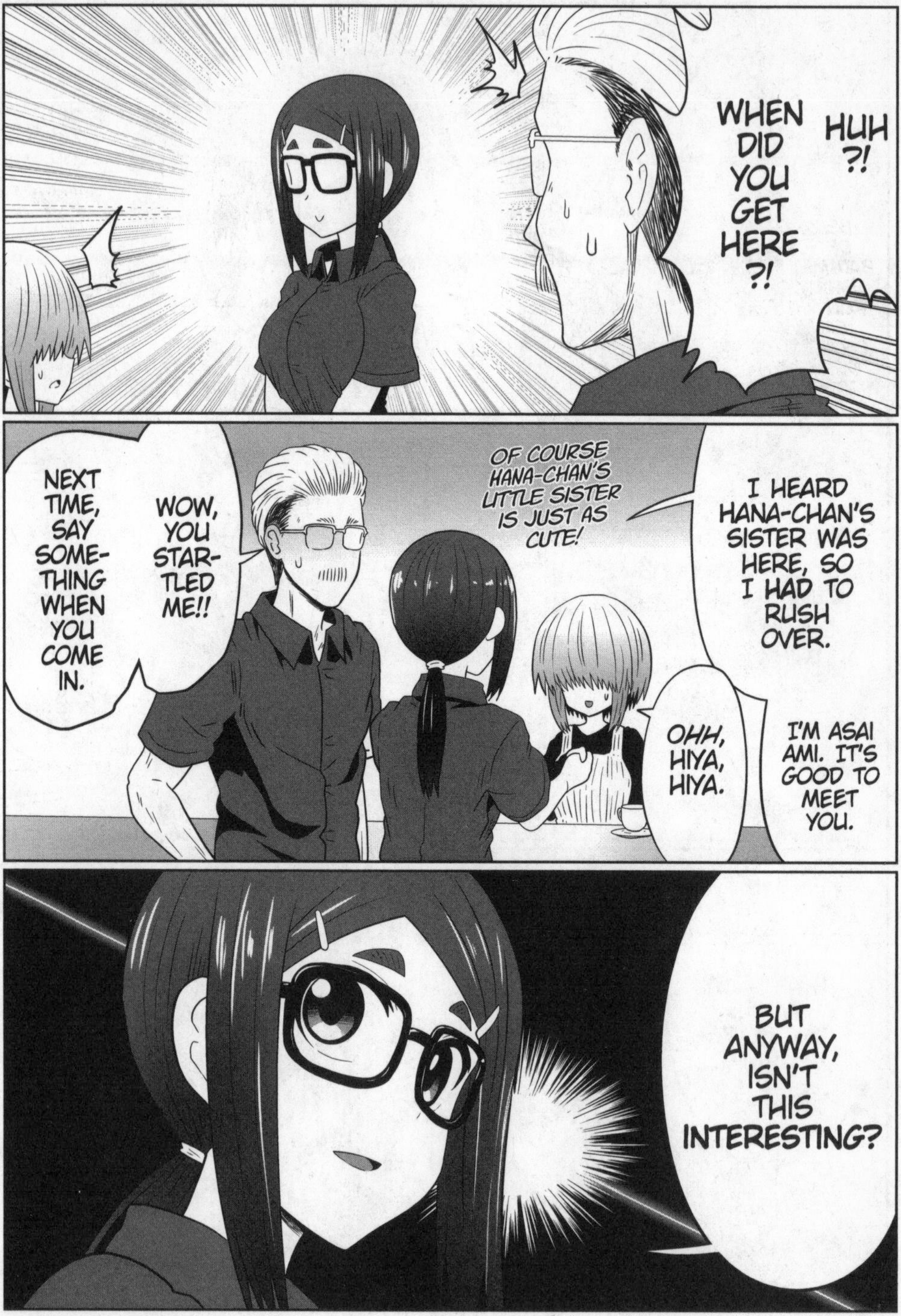
HUH?!
WHEN DID YOU GET HERE?!
I HEARD HANA-CHAN'S SISTER WAS HERE, SO I HAD TO RUSH OVER.
I'M ASAI AMI. IT'S GOOD TO MEET YOU.
OF COURSE HANA-CHAN'S LITTLE SISTER IS JUST AS CUTE!
OHH, HIYA, HIYA.
WOW, YOU STARTLED ME!!
NEXT TIME, SAY SOMETHING WHEN YOU COME IN.
BUT ANYWAY, ISN'T THIS INTERESTING?

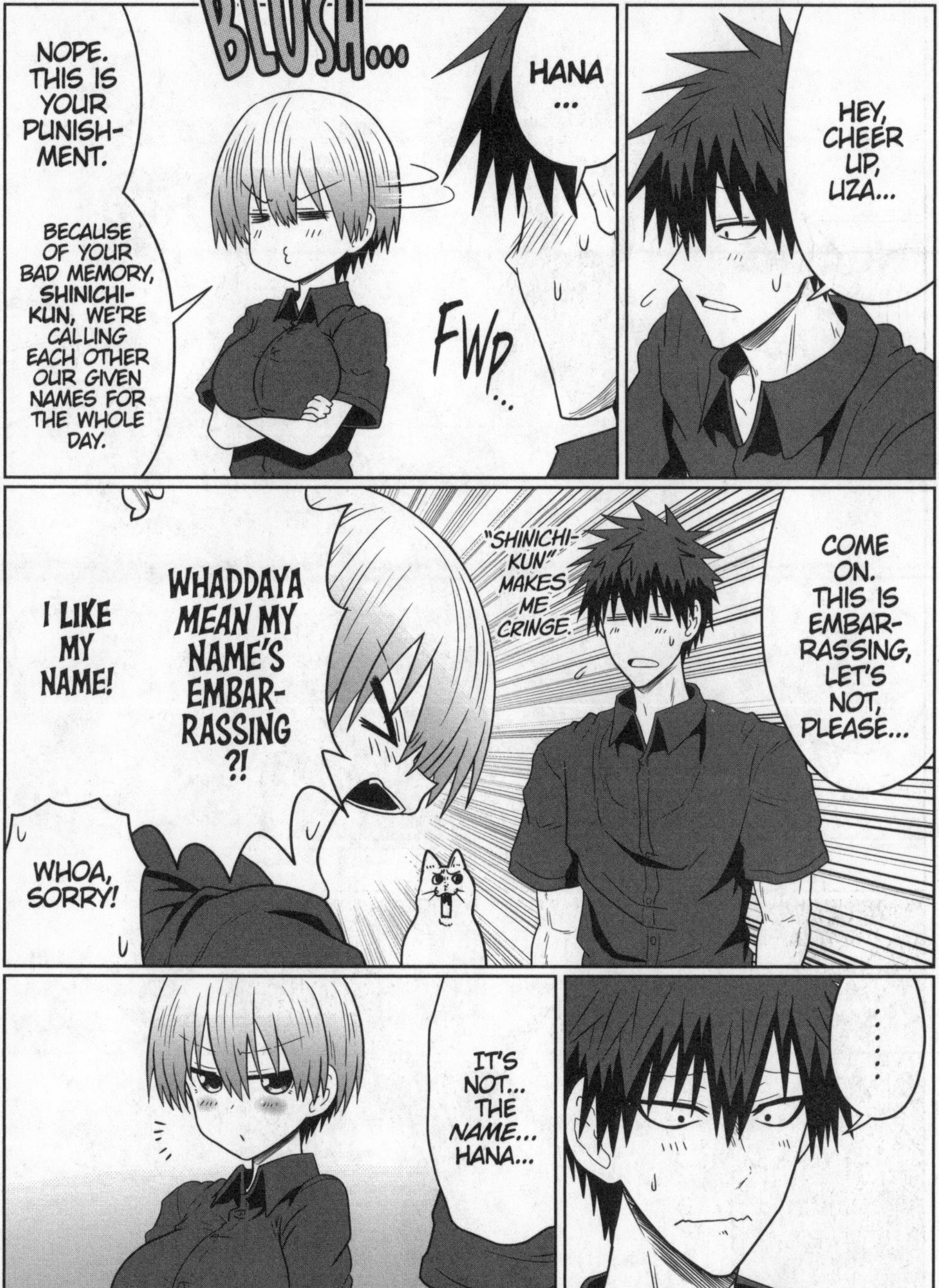
HEY, CHEER UP, UZA...
HANA ...
BLUSH...
NOPE. THIS IS YOUR PUNISH-MENT.
FWP...
BECAUSE OF YOUR BAD MEMORY, SHINICHI-KUN, WE'RE CALLING EACH OTHER OUR GIVEN NAMES FOR THE WHOLE DAY.
COME ON. THIS IS EMBAR-RASSING, LET'S NOT, PLEASE...
"SHINICHI-KUN" MAKES ME CRINGE.
WHADDAYA MEAN MY NAME'S EMBAR-RASSING?!
I LIKE MY NAME!
WHOA, SORRY!
......
IT'S NOT... THE *NAME*... HANA...

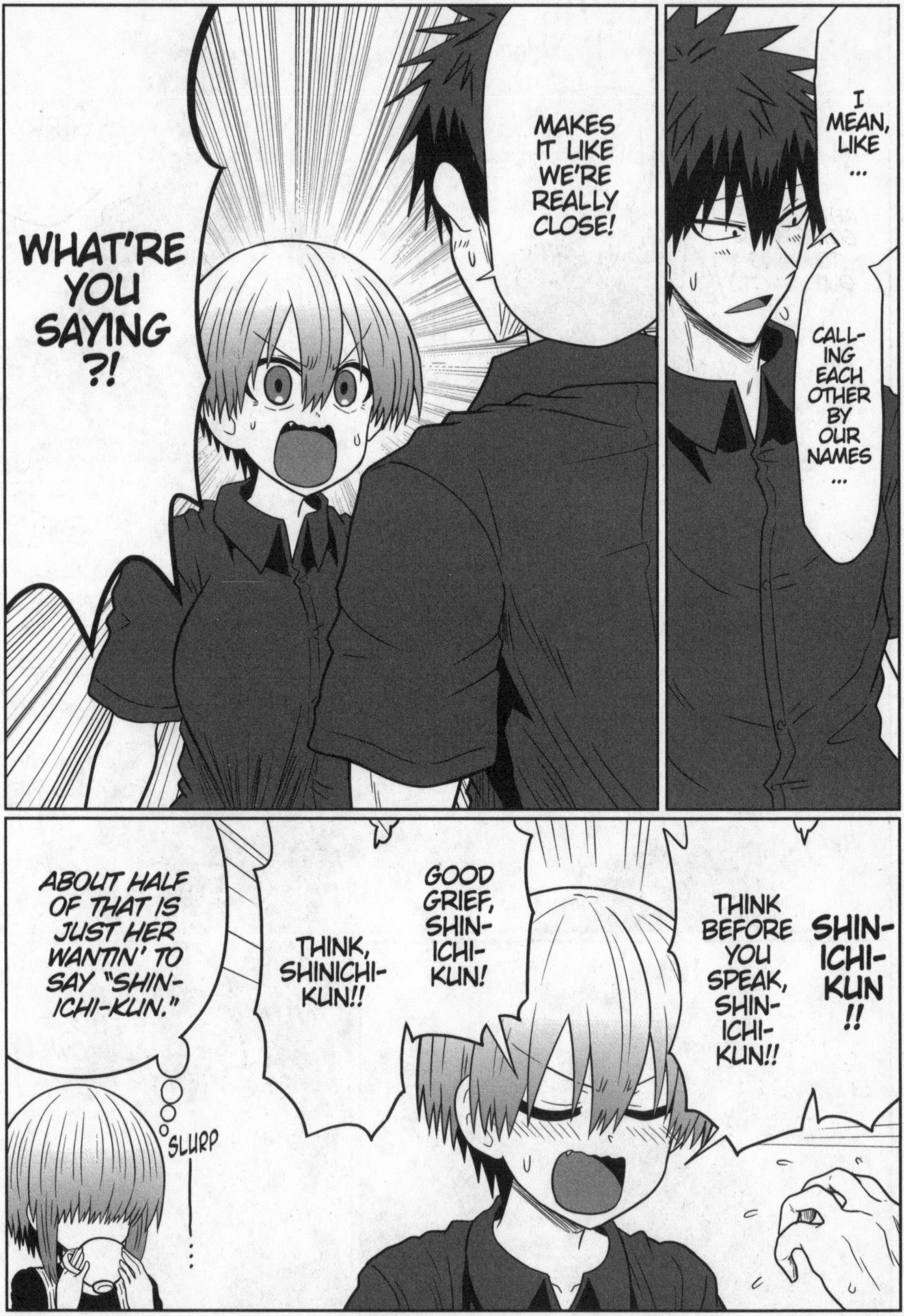
I MEAN, LIKE ...
CALLING EACH OTHER BY OUR NAMES ...
MAKES IT LIKE WE'RE REALLY CLOSE!
WHAT'RE YOU SAYING ?!
SHIN-ICHI-KUN !!
THINK BEFORE YOU SPEAK, SHIN-ICHI-KUN!!
GOOD GRIEF, SHIN-ICHI-KUN!
THINK, SHINICHI-KUN!!
ABOUT HALF OF THAT IS JUST HER WANTIN' TO SAY "SHIN-ICHI-KUN."
SLURP

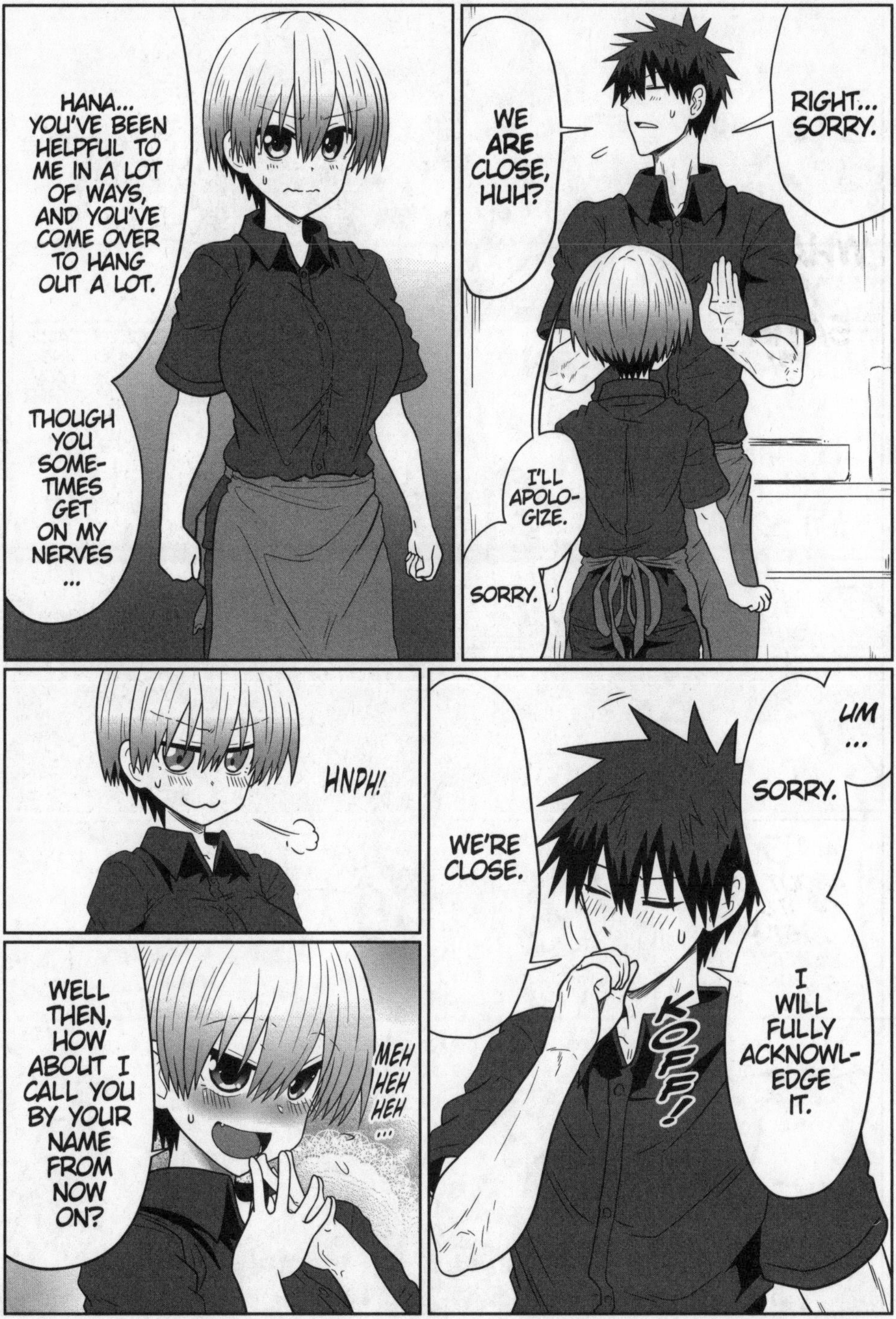
RIGHT... SORRY.
WE ARE CLOSE, HUH?
I'LL APOLOGIZE.
SORRY.
HANA... YOU'VE BEEN HELPFUL TO ME IN A LOT OF WAYS, AND YOU'VE COME OVER TO HANG OUT A LOT.
THOUGH YOU SOME-TIMES GET ON MY NERVES ...
UM ...
SORRY.
WE'RE CLOSE.
I WILL FULLY ACKNOWL-EDGE IT.
KOFF!
HNPH!
WELL THEN, HOW ABOUT I CALL YOU BY YOUR NAME FROM NOW ON?
MEH HEH HEH ...

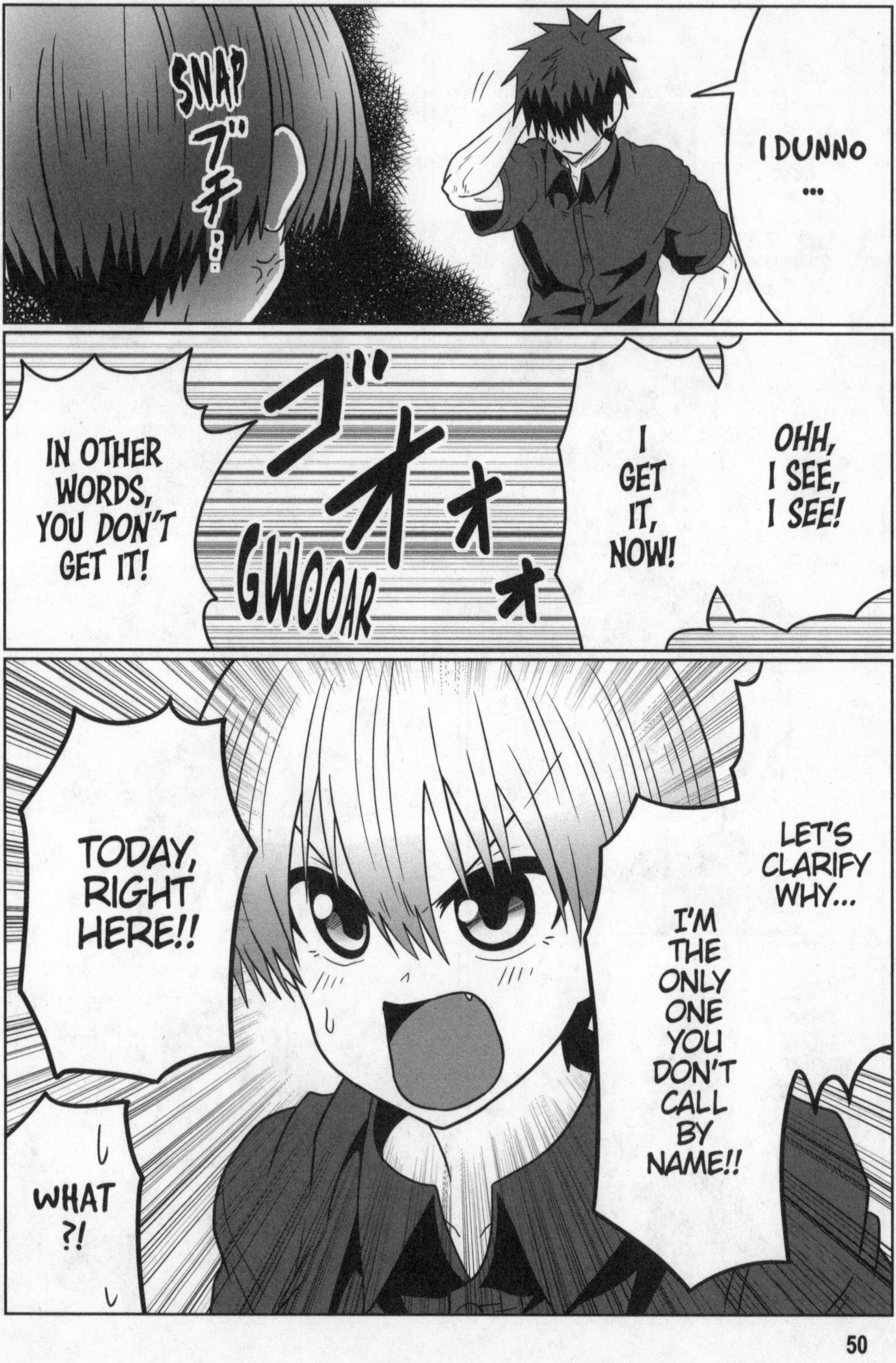
I DUNNO ...
SNAP
ブチ!!
OHH, I SEE, I SEE!
I GET IT, NOW!
ゴオォォ
GWOOAR
IN OTHER WORDS, YOU DON'T GET IT!
LET'S CLARIFY WHY...
I'M THE ONLY ONE YOU DON'T CALL BY NAME!!
TODAY, RIGHT HERE!!
WHAT?!

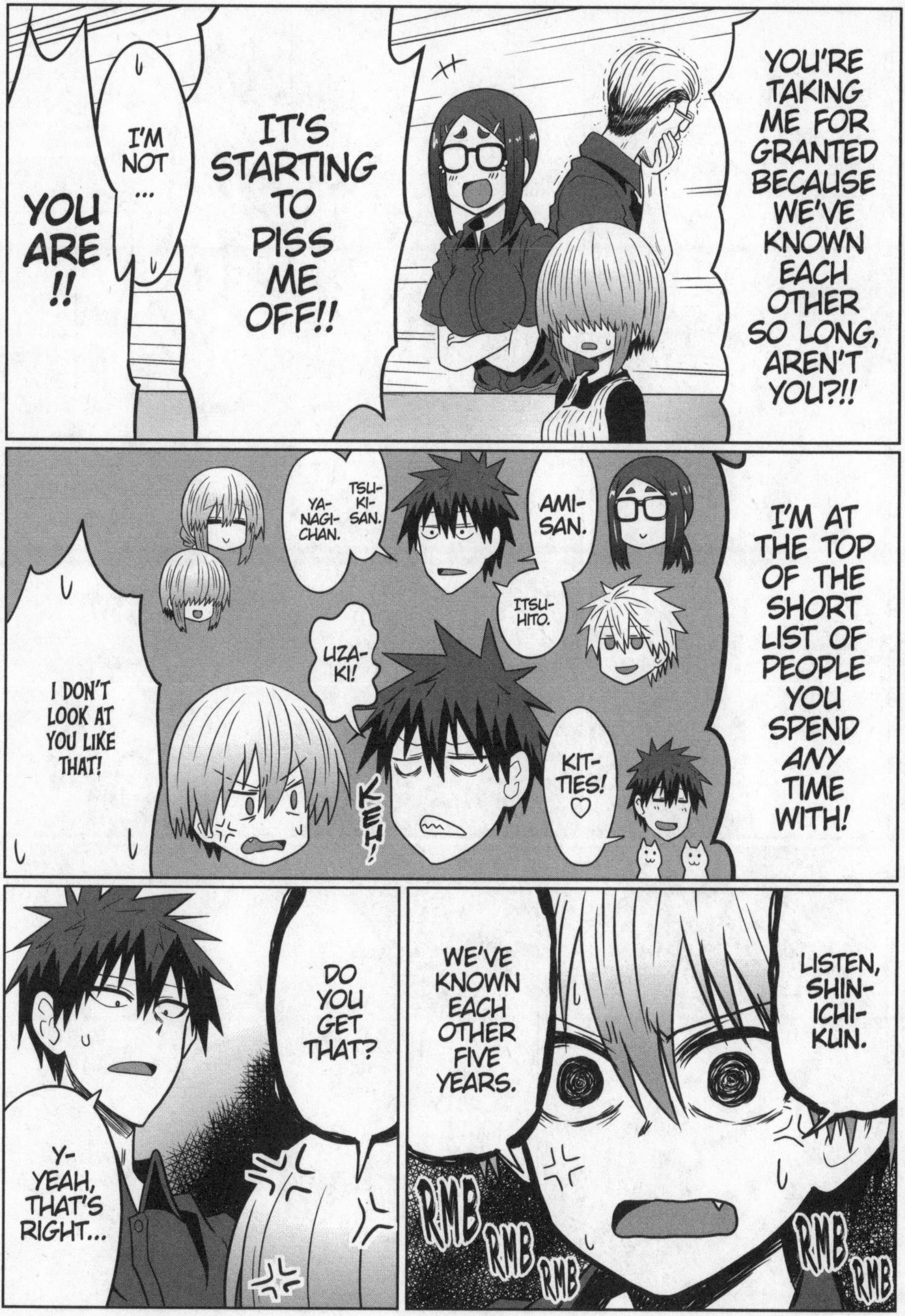
YOU'RE TAKING ME FOR GRANTED BECAUSE WE'VE KNOWN EACH OTHER SO LONG, AREN'T YOU?!!
IT'S STARTING TO PISS ME OFF!!
I'M NOT ...
YOU ARE !!
I'M AT THE TOP OF THE SHORT LIST OF PEOPLE YOU SPEND ANY TIME WITH!
AMI-SAN.
TSU-KI-SAN.
YA-NAGI-CHAN.
ITSU-HITO.
UZA-KI!
KEH!
KIT-TIES! ♡
I DON'T LOOK AT YOU LIKE THAT!
LISTEN, SHIN-ICHI-KUN.
WE'VE KNOWN EACH OTHER FIVE YEARS.
RMB RMB RMB RMB RMB
DO YOU GET THAT?
Y-YEAH, THAT'S RIGHT...

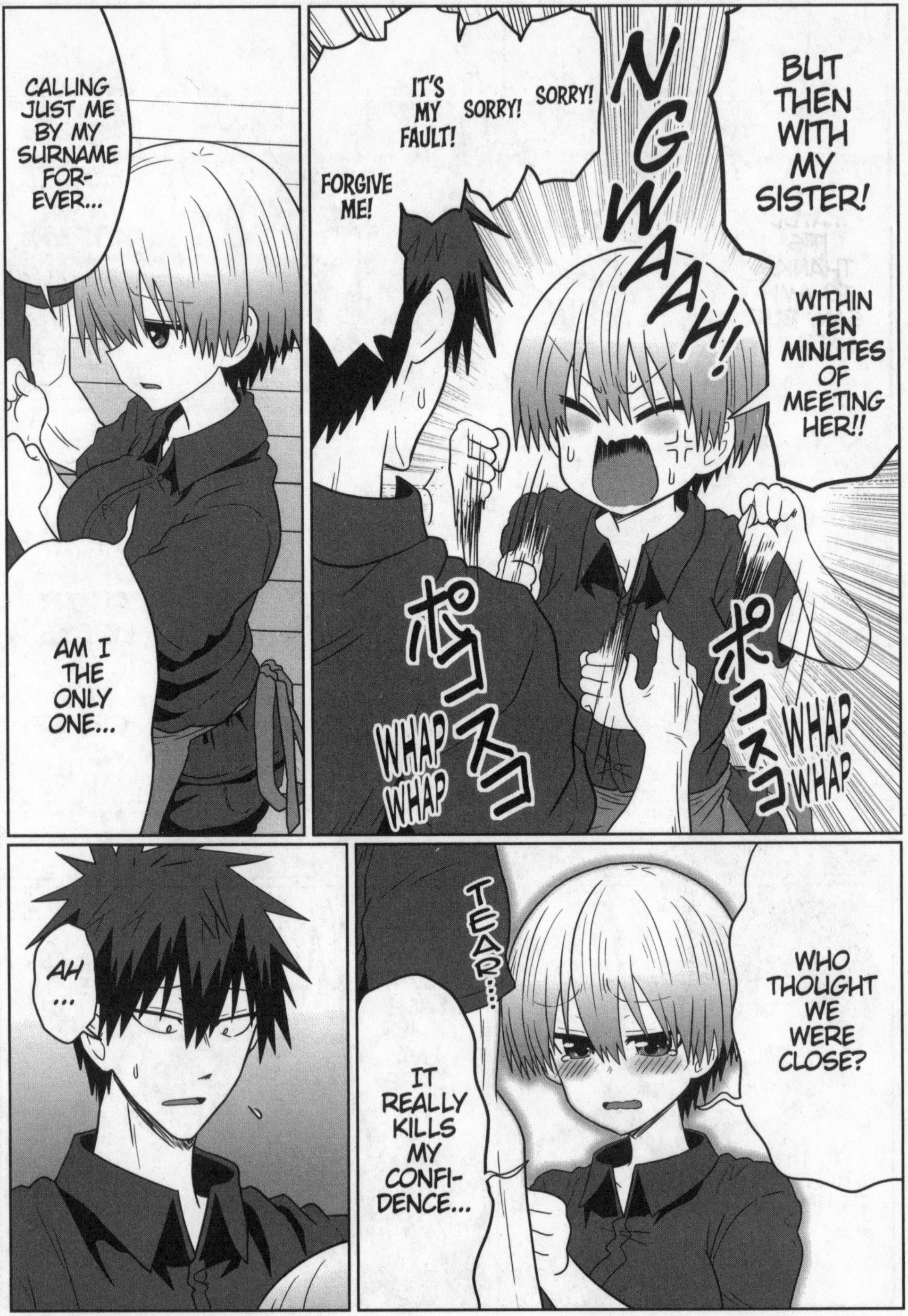
BUT THEN WITH MY SISTER!
WITHIN TEN MINUTES OF MEETING HER!!
NGWAAH!
SORRY!
SORRY!
IT'S MY FAULT!
FORGIVE ME!
ポコスコ
WHAP WHAP
ポコスコ
WHAP WHAP
CALLING JUST ME BY MY SURNAME FOR-EVER...
AM I THE ONLY ONE...
WHO THOUGHT WE WERE CLOSE?
IT REALLY KILLS MY CONFI-DENCE...
TEAR...
AH...

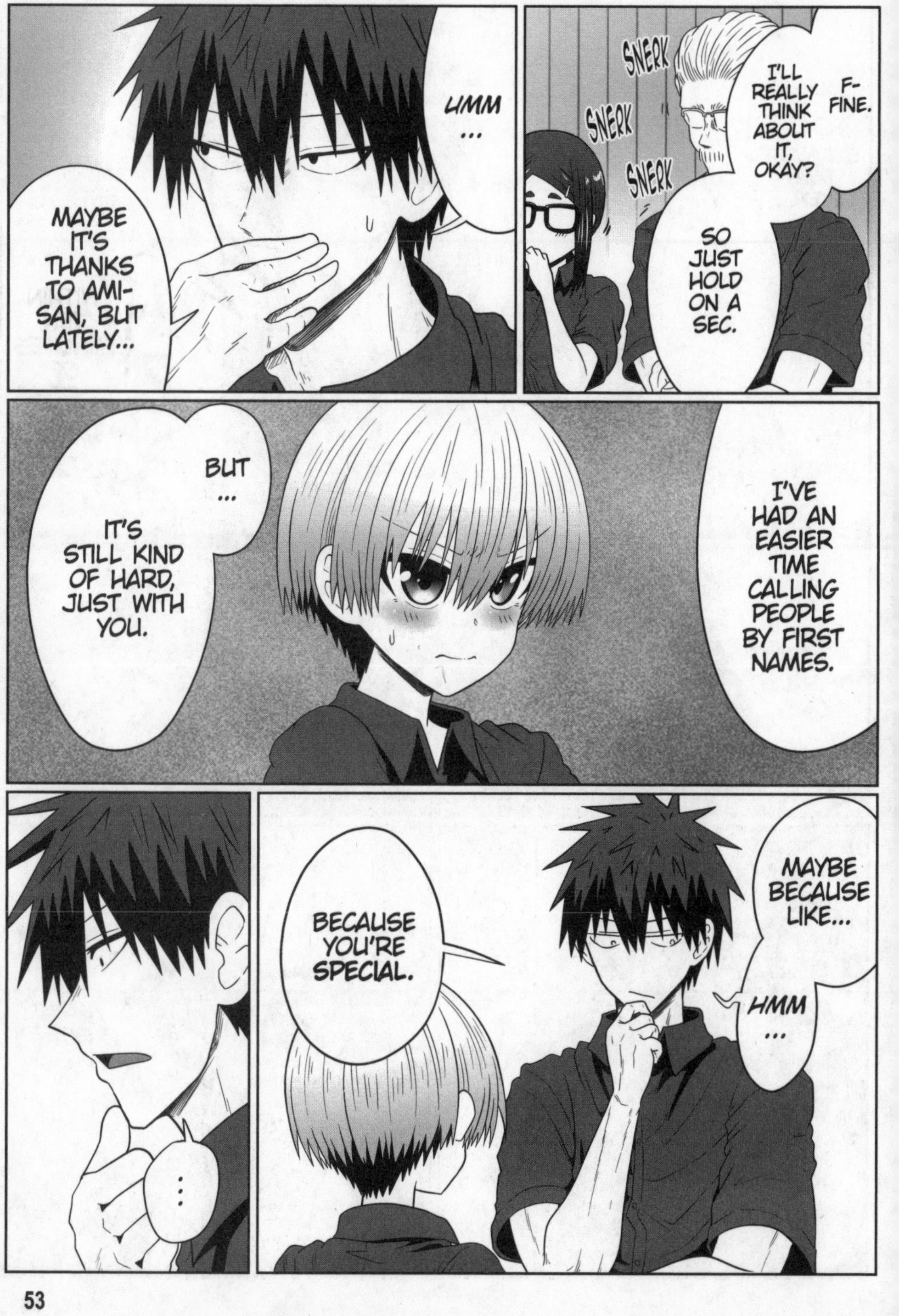
F-FINE.
I'LL REALLY THINK ABOUT IT, OKAY?
SNERK
SNERK
SNERK
SO JUST HOLD ON A SEC.
UMM ...
MAYBE IT'S THANKS TO AMI-SAN, BUT LATELY...
I'VE HAD AN EASIER TIME CALLING PEOPLE BY FIRST NAMES.
BUT ...
IT'S STILL KIND OF HARD, JUST WITH YOU.
MAYBE BECAUSE LIKE...
HMM ...
BECAUSE YOU'RE SPECIAL.
...

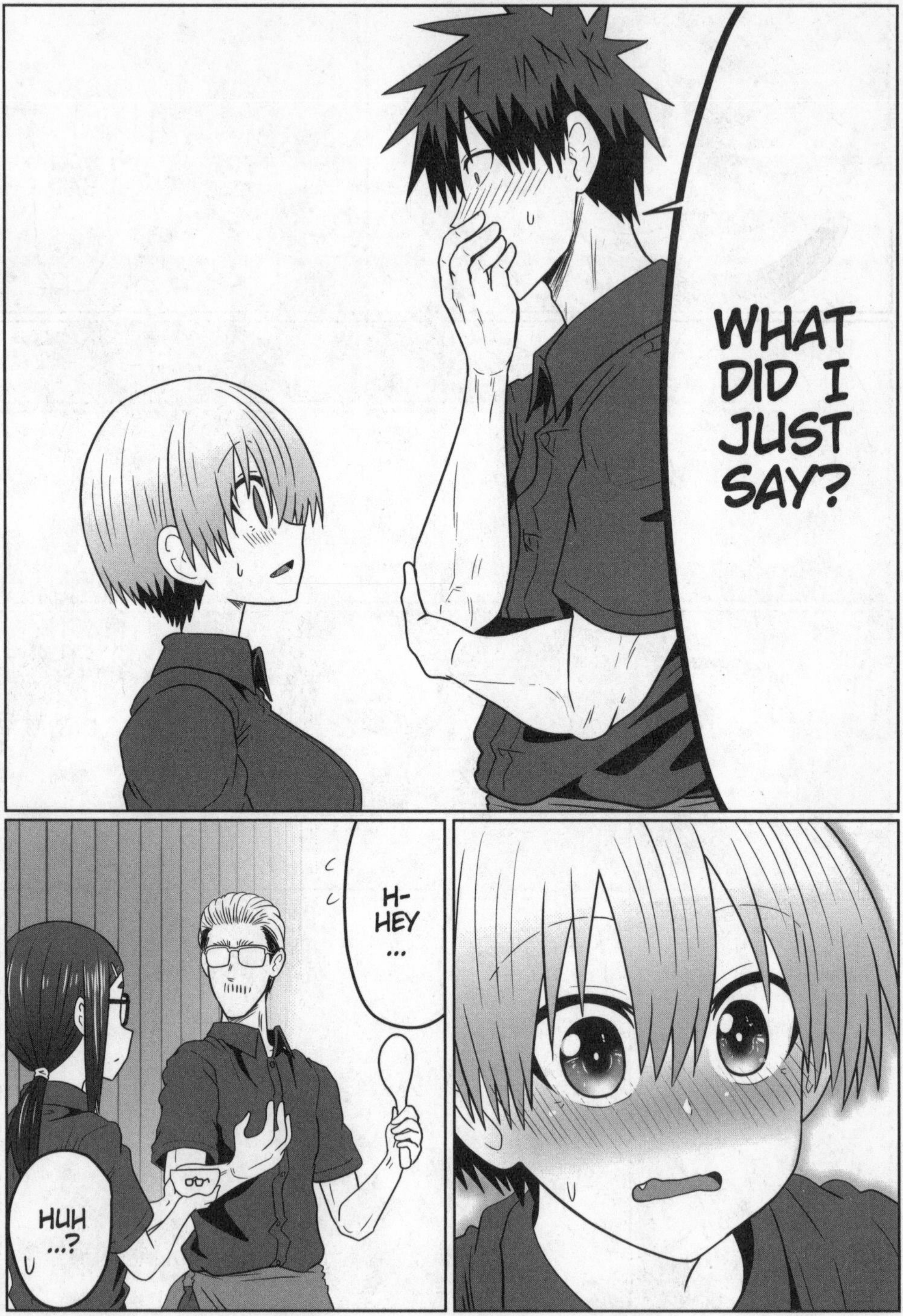
WHAT DID I JUST SAY?
H- HEY ...
HUH ...?

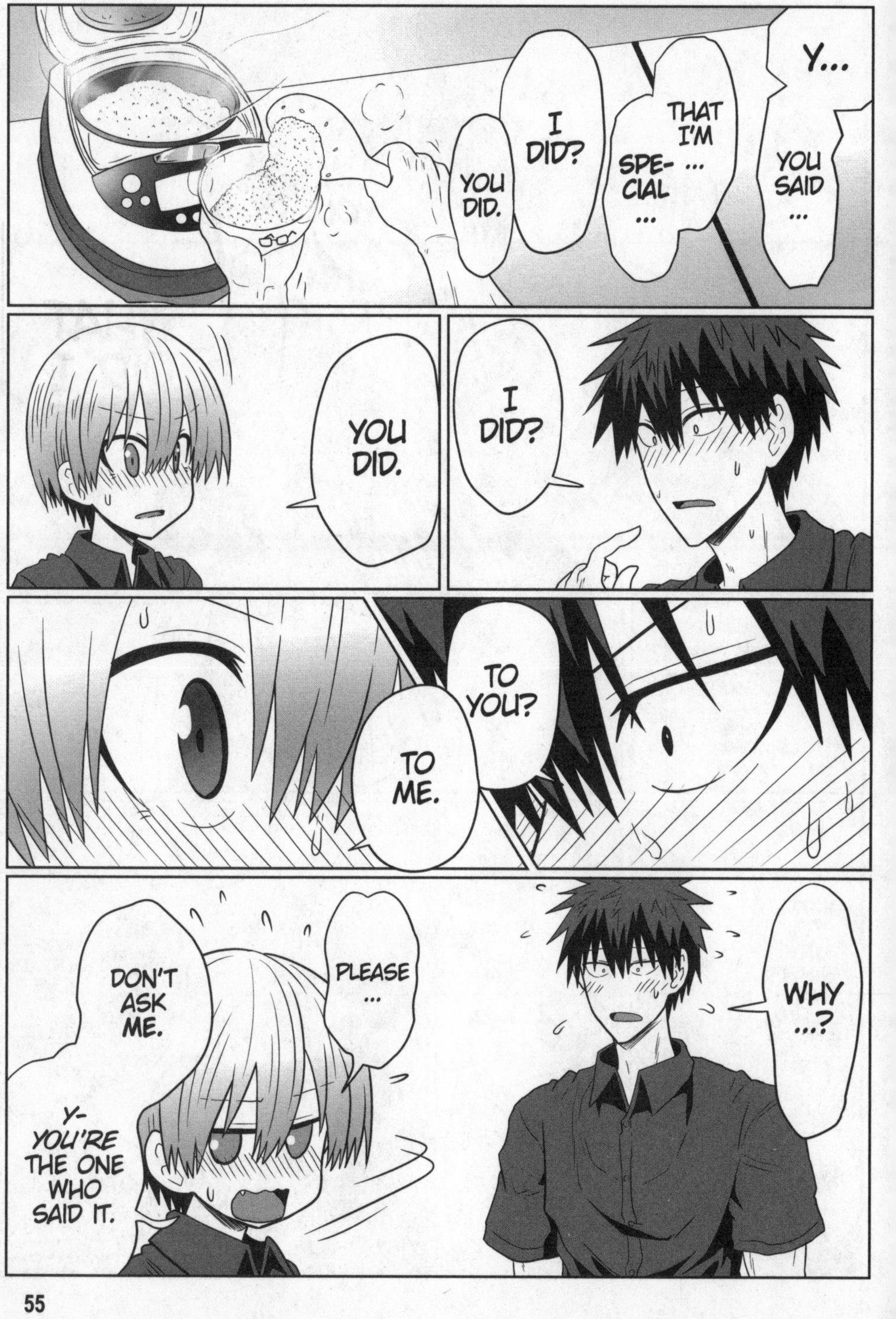

Y... YOU SAID ...
THAT I'M ... SPE-CIAL ...
I DID?
YOU DID.
I DID?
YOU DID.
TO YOU?
TO ME.
WHY ...?
PLEASE ...
DON'T ASK ME.
Y- YOU'RE THE ONE WHO SAID IT.

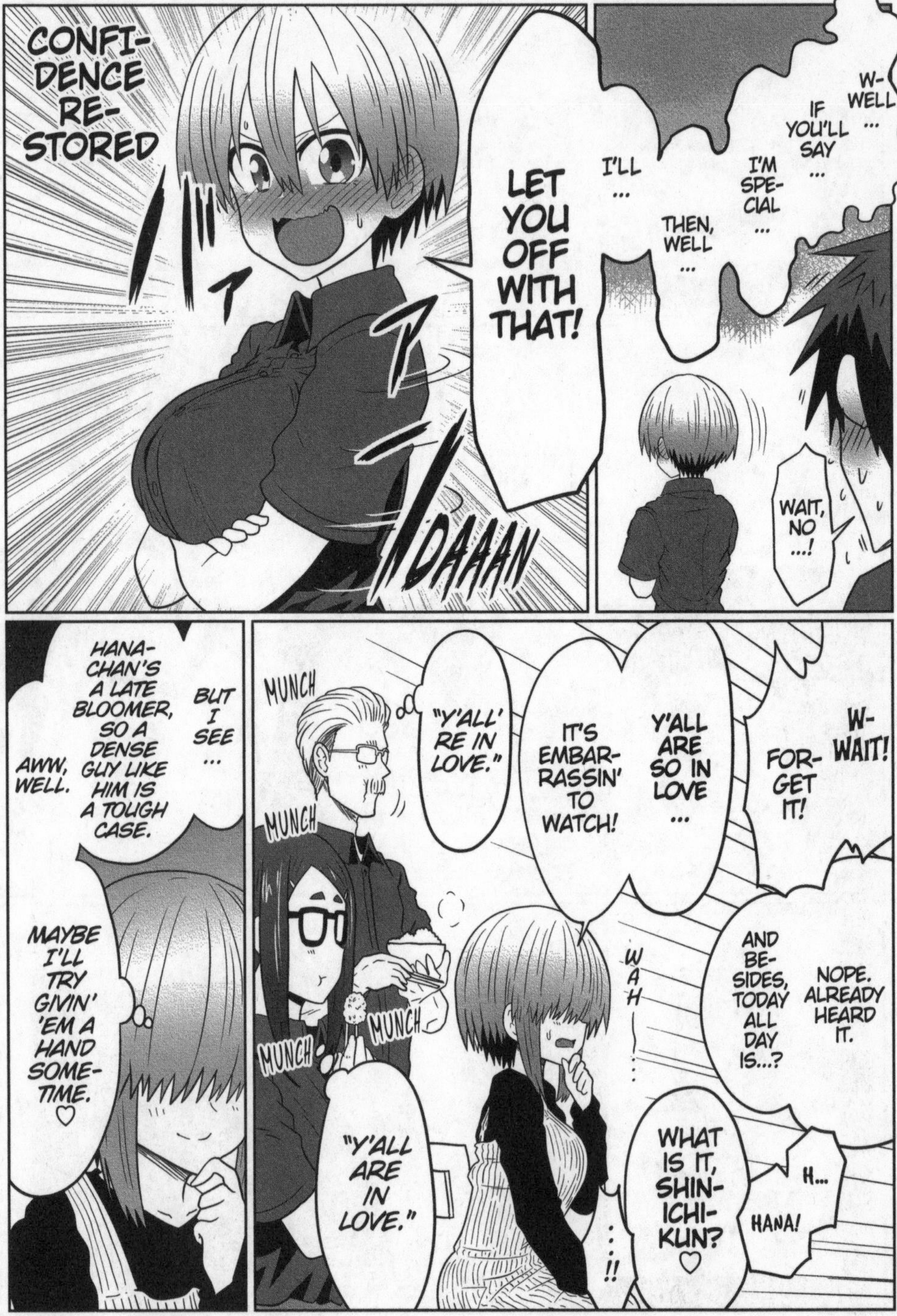
W-WELL...
IF YOU'LL SAY...
I'M SPECIAL...
THEN, WELL...
I'LL...
WAIT, NO...!
LET YOU OFF WITH THAT!
CONFIDENCE RESTORED
DAAAN
W-WAIT!
FORGET IT!
Y'ALL ARE SO IN LOVE...
IT'S EMBARRASSIN' TO WATCH!
"Y'ALL'RE IN LOVE."
MUNCH
MUNCH
NOPE. ALREADY HEARD IT.
AND BESIDES, TODAY ALL DAY IS...?
WAH......
MUNCH
MUNCH
H...
HANA!
WHAT IS IT, SHINICHI-KUN? ♡
...!!
"Y'ALL ARE IN LOVE."
BUT I SEE...
HANA-CHAN'S A LATE BLOOMER, SO A DENSE GUY LIKE HIM IS A TOUGH CASE.
AWW, WELL.
MAYBE I'LL TRY GIVIN' 'EM A HAND SOMETIME. ♡

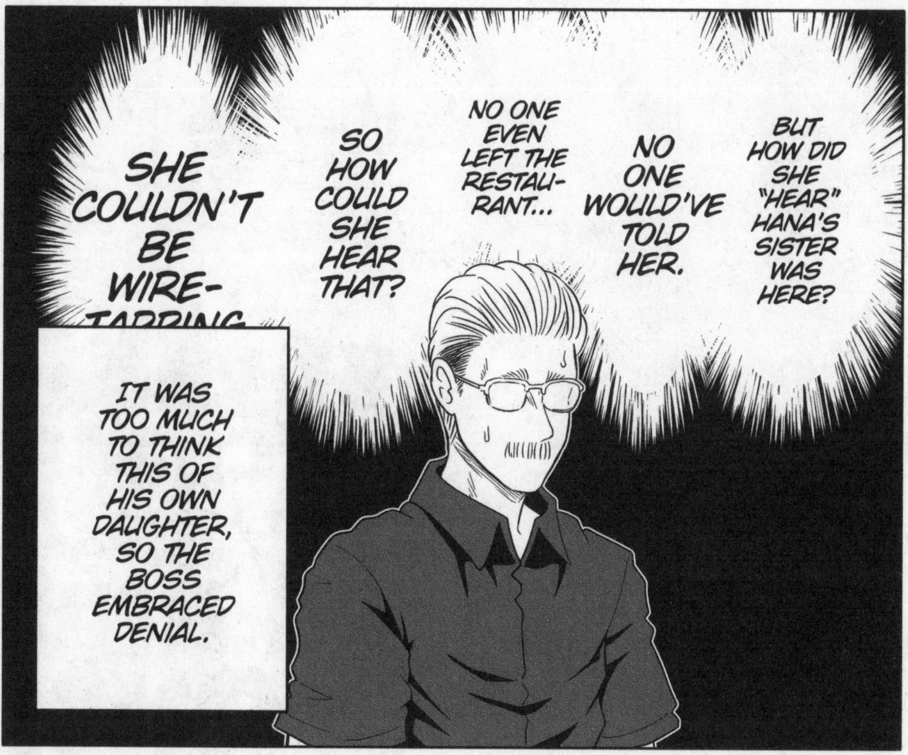
BUT HOW DID SHE "HEAR" HANA'S SISTER WAS HERE?
NO ONE WOULD'VE TOLD HER.
NO ONE EVEN LEFT THE RESTAU-RANT...
SO HOW COULD SHE HEAR THAT?
SHE COULDN'T BE WIRE-
IT WAS TOO MUCH TO THINK THIS OF HIS OWN DAUGHTER, SO THE BOSS EMBRACED DENIAL.

Uzaki-chan Wants to Hang Out!

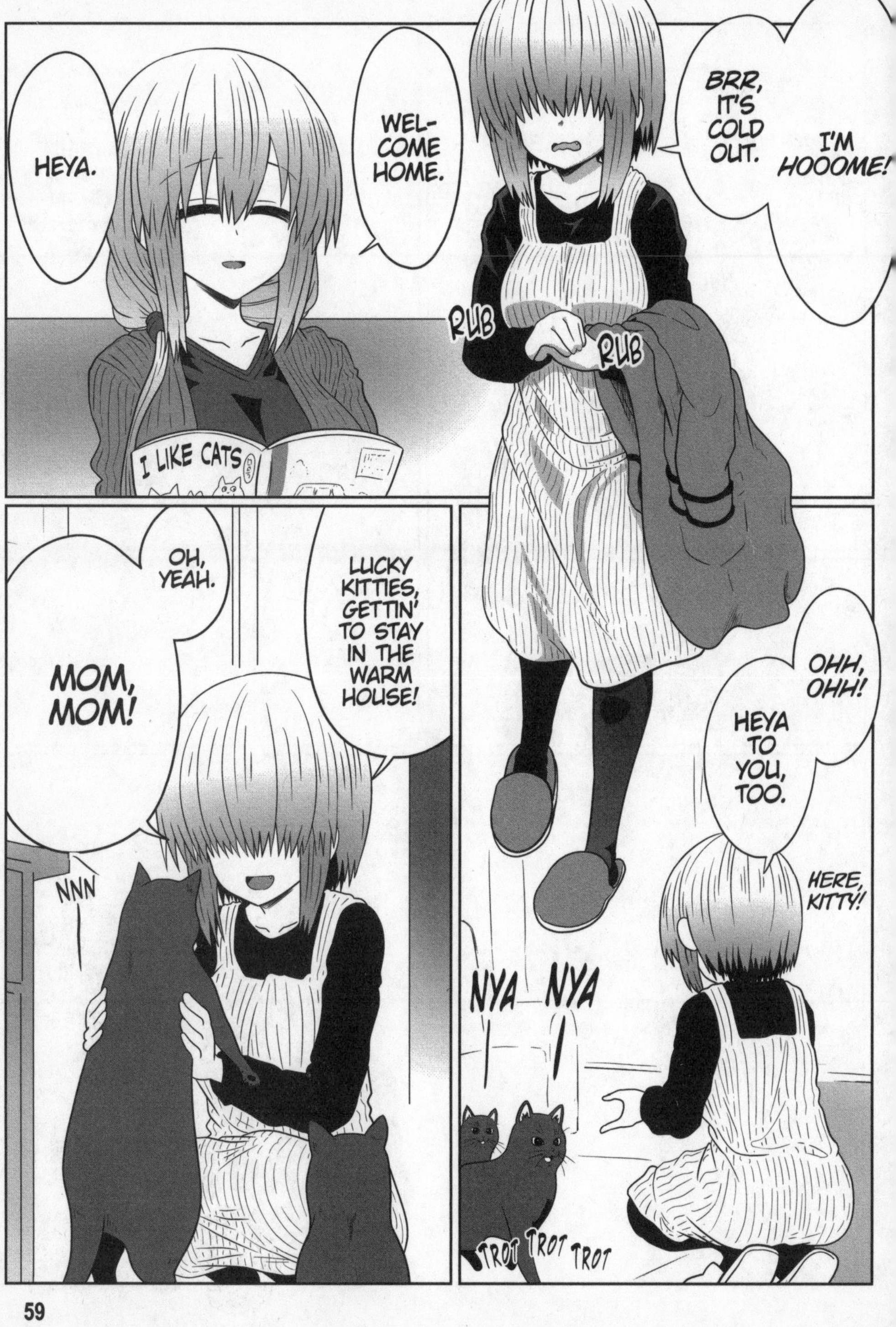
I'M HOOOME!
BRR, IT'S COLD OUT.
RUB
RUB
WEL-COME HOME.
HEYA.
I LIKE CATS
HERE, KITTY!
OHH, OHH!
HEYA TO YOU, TOO.
NYA NYA
TROT TROT TROT
LUCKY KITTIES, GETTIN' TO STAY IN THE WARM HOUSE!
OH, YEAH.
MOM, MOM!
NNN

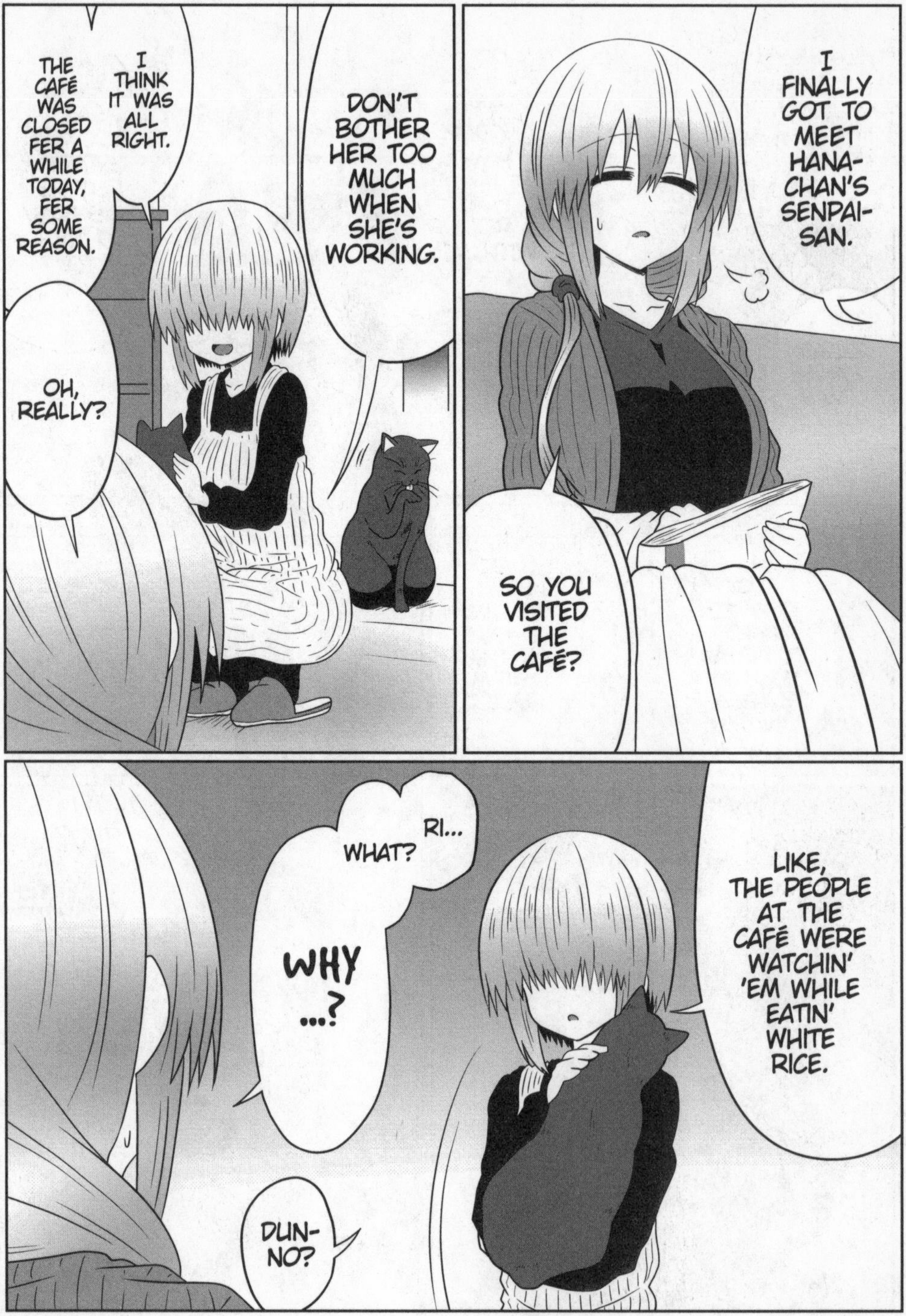
I FINALLY GOT TO MEET HANA-CHAN'S SENPAI-SAN.
SO YOU VISITED THE CAFÉ?
DON'T BOTHER HER TOO MUCH WHEN SHE'S WORKING.
I THINK IT WAS ALL RIGHT.
THE CAFÉ WAS CLOSED FER A WHILE TODAY, FER SOME REASON.
OH, REALLY?
LIKE, THE PEOPLE AT THE CAFÉ WERE WATCHIN' 'EM WHILE EATIN' WHITE RICE.
RI... WHAT?
WHY ...?
DUN-NO?

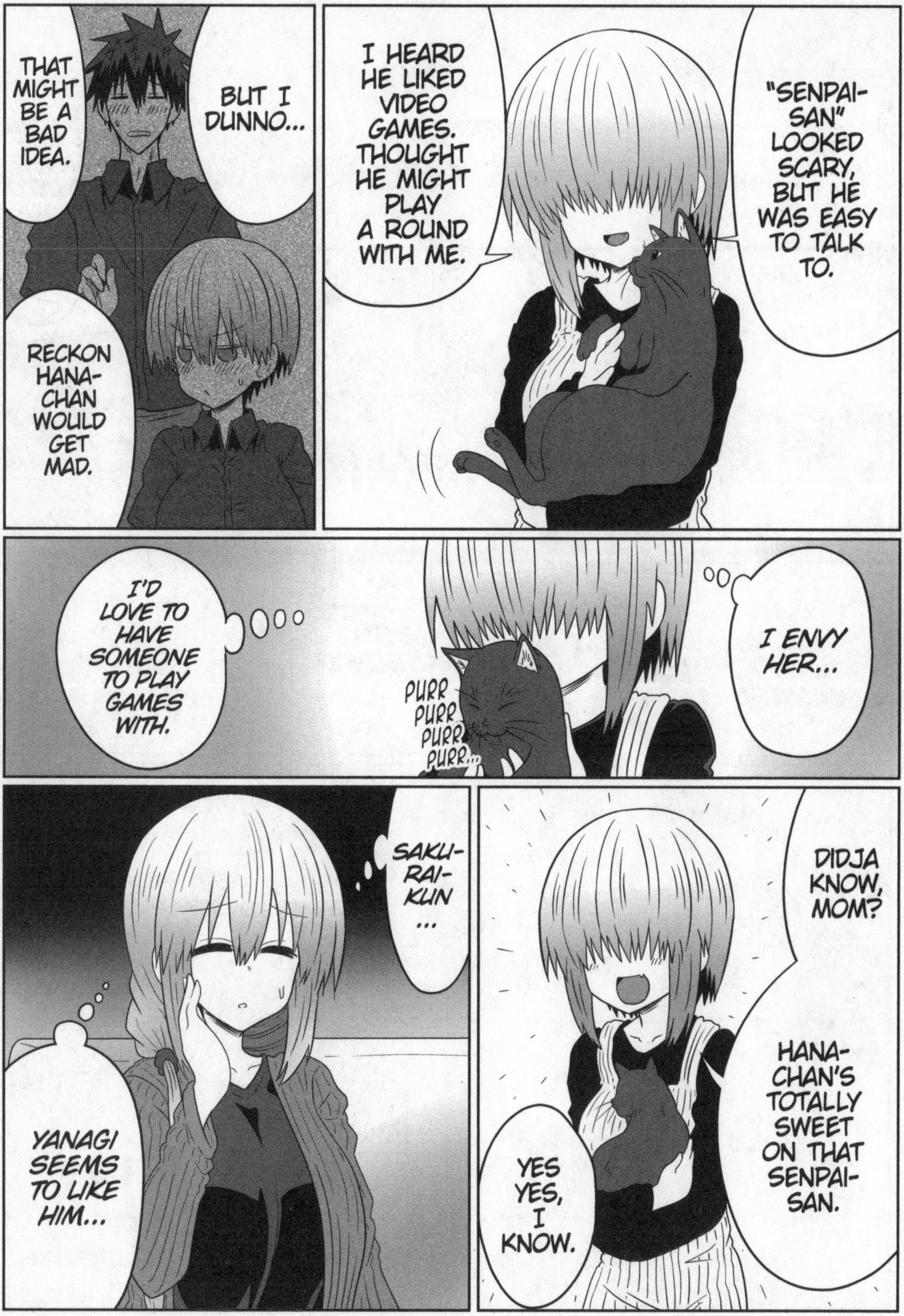
"SENPAI-SAN" LOOKED SCARY, BUT HE WAS EASY TO TALK TO.
I HEARD HE LIKED VIDEO GAMES. THOUGHT HE MIGHT PLAY A ROUND WITH ME.
BUT I DUNNO...
THAT MIGHT BE A BAD IDEA.
RECKON HANA-CHAN WOULD GET MAD.
I ENVY HER...
PURR PURR PURR PURR...
I'D LOVE TO HAVE SOMEONE TO PLAY GAMES WITH.
DIDJA KNOW, MOM?
HANA-CHAN'S TOTALLY SWEET ON THAT SENPAI-SAN.
YES YES, I KNOW.
SAKURAI-KUN...
YANAGI SEEMS TO LIKE HIM...

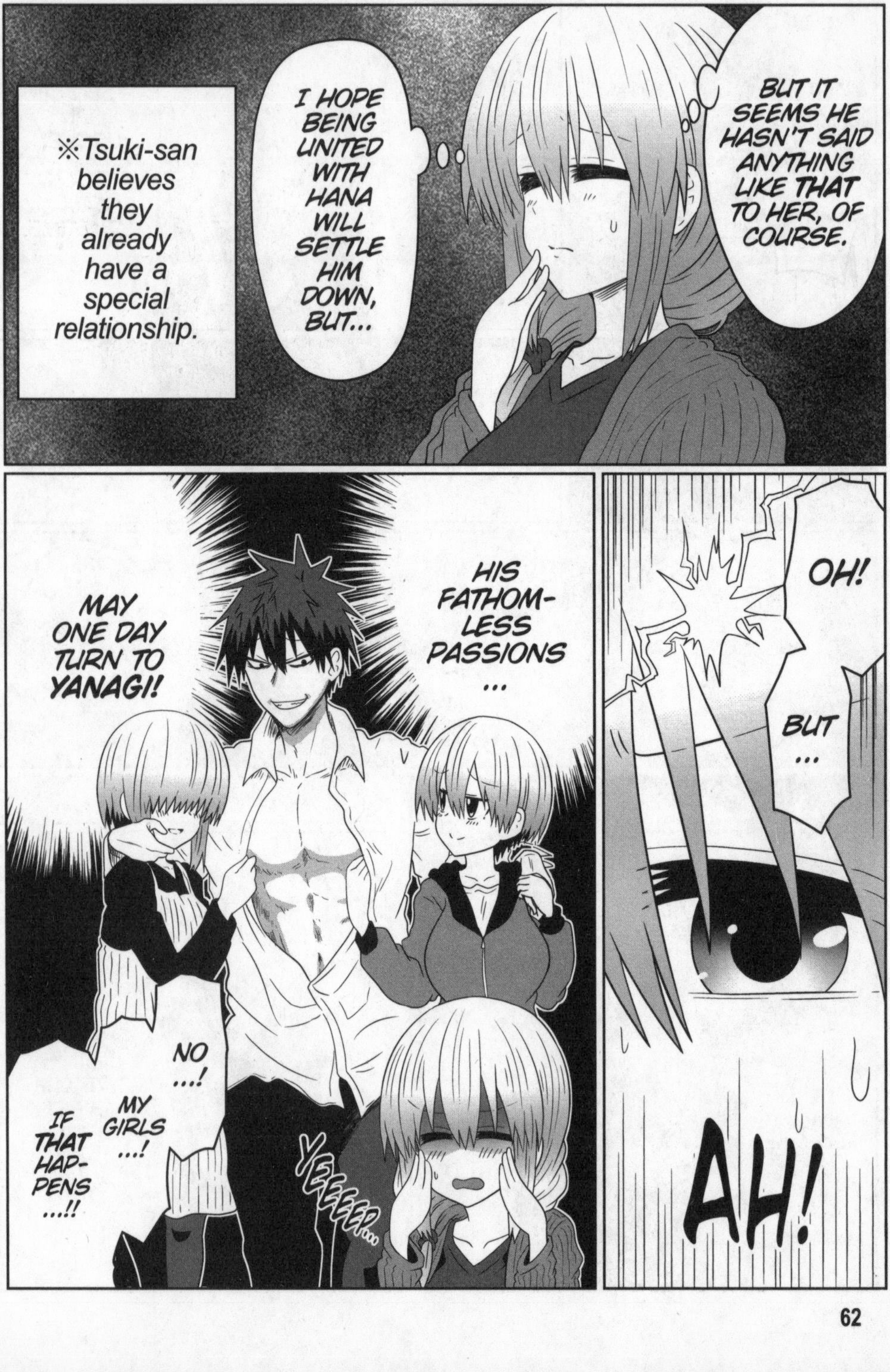
BUT IT SEEMS HE HASN'T SAID ANYTHING LIKE THAT TO HER, OF COURSE.
I HOPE BEING UNITED WITH HANA WILL SETTLE HIM DOWN, BUT...
※Tsuki-san believes they already have a special relationship.
OH!
BUT ...
AH!
HIS FATHOM-LESS PASSIONS ...
MAY ONE DAY TURN TO YANAGI!
NO ...!
MY GIRLS ...!
IF THAT HAP-PENS ...!!
YEEEEEP...

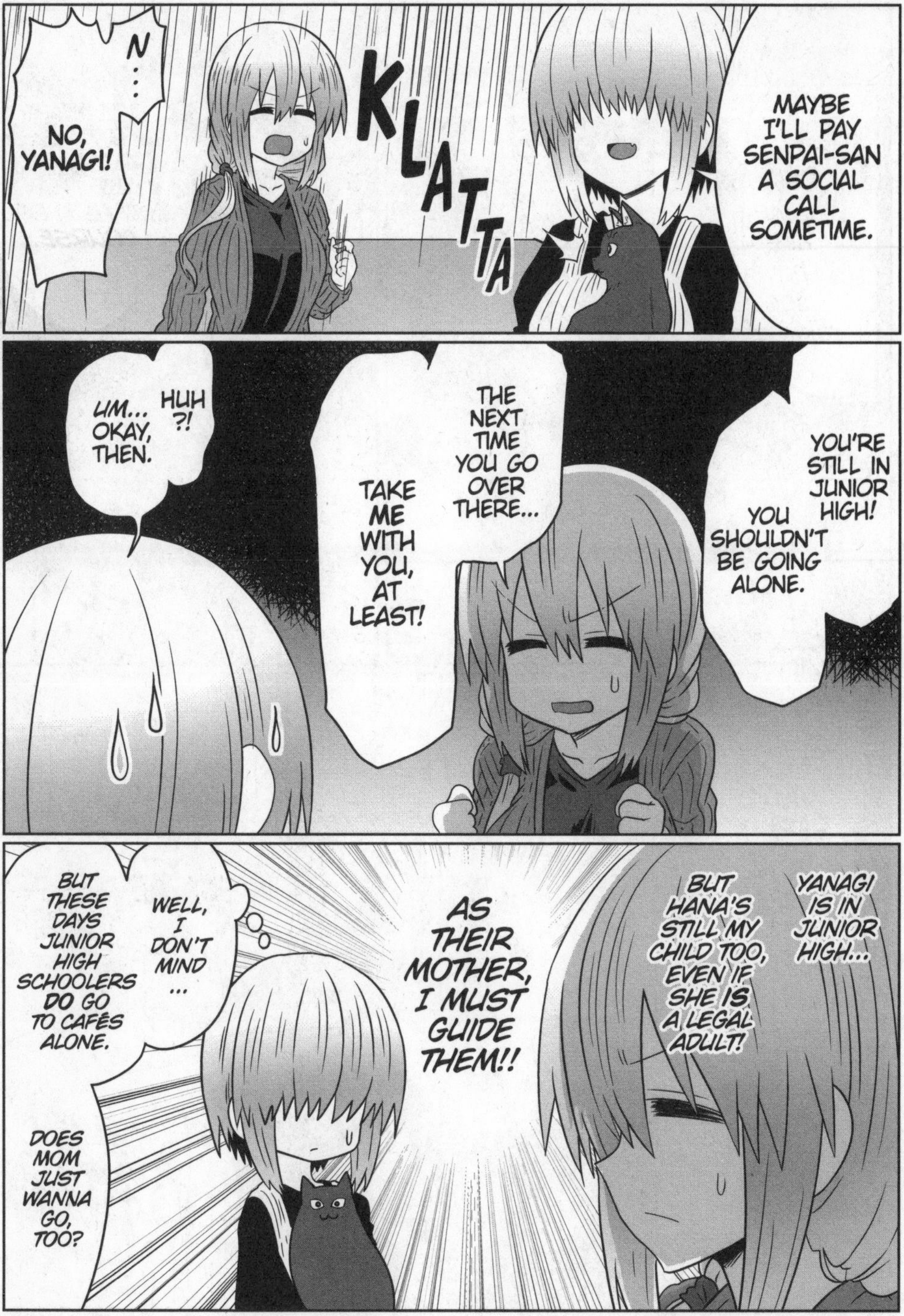
MAYBE I'LL PAY SENPAI-SAN A SOCIAL CALL SOMETIME.
KLATTA
N... NO, YANAGI!
YOU'RE STILL IN JUNIOR HIGH!
YOU SHOULDN'T BE GOING ALONE.
THE NEXT TIME YOU GO OVER THERE...
TAKE ME WITH YOU, AT LEAST!
HUH?!
UM... OKAY, THEN.
YANAGI IS IN JUNIOR HIGH...
BUT HANA'S STILL MY CHILD TOO, EVEN IF SHE IS A LEGAL ADULT!
AS THEIR MOTHER, I MUST GUIDE THEM!!
WELL, I DON'T MIND...
BUT THESE DAYS JUNIOR HIGH SCHOOLERS DO GO TO CAFÉS ALONE.
DOES MOM JUST WANNA GO, TOO?

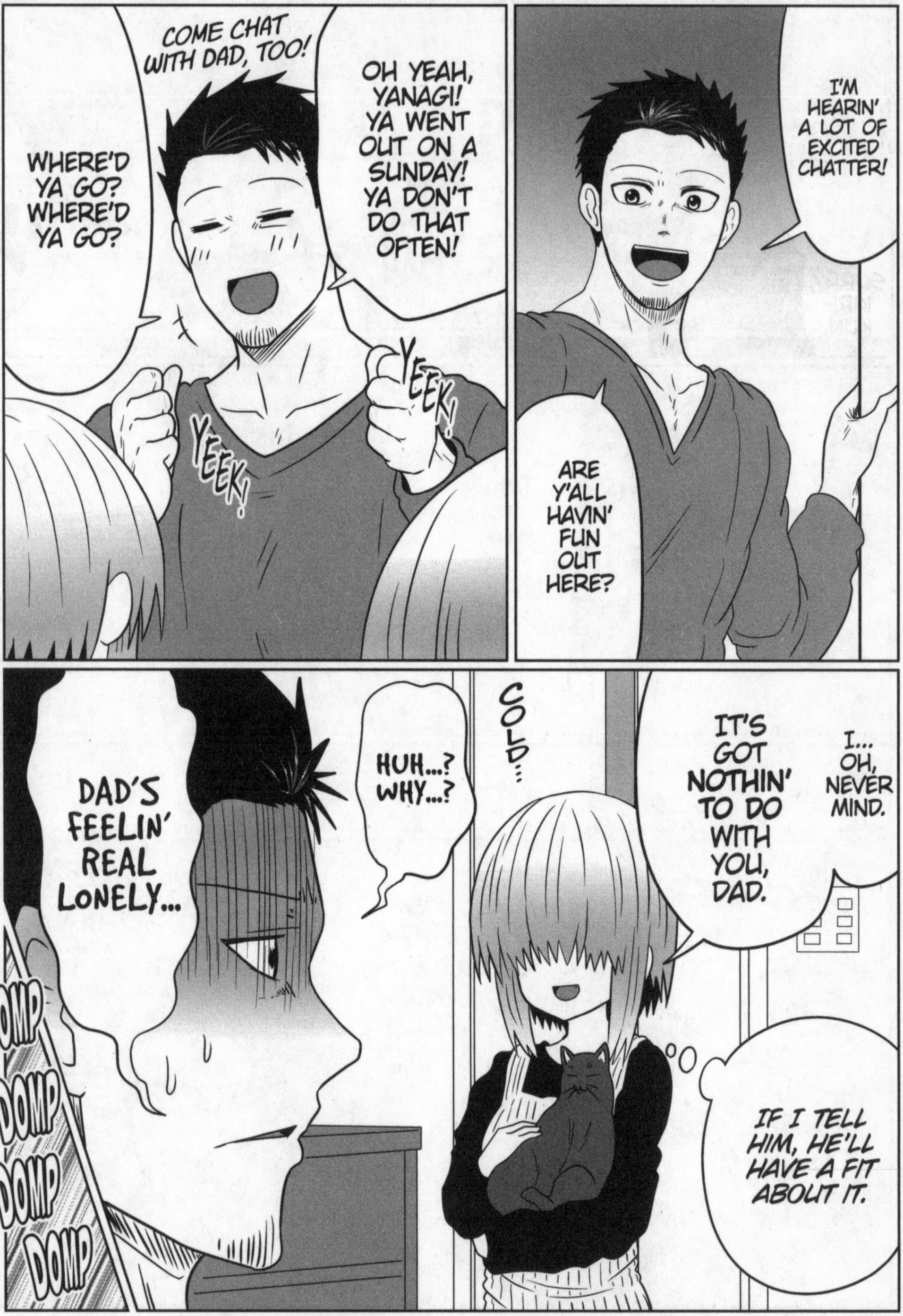
I'M HEARIN' A LOT OF EXCITED CHATTER!
ARE Y'ALL HAVIN' FUN OUT HERE?
OH YEAH, YANAGI! YA WENT OUT ON A SUNDAY! YA DON'T DO THAT OFTEN!
COME CHAT WITH DAD, TOO!
WHERE'D YA GO? WHERE'D YA GO?
YEEK!
YEEK!
I... OH, NEVER MIND.
IT'S GOT NOTHIN' TO DO WITH YOU, DAD.
IF I TELL HIM, HE'LL HAVE A FIT ABOUT IT.
COLD...
HUH...? WHY...?
DAD'S FEELIN' REAL LONELY...
DOMP DOMP DOMP DOMP DOMP

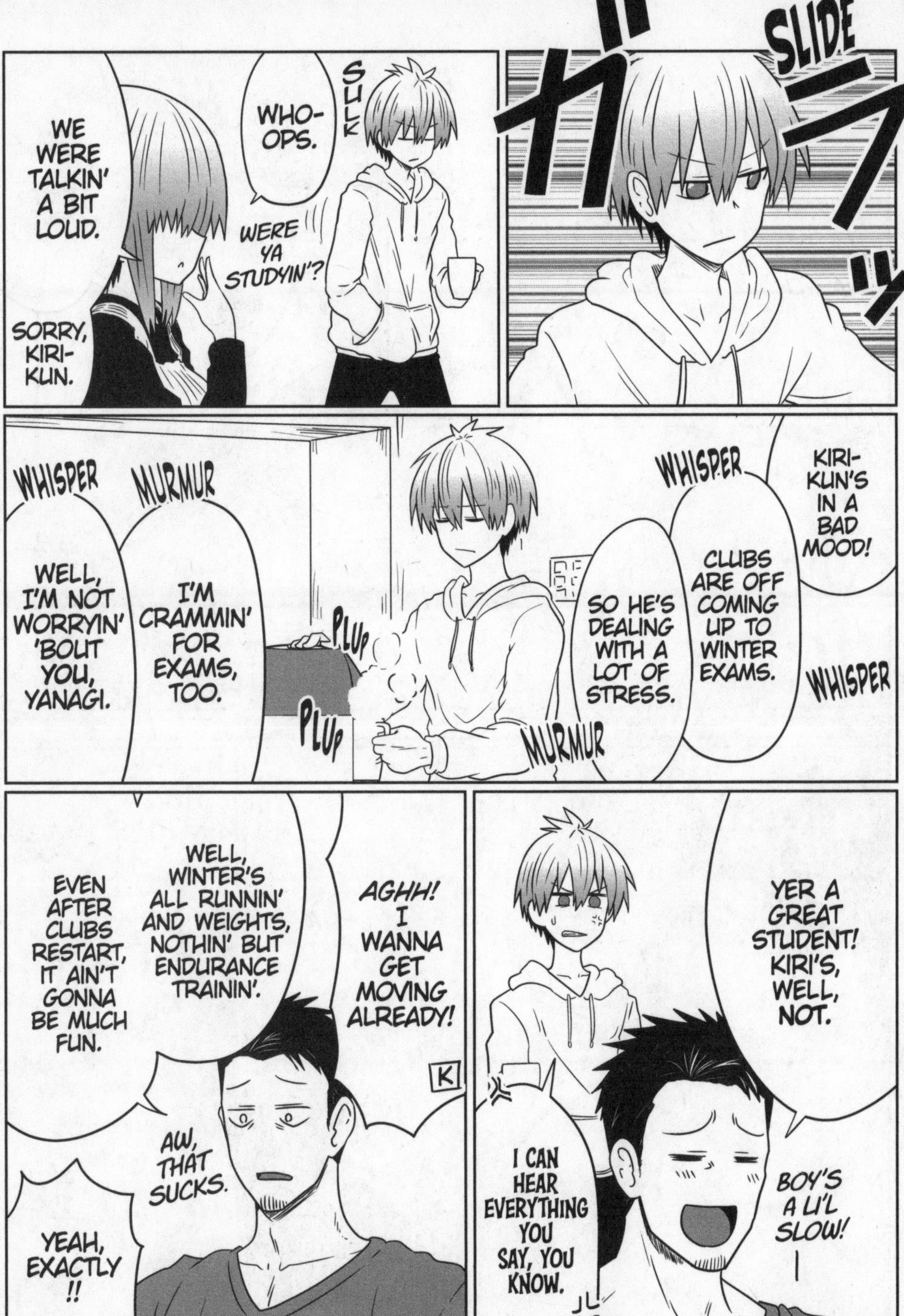
SLIDE
ガラッ
SULK
WHO-OPS.
WERE YA STUDYIN'?
WE WERE TALKIN' A BIT LOUD.
SORRY, KIRI-KUN.
KIRI-KUN'S IN A BAD MOOD!
WHISPER
CLUBS ARE OFF COMING UP TO WINTER EXAMS.
WHISPER
SO HE'S DEALING WITH A LOT OF STRESS.
MURMUR
PLUP
PLUP
MURMUR
I'M CRAMMIN' FOR EXAMS, TOO.
WHISPER
WELL, I'M NOT WORRYIN' 'BOUT YOU, YANAGI.
YER A GREAT STUDENT! KIRI'S, WELL, NOT.
BOY'S A LI'L SLOW!
I CAN HEAR EVERYTHING YOU SAY, YOU KNOW.
AGHH! I WANNA GET MOVING ALREADY!
WELL, WINTER'S ALL RUNNIN' AND WEIGHTS, NOTHIN' BUT ENDURANCE TRAININ'.
EVEN AFTER CLUBS RESTART, IT AIN'T GONNA BE MUCH FUN.
K
AW, THAT SUCKS.
YEAH, EXACTLY!!

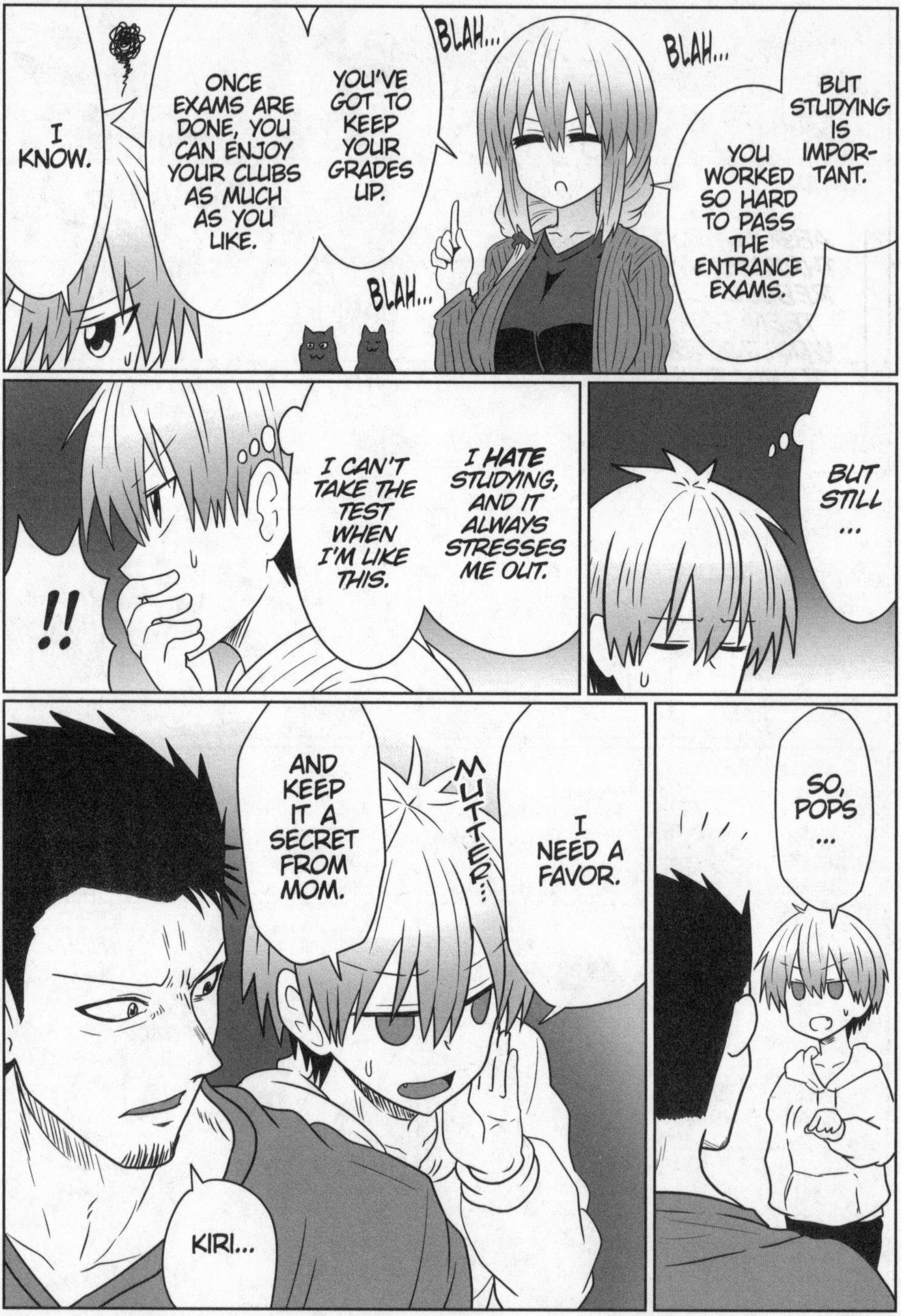
BLAH...
BLAH...
BUT STUDYING IS IMPORTANT.
YOU WORKED SO HARD TO PASS THE ENTRANCE EXAMS.
BLAH...
YOU'VE GOT TO KEEP YOUR GRADES UP.
ONCE EXAMS ARE DONE, YOU CAN ENJOY YOUR CLUBS AS MUCH AS YOU LIKE.
I KNOW.
BUT STILL ...
I HATE STUDYING, AND IT ALWAYS STRESSES ME OUT.
I CAN'T TAKE THE TEST WHEN I'M LIKE THIS.
!!
SO, POPS ...
I NEED A FAVOR.
MUTTER...
AND KEEP IT A SECRET FROM MOM.
KIRI...

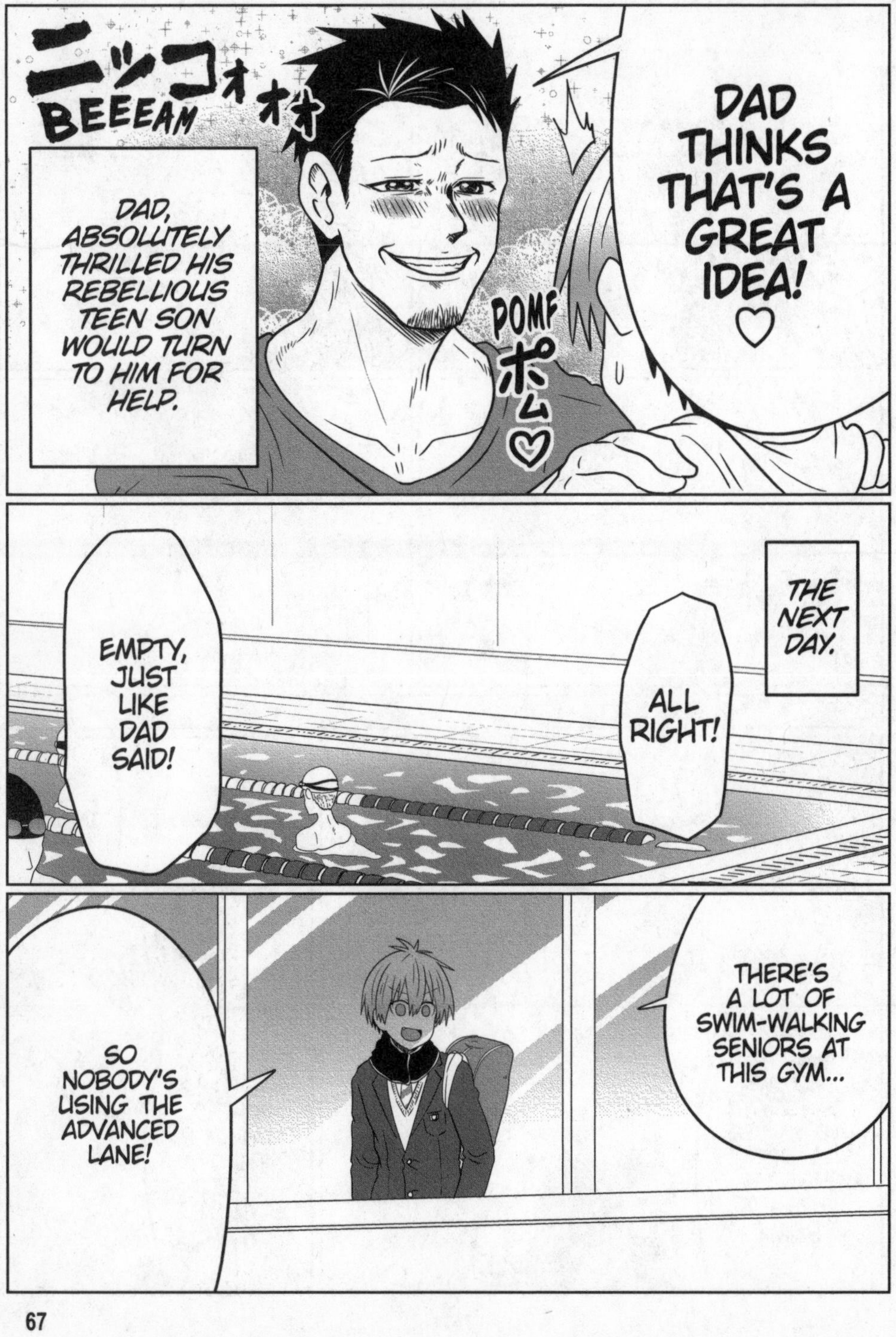
DAD THINKS THAT'S A GREAT IDEA! ♡
ニッコオオオ
BEEEEAM
POMF
ポム♡
DAD, ABSOLUTELY THRILLED HIS REBELLIOUS TEEN SON WOULD TURN TO HIM FOR HELP.
THE NEXT DAY.
ALL RIGHT!
EMPTY, JUST LIKE DAD SAID!
THERE'S A LOT OF SWIM-WALKING SENIORS AT THIS GYM...
SO NOBODY'S USING THE ADVANCED LANE!

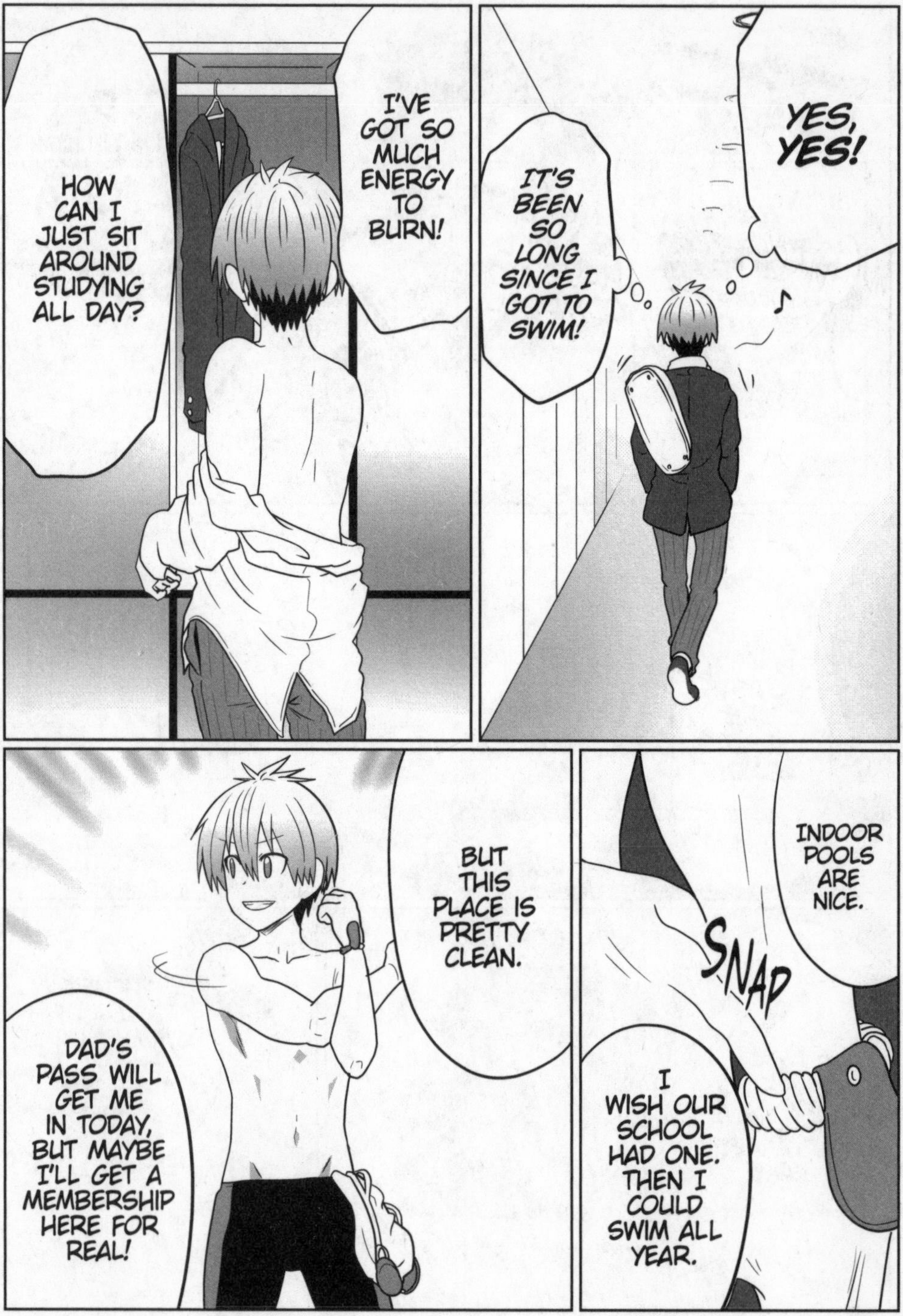
YES, YES!
IT'S BEEN SO LONG SINCE I GOT TO SWIM!
I'VE GOT SO MUCH ENERGY TO BURN!
HOW CAN I JUST SIT AROUND STUDYING ALL DAY?
INDOOR POOLS ARE NICE.
SNAP
I WISH OUR SCHOOL HAD ONE. THEN I COULD SWIM ALL YEAR.
BUT THIS PLACE IS PRETTY CLEAN.
DAD'S PASS WILL GET ME IN TODAY, BUT MAYBE I'LL GET A MEMBERSHIP HERE FOR REAL!

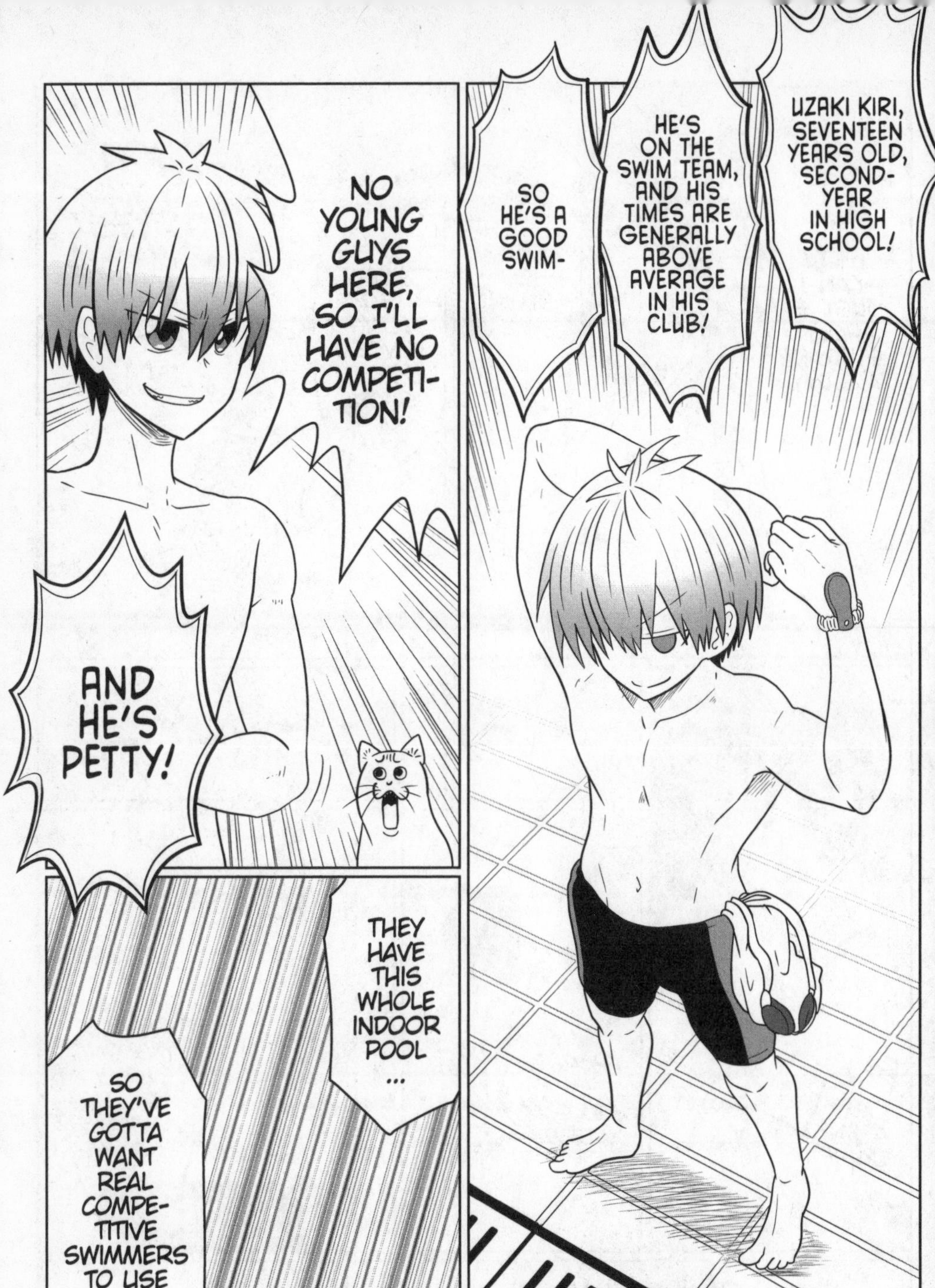
UZAKI KIRI, SEVENTEEN YEARS OLD, SECOND-YEAR IN HIGH SCHOOL!
HE'S ON THE SWIM TEAM, AND HIS TIMES ARE GENERALLY ABOVE AVERAGE IN HIS CLUB!
SO HE'S A GOOD SWIM-
NO YOUNG GUYS HERE, SO I'LL HAVE NO COMPETITION!
AND HE'S PETTY!
THEY HAVE THIS WHOLE INDOOR POOL ...
SO THEY'VE GOTTA WANT REAL COMPETITIVE SWIMMERS TO USE IT!

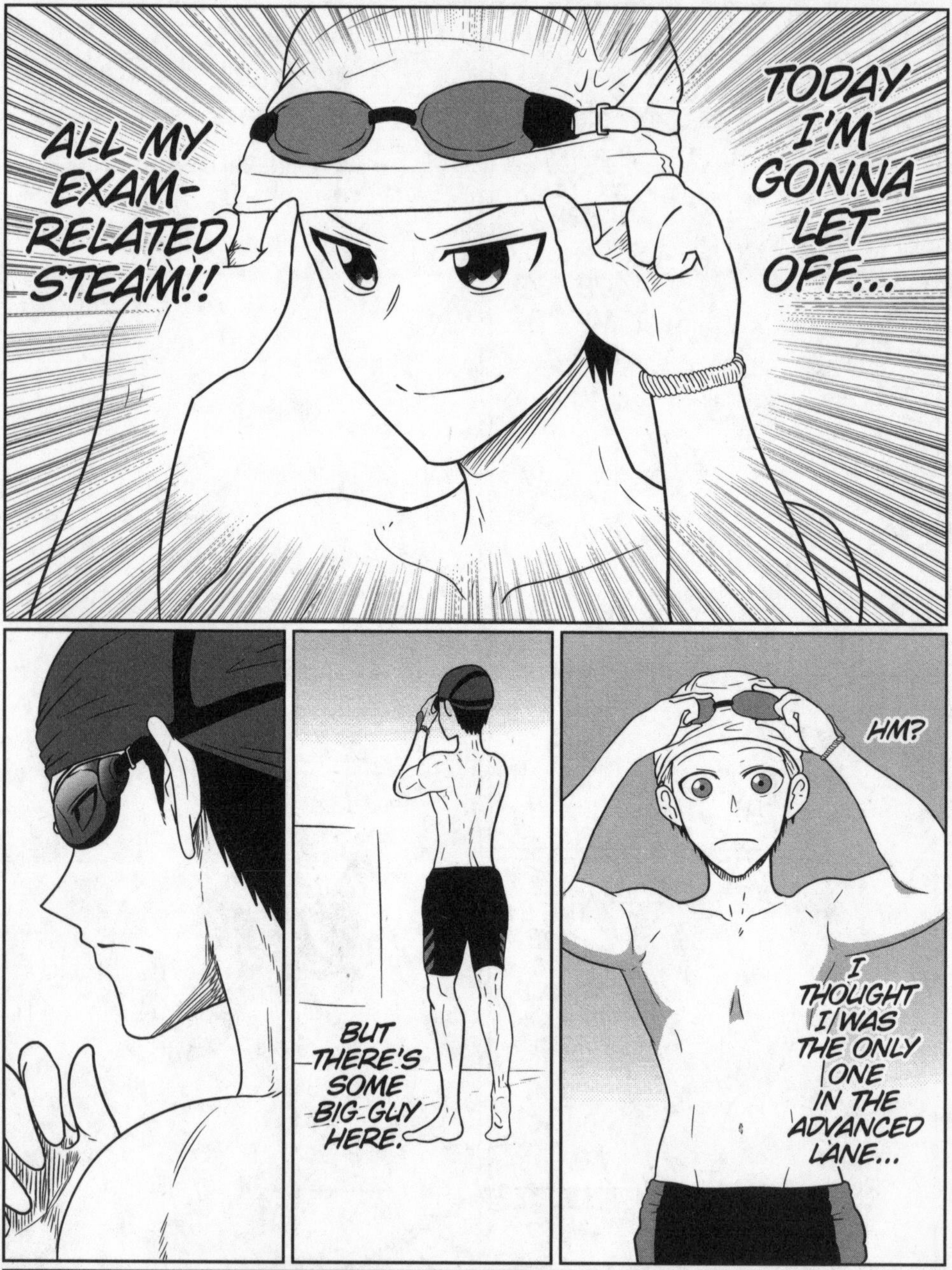
TODAY I'M GONNA LET OFF...
ALL MY EXAM-RELATED STEAM!!
HM?
I THOUGHT I WAS THE ONLY ONE IN THE ADVANCED LANE...
BUT THERE'S SOME BIG GUY HERE.

Chapter 56:
The Kouhai and Her Brother: Part 1

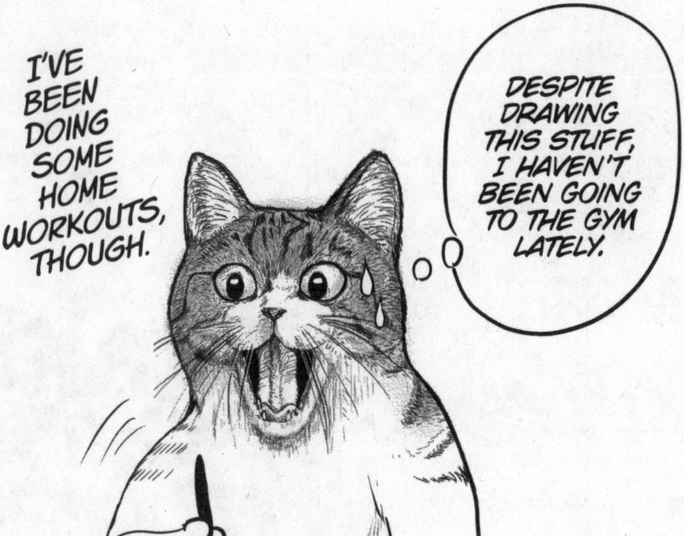
DESPITE DRAWING THIS STUFF, I HAVEN'T BEEN GOING TO THE GYM LATELY.
I'VE BEEN DOING SOME HOME WORKOUTS, THOUGH.

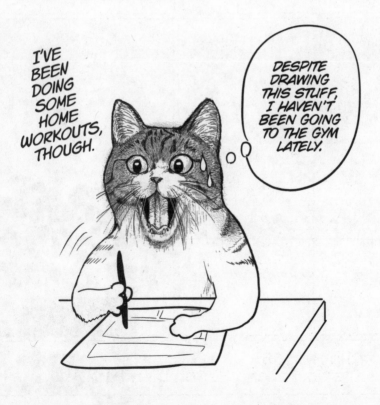

Uzaki-chan ✦
Wants to Hang
Out!

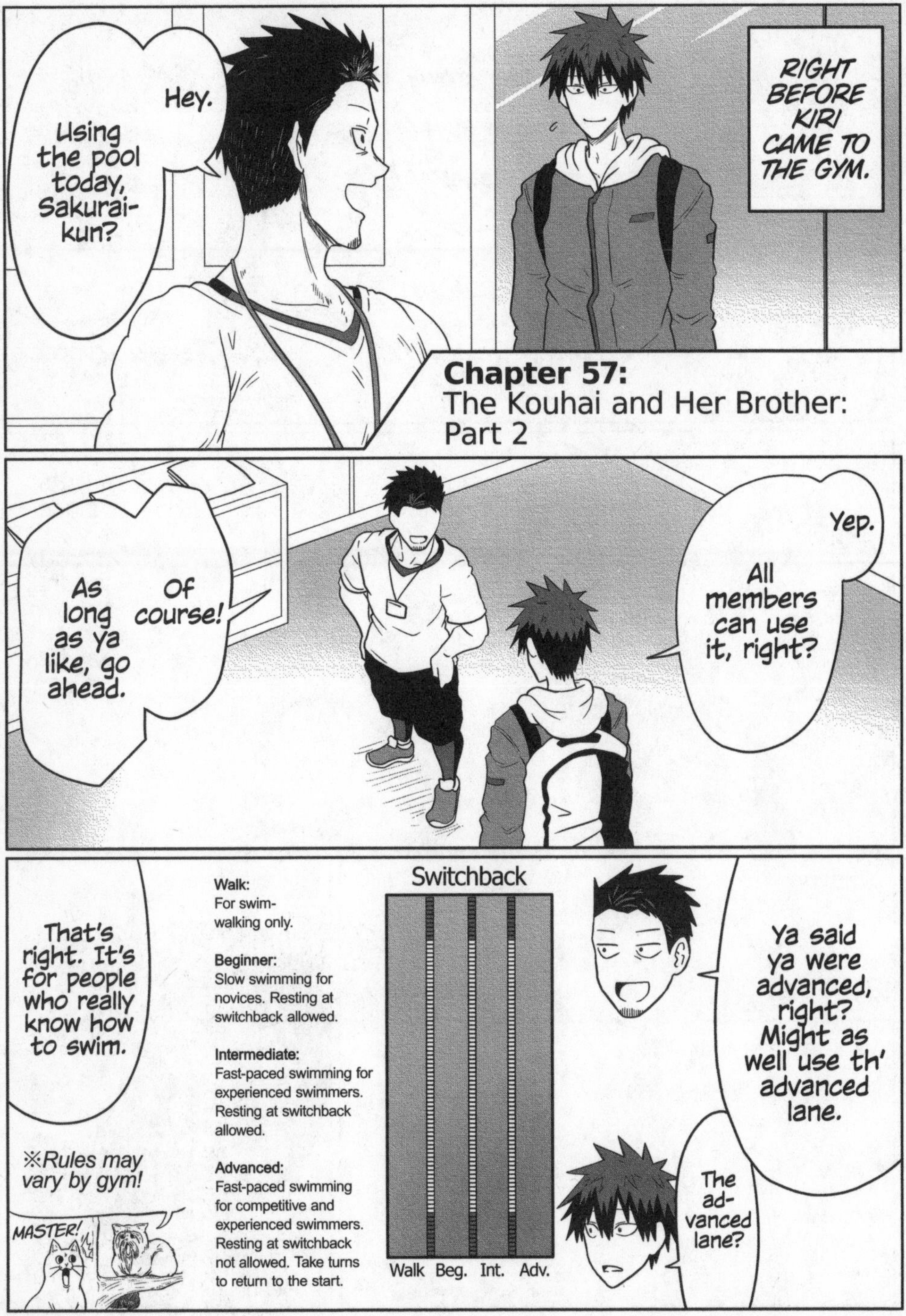
RIGHT BEFORE KIRI CAME TO THE GYM.
Hey. Using the pool today, Sakurai-kun?
Chapter 57:
The Kouhai and Her Brother: Part 2
Yep. All members can use it, right?
Of course! As long as ya like, go ahead.
Ya said ya were advanced, right? Might as well use th' advanced lane.
The ad-vanced lane?
That's right. It's for people who really know how to swim.
Switchback
Walk Beg. Int. Adv.
Walk: For swim-walking only.
Beginner: Slow swimming for novices. Resting at switchback allowed.
Intermediate: Fast-paced swimming for experienced swimmers. Resting at switchback allowed.
Advanced: Fast-paced swimming for competitive and experienced swimmers. Resting at switchback not allowed. Take turns to return to the start.
※Rules may vary by gym!
MASTER!

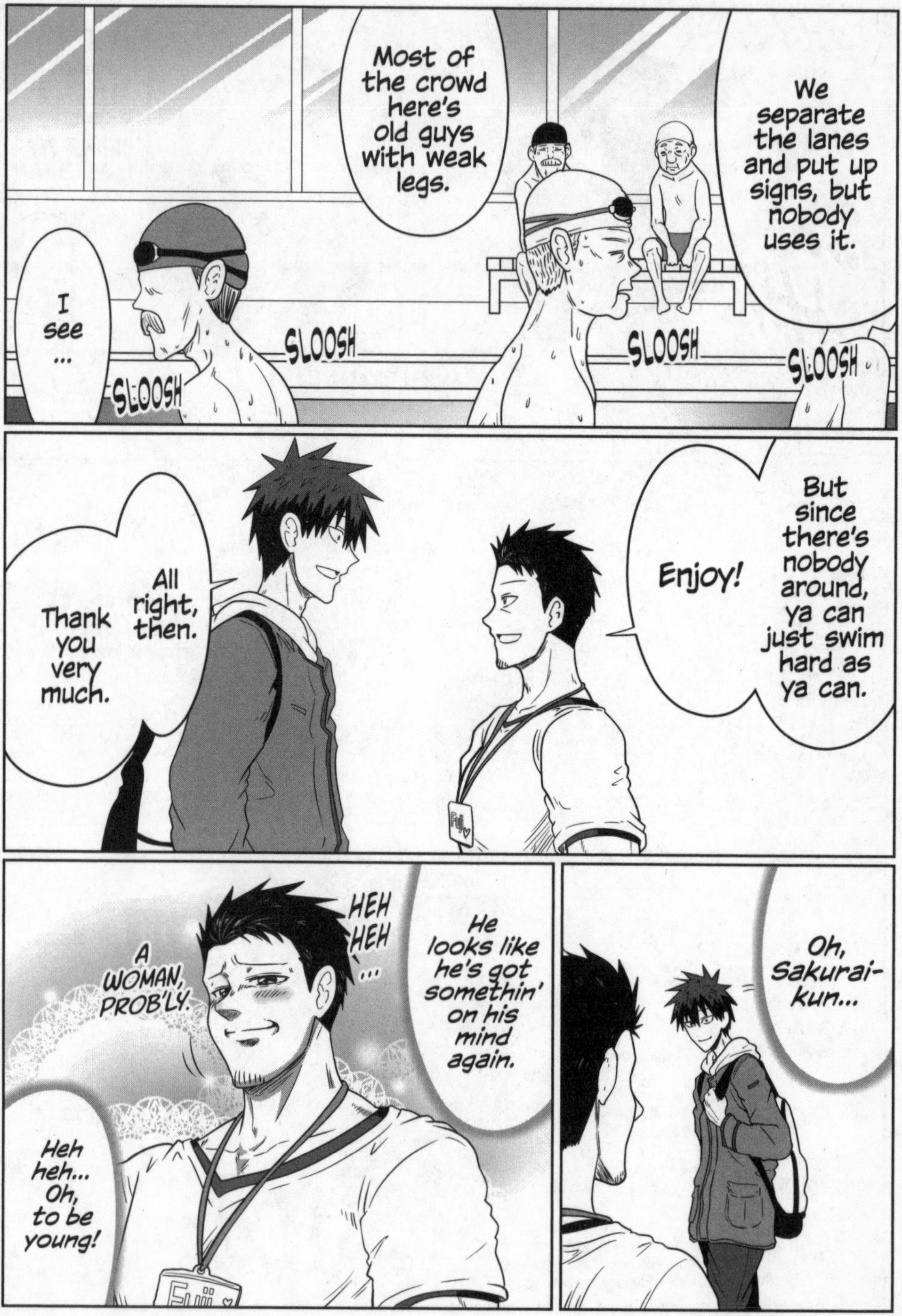
We separate the lanes and put up signs, but nobody uses it.
Most of the crowd here's old guys with weak legs.
SLOOSH
SLOOSH
SLOOSH
I see ...
SLOOSH
But since there's nobody around, ya can just swim hard as ya can.
Enjoy!
All right, then.
Thank you very much.
Oh, Sakurai-kun...
He looks like he's got somethin' on his mind again.
HEH HEH ...
A WOMAN, PROB'LY.
Heh heh... Oh, to be young!

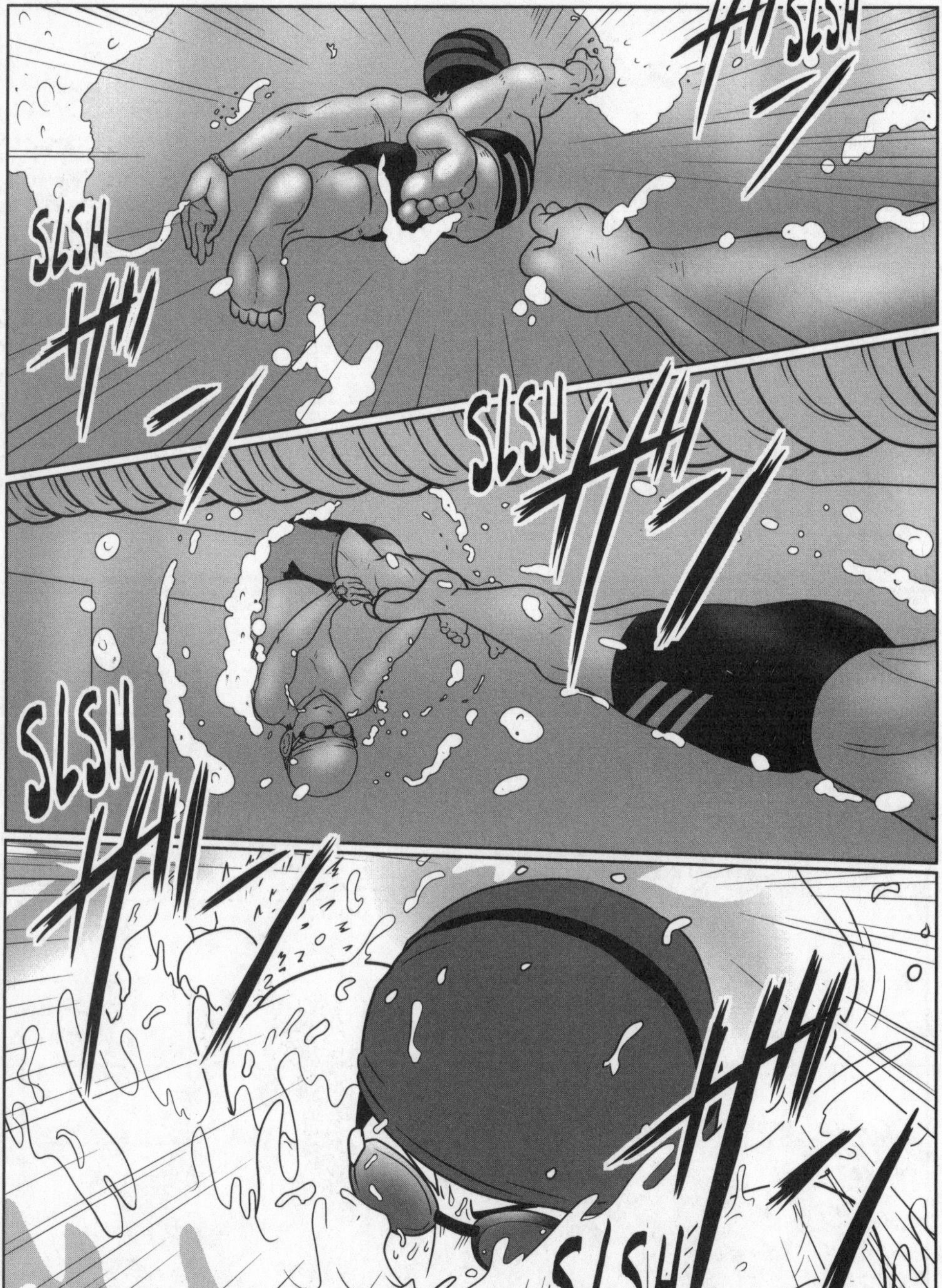
SLSH
SLSH
SLSH
SLSH
SLSH

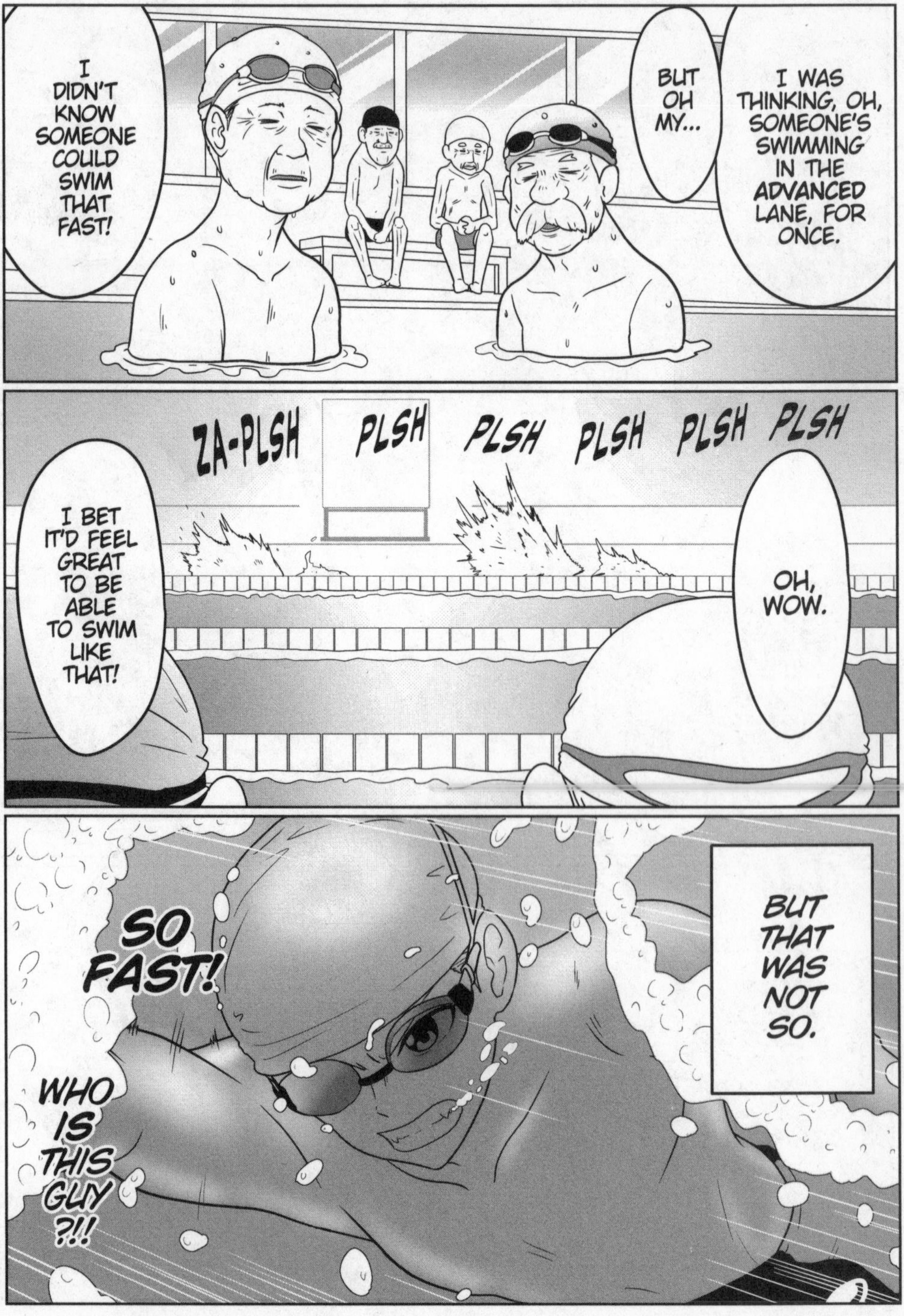
I WAS THINKING, OH, SOMEONE'S SWIMMING IN THE ADVANCED LANE, FOR ONCE.
BUT OH MY...
I DIDN'T KNOW SOMEONE COULD SWIM THAT FAST!
PLSH
PLSH
PLSH
PLSH
PLSH
ZA-PLSH
OH, WOW.
I BET IT'D FEEL GREAT TO BE ABLE TO SWIM LIKE THAT!
BUT THAT WAS NOT SO.
SO FAST!
WHO IS THIS GUY ?!!

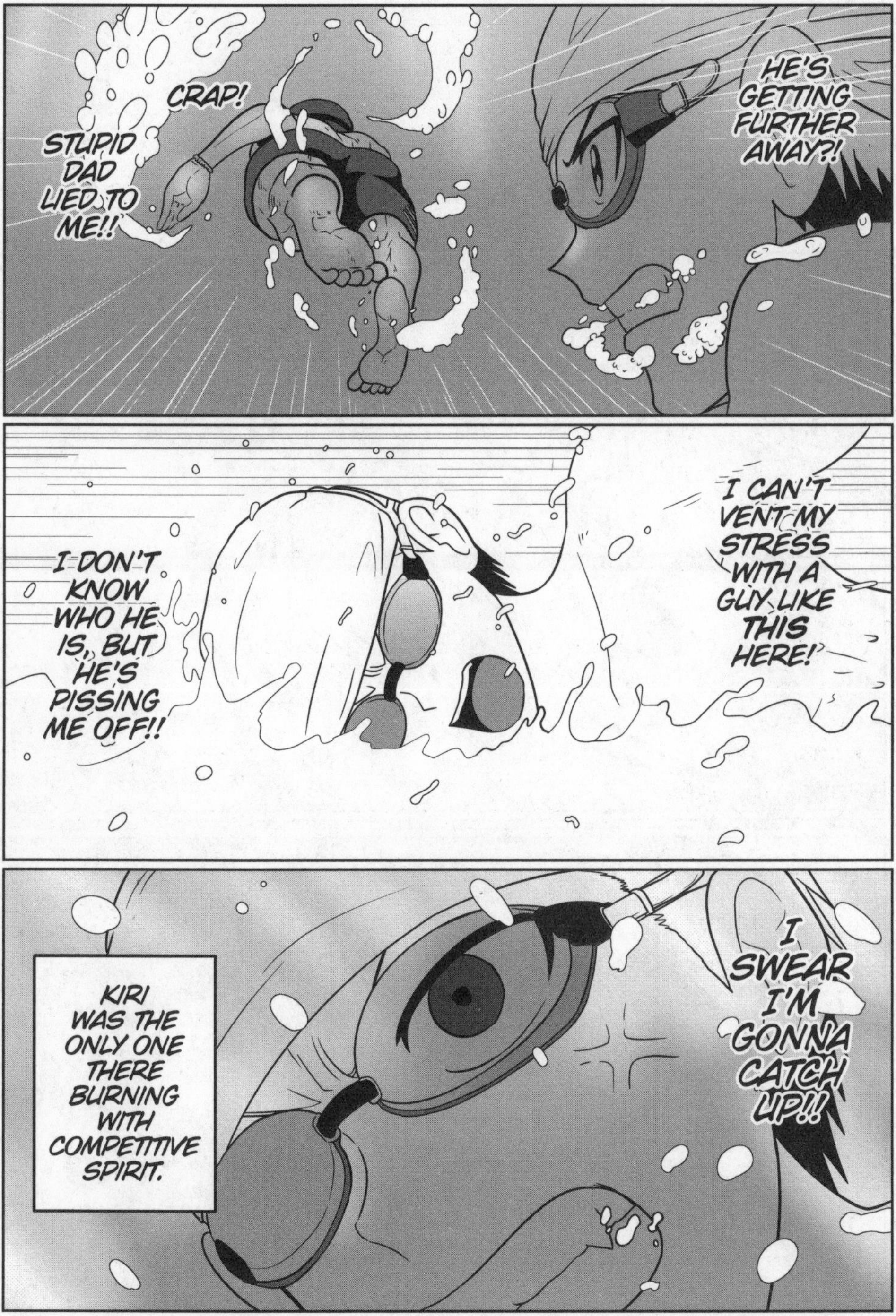
HE'S GETTING FURTHER AWAY?!
CRAP!
STUPID DAD LIED TO ME!!
I CAN'T VENT MY STRESS WITH A GUY LIKE THIS HERE!
I DON'T KNOW WHO HE IS, BUT HE'S PISSING ME OFF!!
I SWEAR I'M GONNA CATCH UP!!
KIRI WAS THE ONLY ONE THERE BURNING WITH COMPETITIVE SPIRIT.

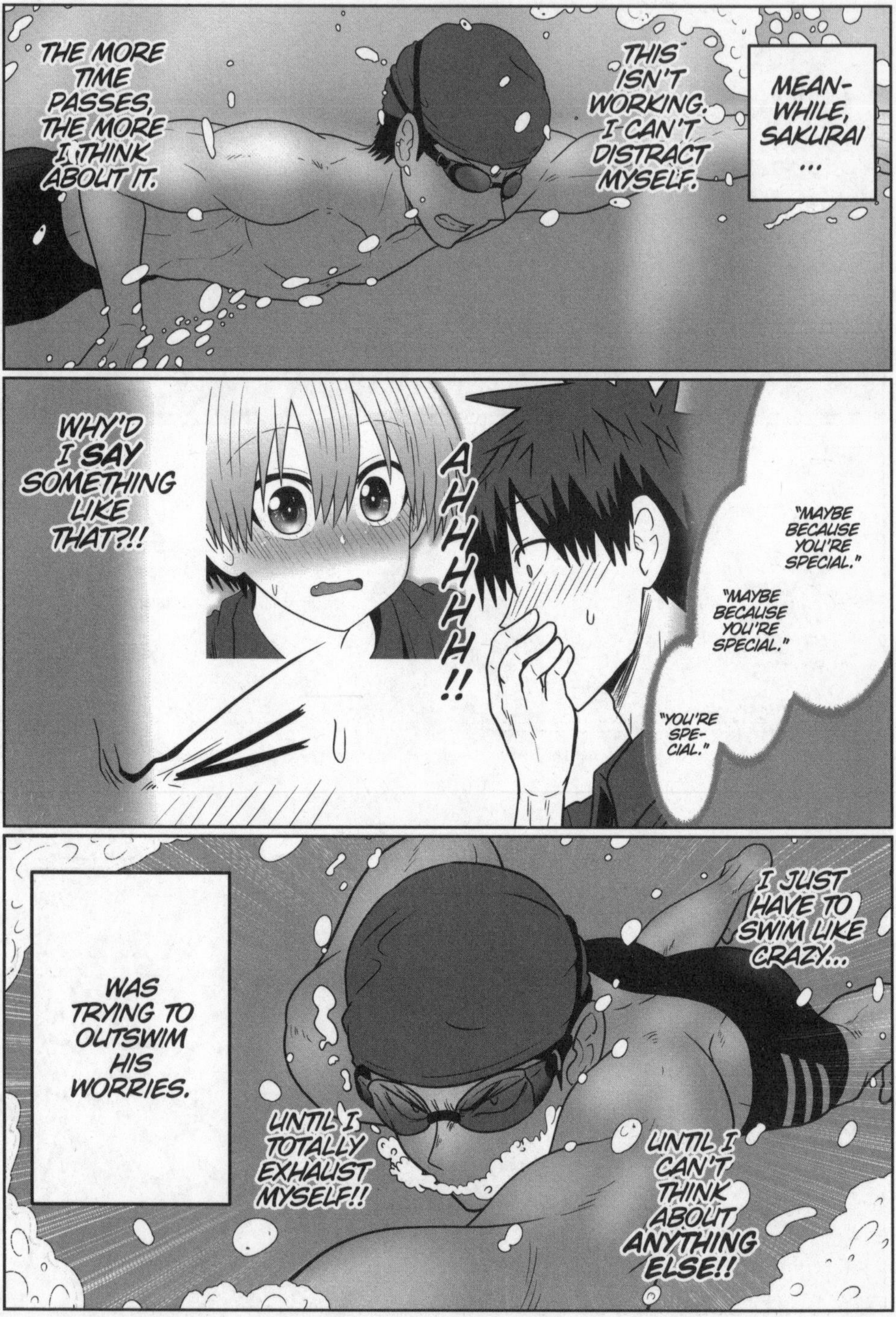
MEAN-WHILE, SAKURAI ...
THIS ISN'T WORKING. I CAN'T DISTRACT MYSELF.
THE MORE TIME PASSES, THE MORE I THINK ABOUT IT.
"MAYBE BECAUSE YOU'RE SPECIAL."
"MAYBE BECAUSE YOU'RE SPECIAL."
"YOU'RE SPE-CIAL."
AHHHHHH!!
WHY'D I SAY SOMETHING LIKE THAT?!!
I JUST HAVE TO SWIM LIKE CRAZY...
UNTIL I CAN'T THINK ABOUT ANYTHING ELSE!!
UNTIL I TOTALLY EXHAUST MYSELF!!
WAS TRYING TO OUTSWIM HIS WORRIES.

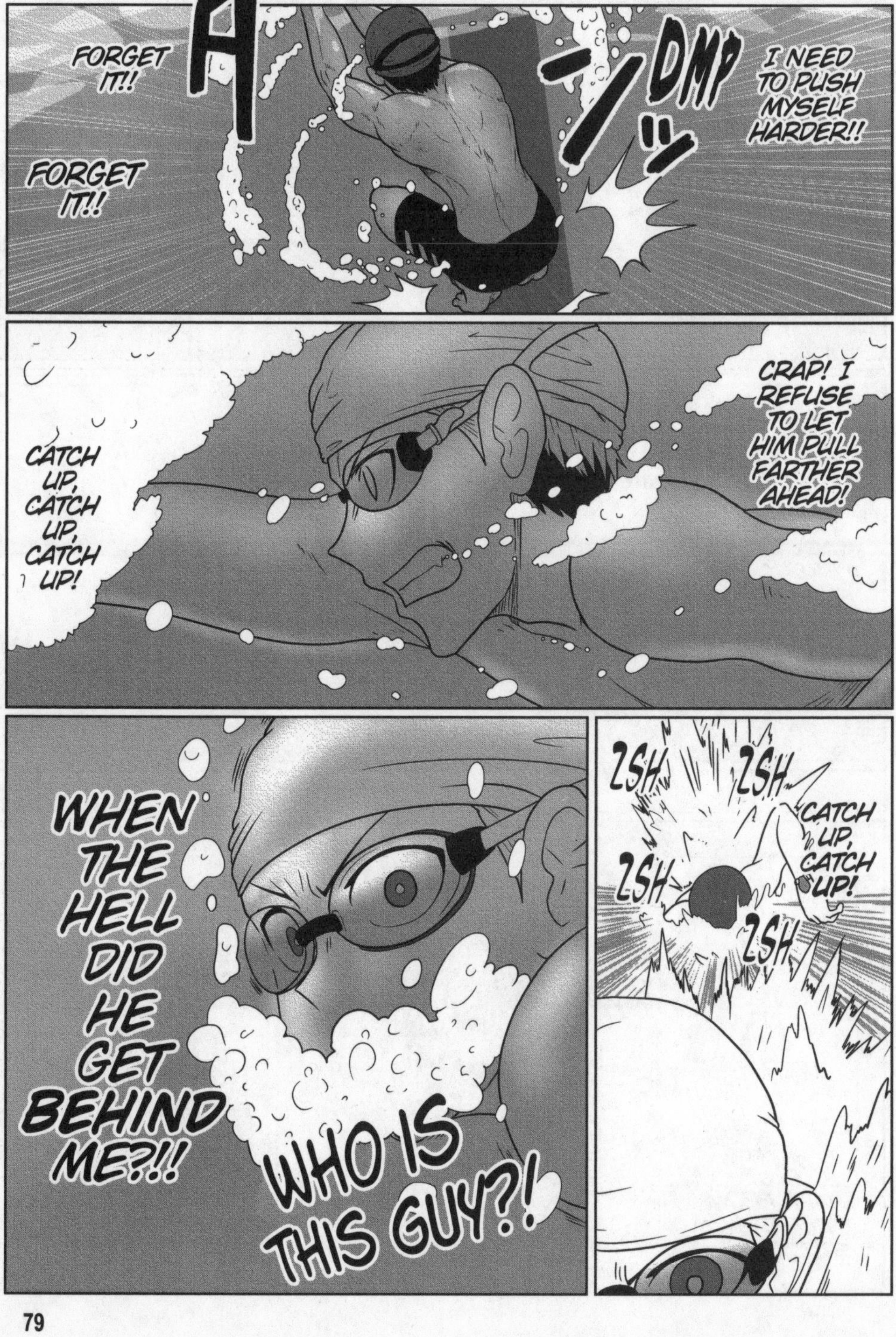
I NEED TO PUSH MYSELF HARDER!!
DMP
FORGET IT!!
FORGET IT!!
CRAP! I REFUSE TO LET HIM PULL FARTHER AHEAD!
CATCH UP, CATCH UP, CATCH UP!
ZSH
ZSH
CATCH UP, CATCH UP!
ZSH
ZSH
WHEN THE HELL DID HE GET BEHIND ME?!!
WHO IS THIS GUY?!

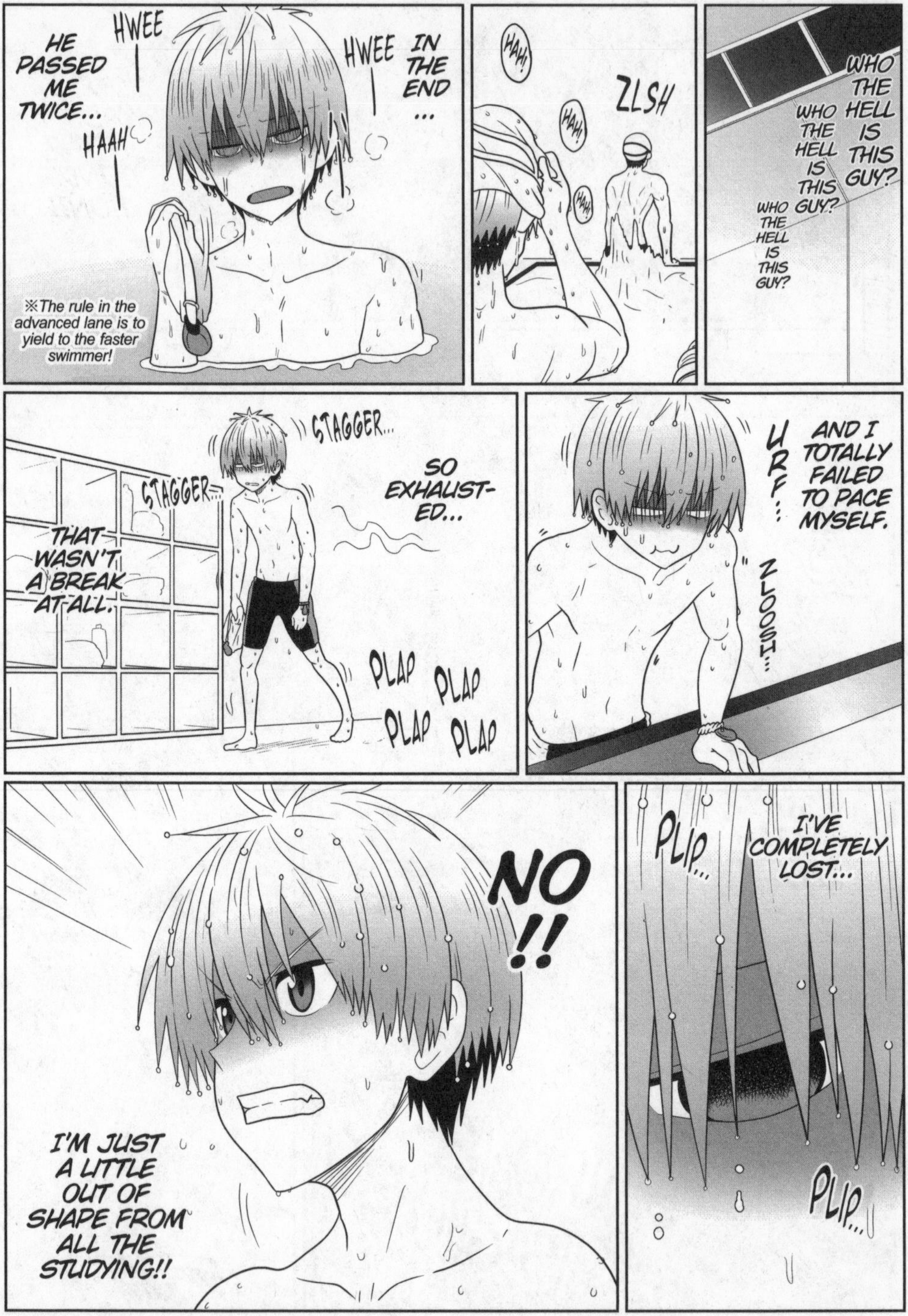
WHO THE HELL IS THIS GUY?
WHO THE HELL IS THIS GUY?
WHO THE HELL IS THIS GUY?
HAH!
HAH!
HAH!
ZLSH
IN THE END ...
HWEE
HWEE
HE PASSED ME TWICE...
HAAH
※The rule in the advanced lane is to yield to the faster swimmer!
AND I TOTALLY FAILED TO PACE MYSELF.
URF...
ZLOOSH...
STAGGER...
SO EXHAUST-ED...
STAGGER...
THAT WASN'T A BREAK AT ALL.
PLAP
PLAP
PLAP
PLAP
I'VE COMPLETELY LOST...
PLIP...
PLIP...
NO!!
I'M JUST A LITTLE OUT OF SHAPE FROM ALL THE STUDYING!!

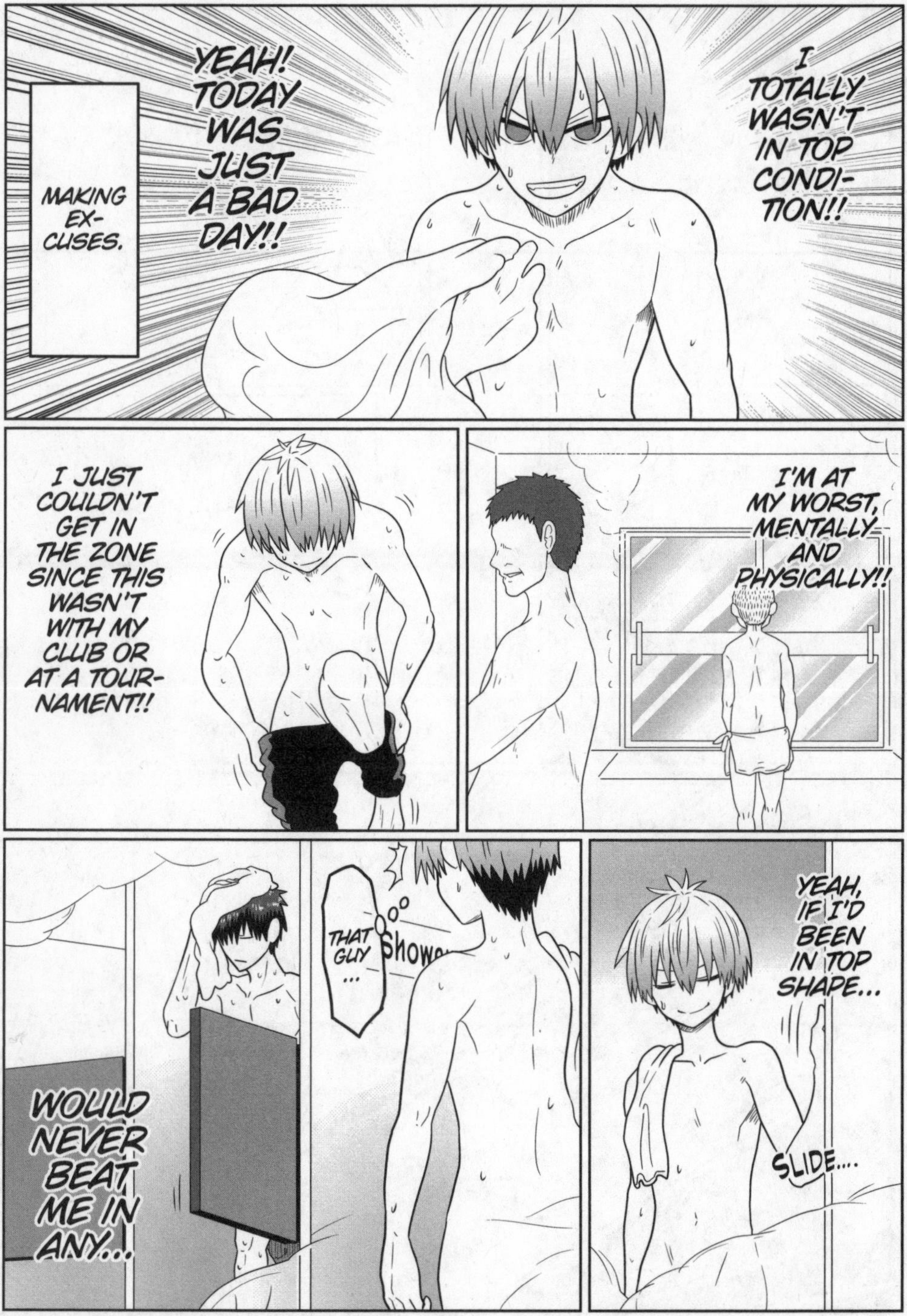
I TOTALLY WASN'T IN TOP CONDITION!!
YEAH! TODAY WAS JUST A BAD DAY!!
MAKING EXCUSES.
I'M AT MY WORST, MENTALLY AND PHYSICALLY!!
I JUST COULDN'T GET IN THE ZONE SINCE THIS WASN'T WITH MY CLUB OR AT A TOURNAMENT!!
YEAH, IF I'D BEEN IN TOP SHAPE...
SLIDE....
THAT GUY ...
WOULD NEVER BEAT ME IN ANY...

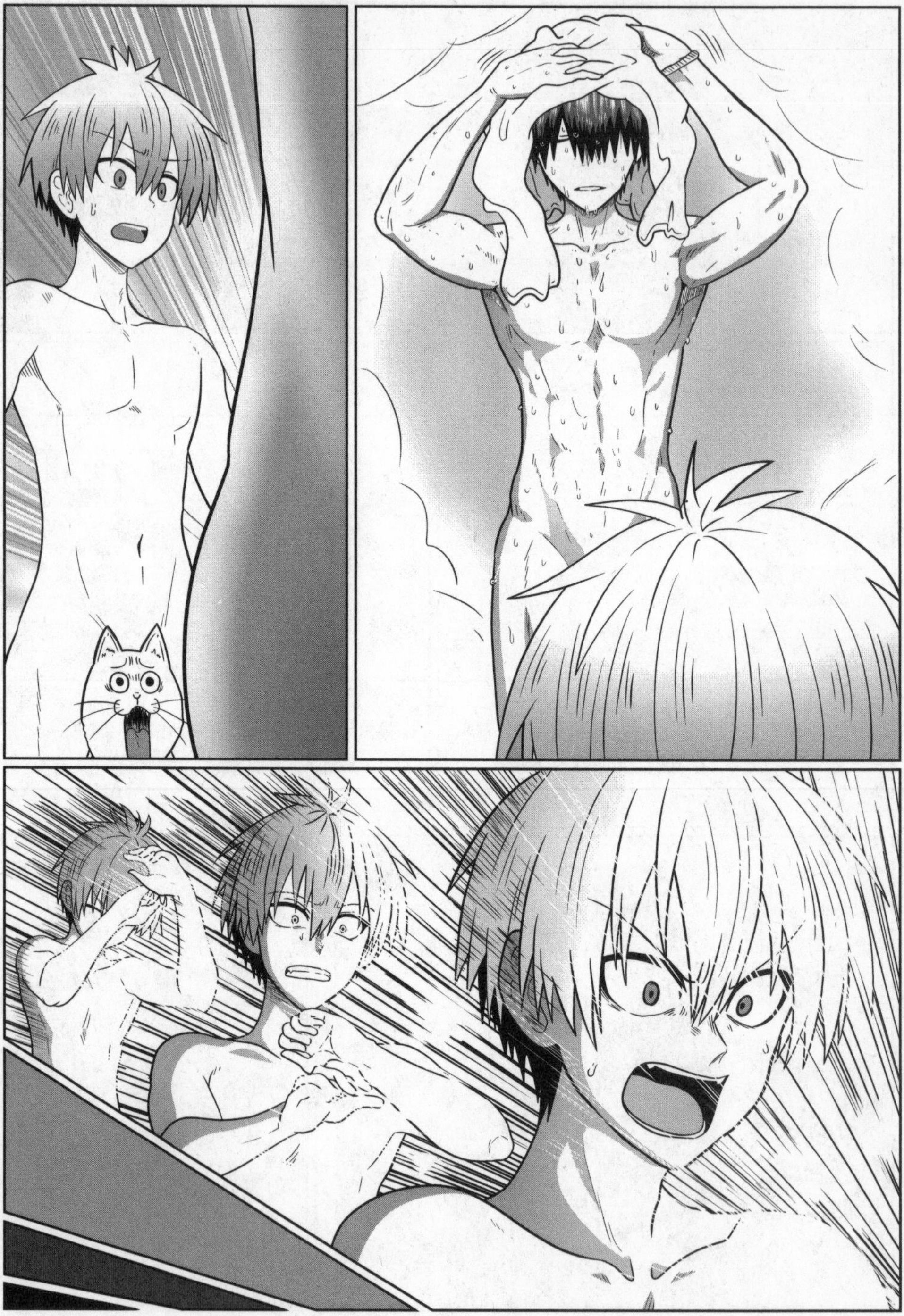

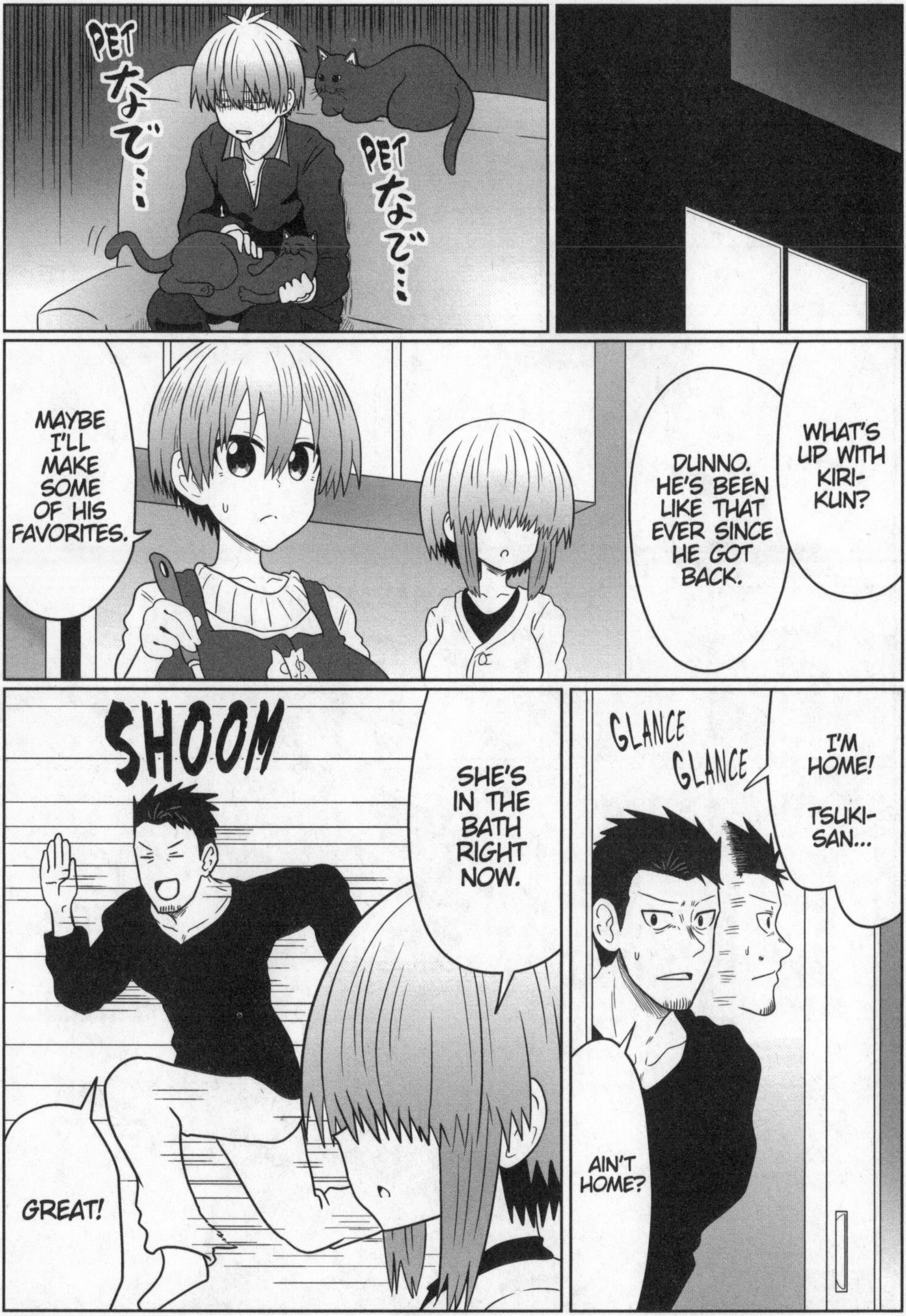
PET なで…
PET なで…
WHAT'S UP WITH KIRI-KUN?
DUNNO. HE'S BEEN LIKE THAT EVER SINCE HE GOT BACK.
MAYBE I'LL MAKE SOME OF HIS FAVORITES.
I'M HOME!
TSUKI-SAN...
GLANCE GLANCE
AIN'T HOME?
SHE'S IN THE BATH RIGHT NOW.
SHOOM
GREAT!

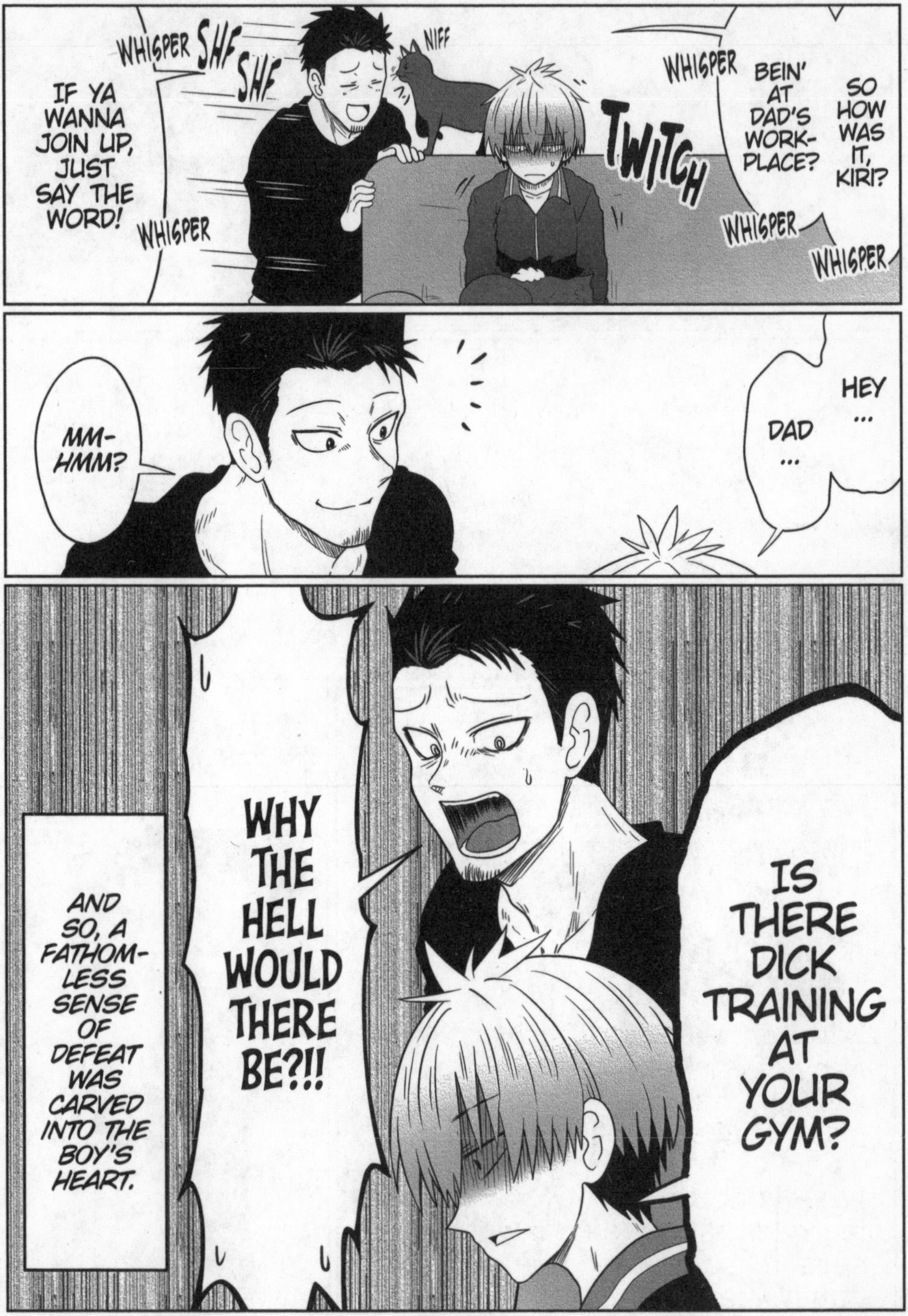

SO HOW WAS IT, KIRI?
BEIN' AT DAD'S WORK-PLACE?
WHISPER
WHISPER
WHISPER
TWITCH
NIFF
SHF SHF
WHISPER
IF YA WANNA JOIN UP, JUST SAY THE WORD!
WHISPER
HEY ...
DAD ...
MM-HMM?
IS THERE DICK TRAINING AT YOUR GYM?
WHY THE HELL WOULD THERE BE?!!
AND SO, A FATHOMLESS SENSE OF DEFEAT WAS CARVED INTO THE BOY'S HEART.

When this chapter (57) was published in *Dra Dra Sharp#*
Magazine, I got a message saying, "It was funny, but I
will refrain from commenting further," and I replied with
just, "That's wise."

I mean, at the time when I was drawing it, I hadn't yet...
learned that the anime was being renewed for a second
season...so I'd been thinking, "I don't have to worry
about keeping this going, I can do whatever..."

Uzaki-chan☆ Wants to Hang Out!

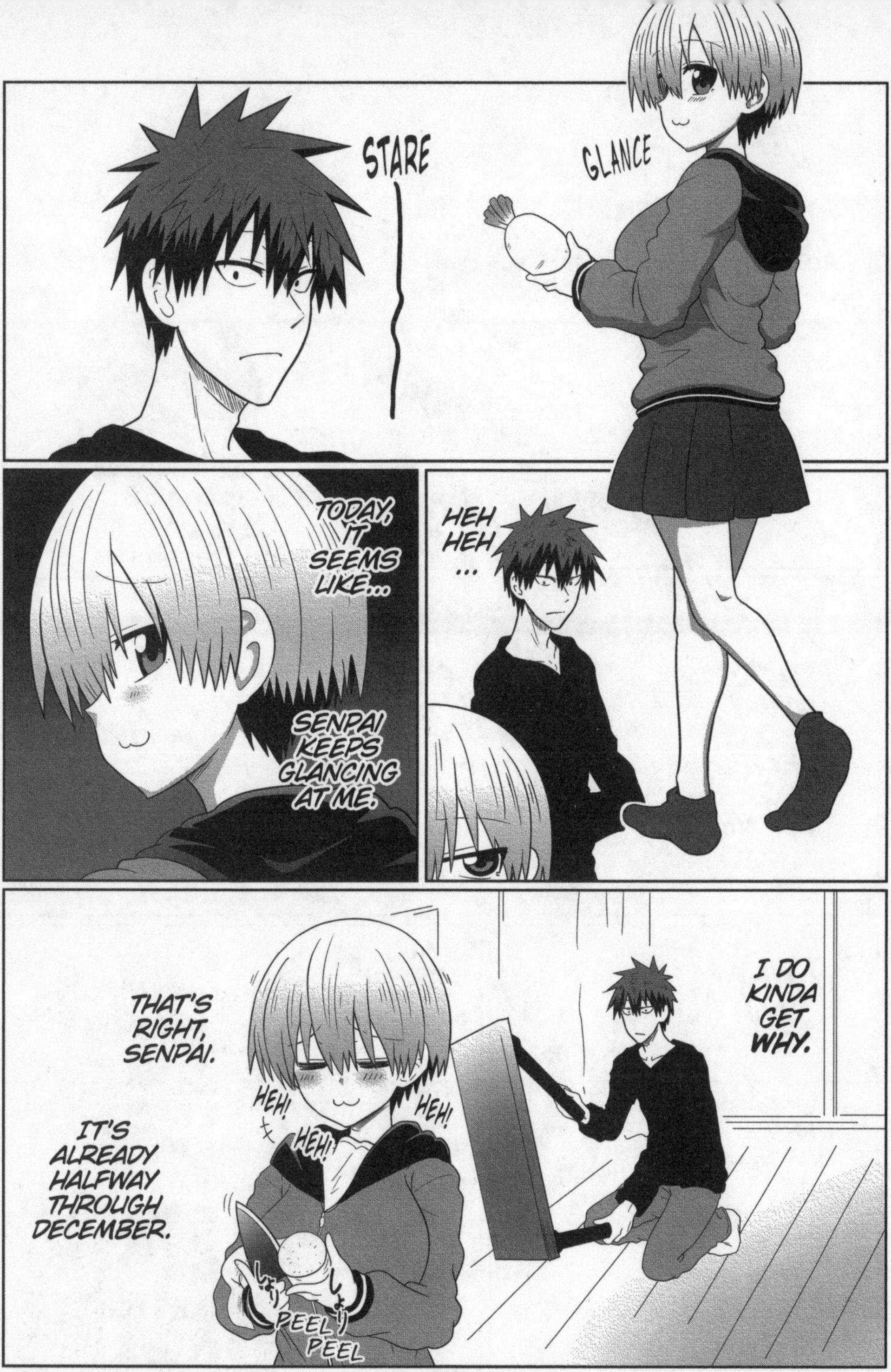
GLANCE
STARE
HEH HEH ...
TODAY, IT SEEMS LIKE...
SENPAI KEEPS GLANCING AT ME.
I DO KINDA GET WHY.
THAT'S RIGHT, SENPAI.
HEH! HEH! HEH!
IT'S ALREADY HALFWAY THROUGH DECEMBER.
しょり しょり
PEEL PEEL

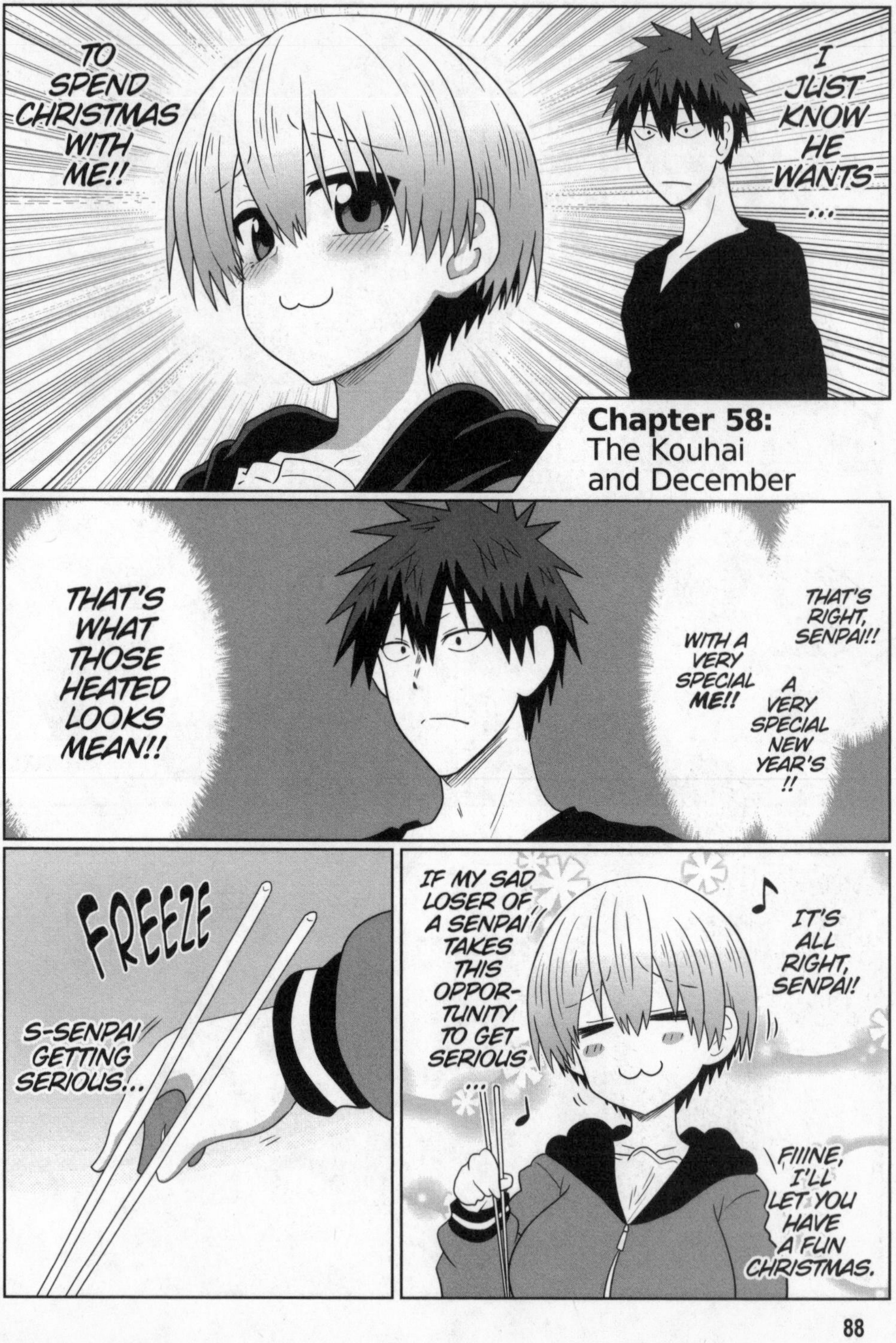
I JUST KNOW HE WANTS...
TO SPEND CHRISTMAS WITH ME!!
Chapter 58: The Kouhai and December
THAT'S RIGHT, SENPAI!!
A VERY SPECIAL NEW YEAR'S!!
WITH A VERY SPECIAL ME!!
THAT'S WHAT THOSE HEATED LOOKS MEAN!!
IT'S ALL RIGHT, SENPAI!
IF MY SAD LOSER OF A SENPAI TAKES THIS OPPORTUNITY TO GET SERIOUS...
FIIINE, I'LL LET YOU HAVE A FUN CHRISTMAS.
FREEZE
S-SENPAI GETTING SERIOUS...

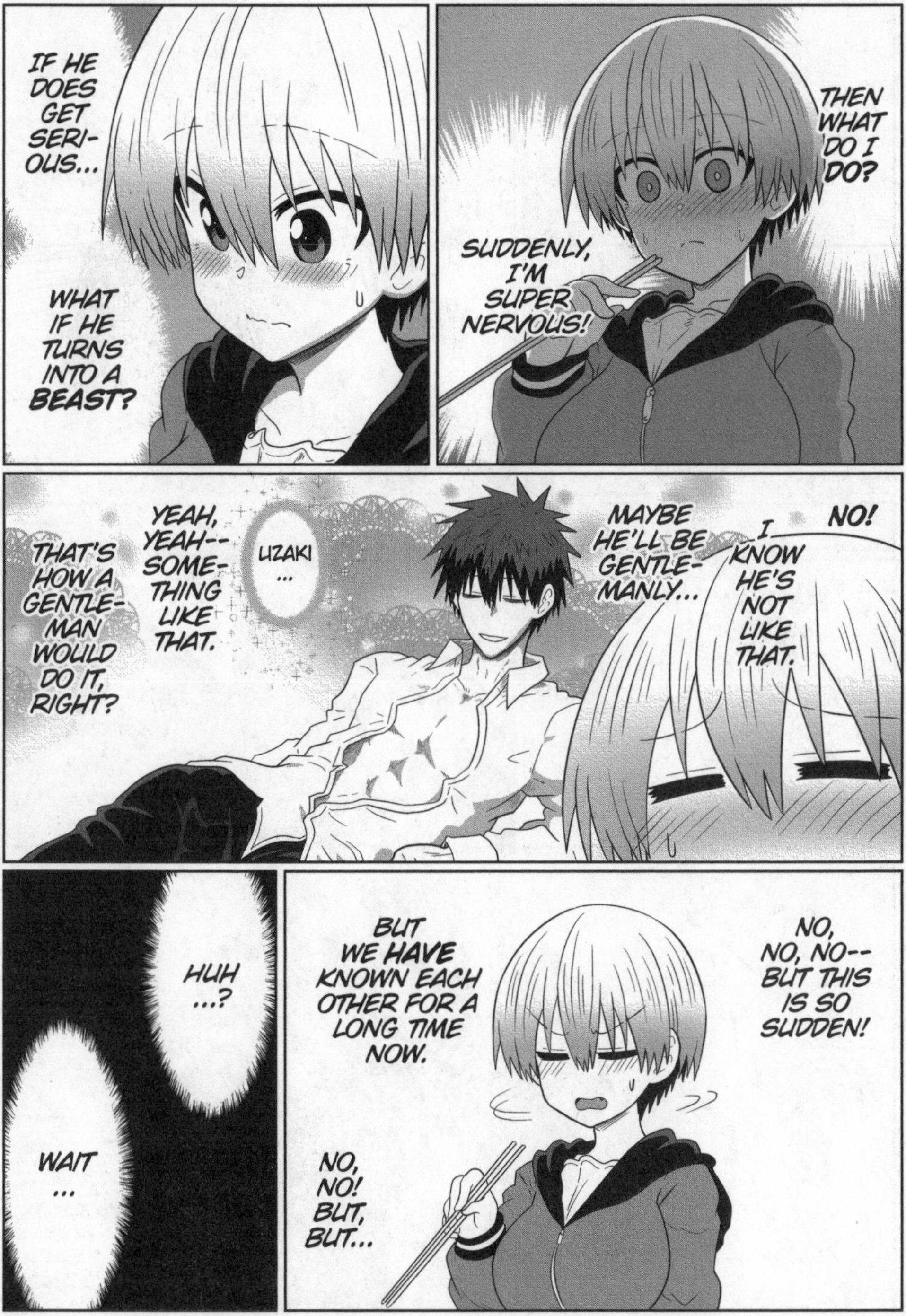
THEN WHAT DO I DO?
SUDDENLY, I'M SUPER NERVOUS!
IF HE DOES GET SERIOUS...
WHAT IF HE TURNS INTO A BEAST?
NO!
I KNOW HE'S NOT LIKE THAT.
MAYBE HE'LL BE GENTLEMANLY...
UZAKI ...
YEAH, YEAH--SOMETHING LIKE THAT.
THAT'S HOW A GENTLEMAN WOULD DO IT, RIGHT?
NO, NO, NO--BUT THIS IS SO SUDDEN!
BUT WE HAVE KNOWN EACH OTHER FOR A LONG TIME NOW.
NO, NO! BUT, BUT...
HUH ...?
WAIT ...

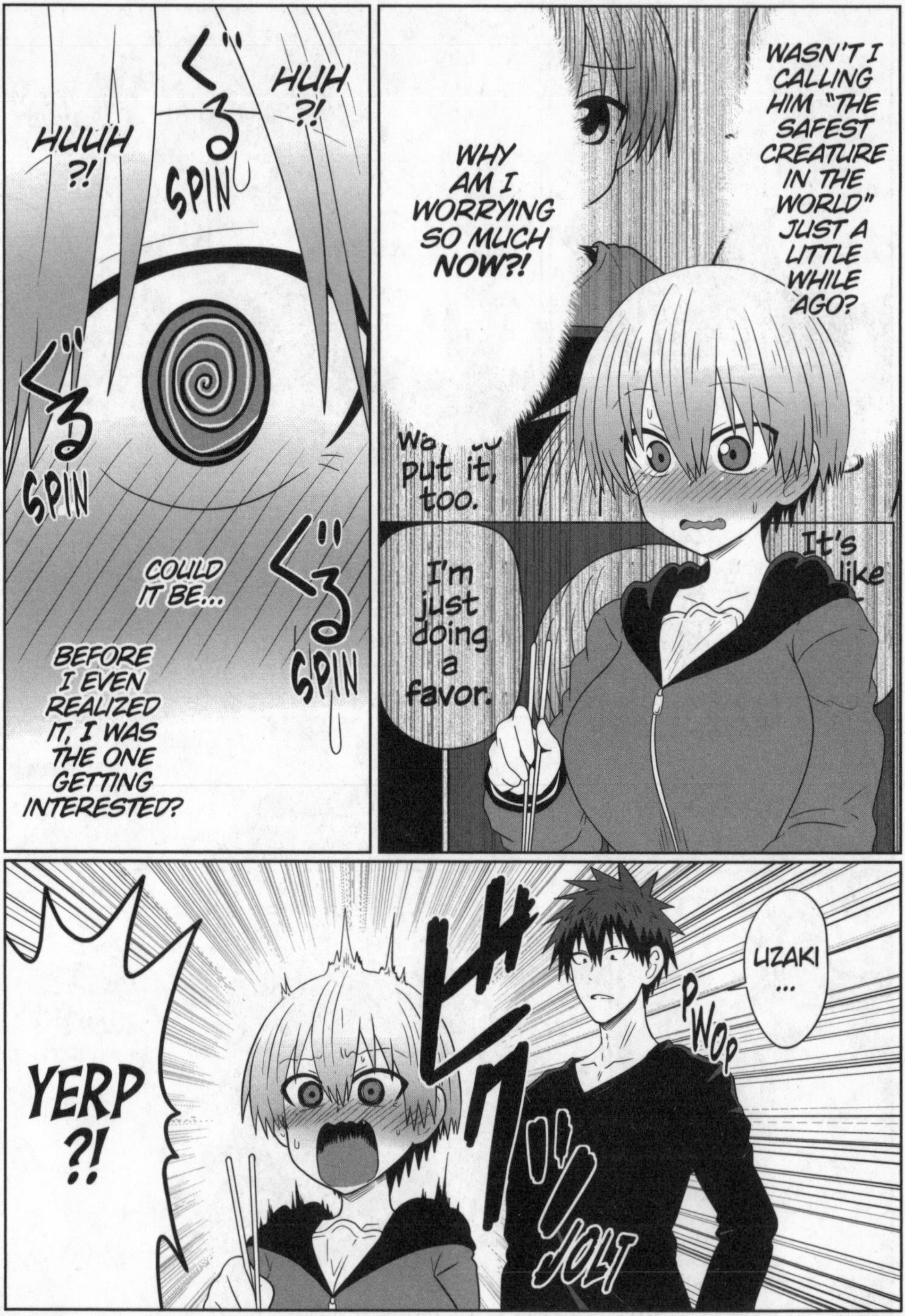
WASN'T I CALLING HIM "THE SAFEST CREATURE IN THE WORLD" JUST A LITTLE WHILE AGO?
WHY AM I WORRYING SO MUCH NOW?!
It's like
put it, too.
I'm just doing a favor.
HUH ?!
ぐる
SPIN
HUUH ?!
ぐる
SPIN
ぐる
SPIN
COULD IT BE...
BEFORE I EVEN REALIZED IT, I WAS THE ONE GETTING INTERESTED?
UZAKI ...
PWOP
ビク
JOLT
YERP ?!

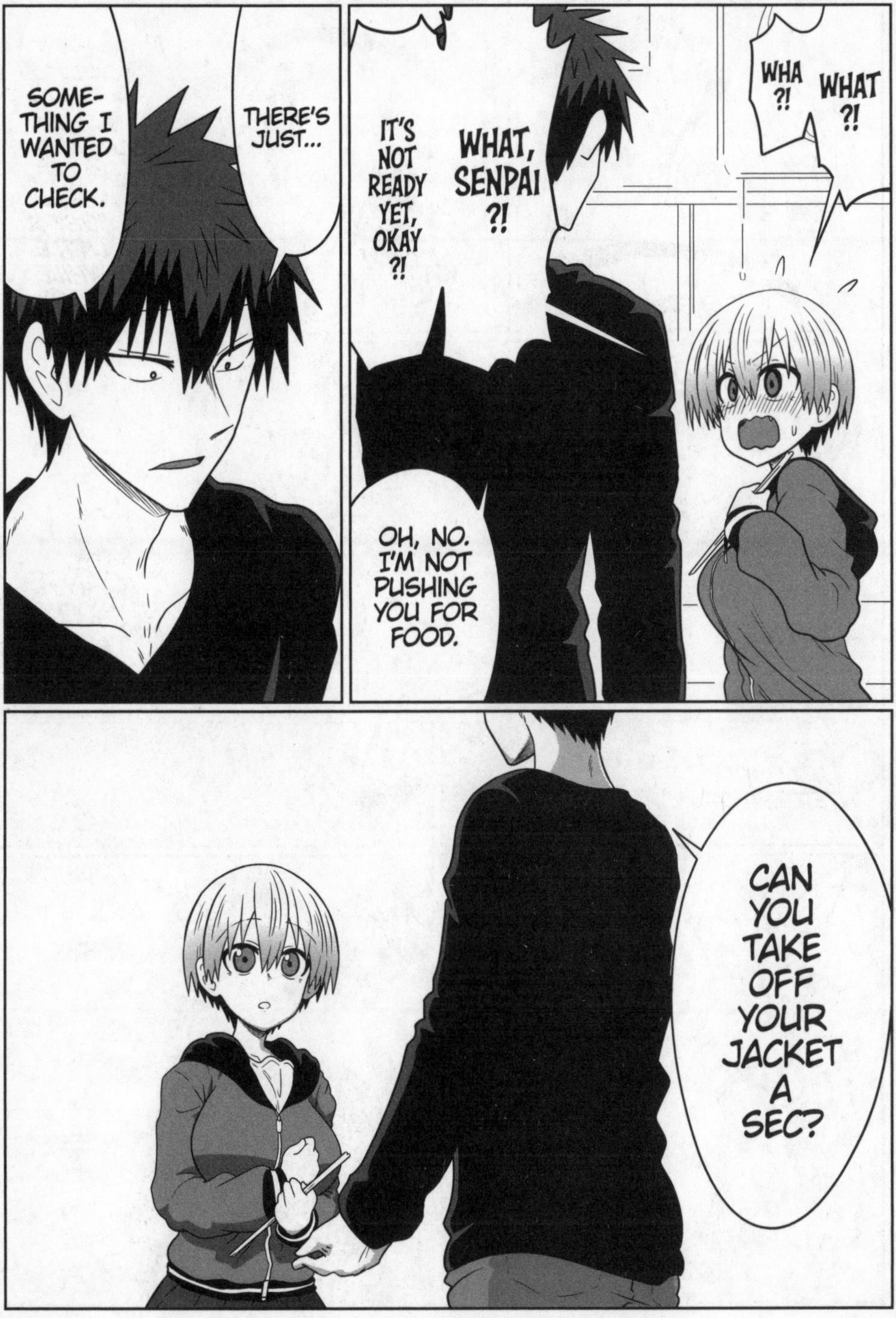

WHAT ?!
WHA ?!
WHAT, SENPAI ?!
IT'S NOT READY YET, OKAY ?!
OH, NO. I'M NOT PUSHING YOU FOR FOOD.
THERE'S JUST...
SOMETHING I WANTED TO CHECK.
CAN YOU TAKE OFF YOUR JACKET A SEC?

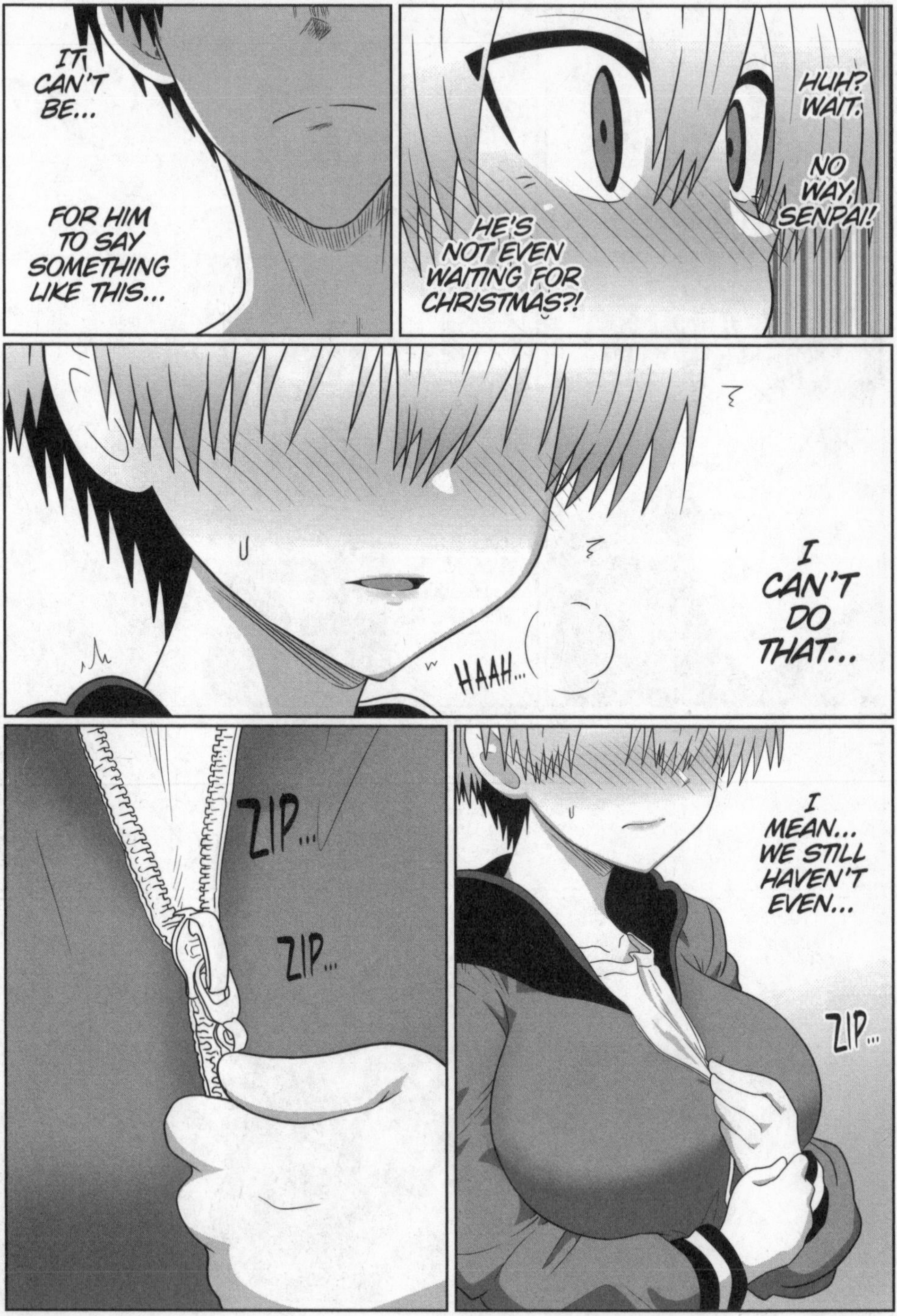
HUH? WAIT.
NO WAY, SENPAI!
HE'S NOT EVEN WAITING FOR CHRISTMAS?!
IT CAN'T BE...
FOR HIM TO SAY SOMETHING LIKE THIS...
I CAN'T DO THAT...
HAAH...
I MEAN... WE STILL HAVEN'T EVEN...
ZIP...
ZIP...
ZIP...

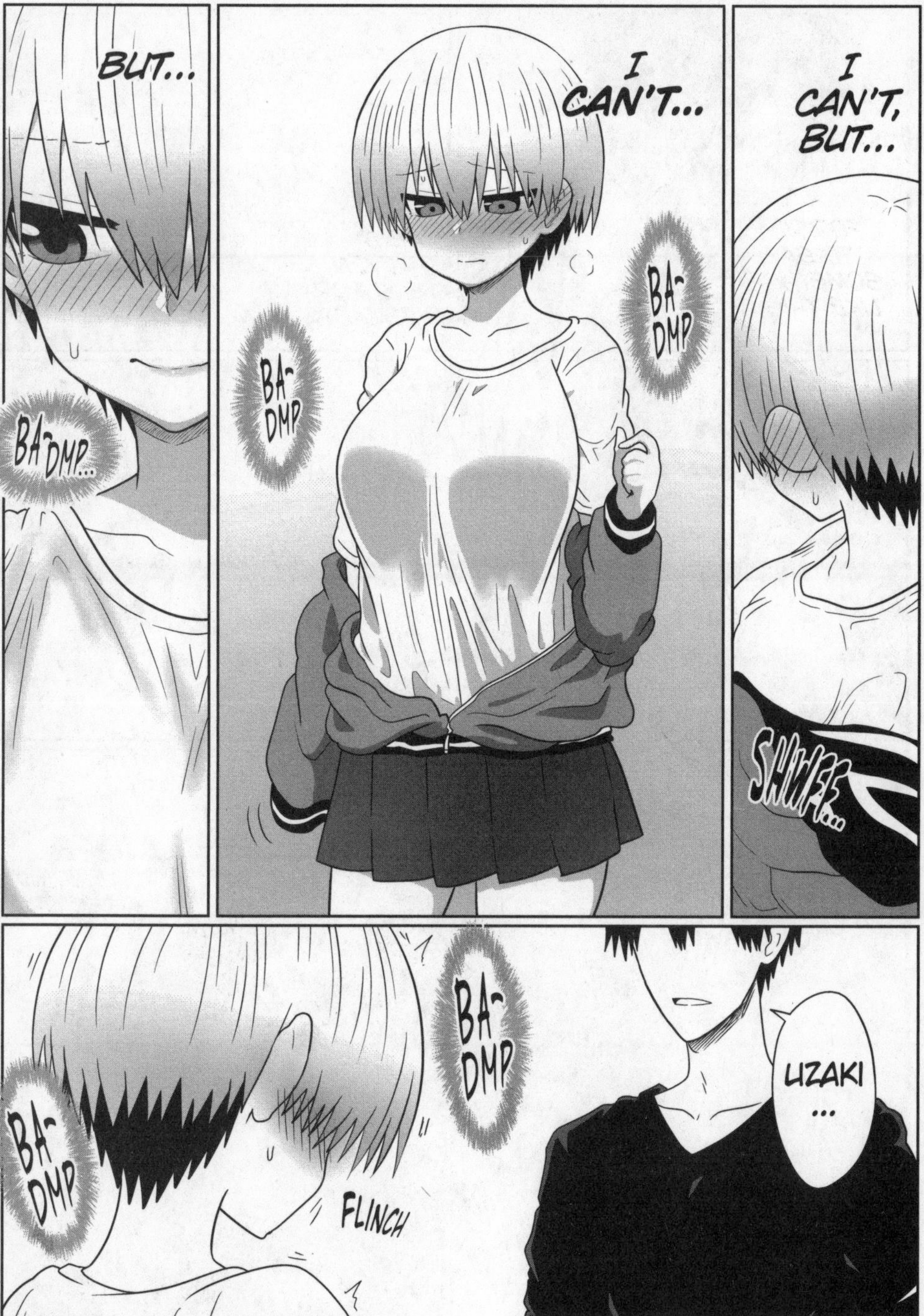
I CAN'T, BUT...
SHWFF...
I CAN'T...
BA-DMP
BA-DMP
BUT...
BA-DMP...
UZAKI ...
BA-DMP
FLINCH
BA-DMP

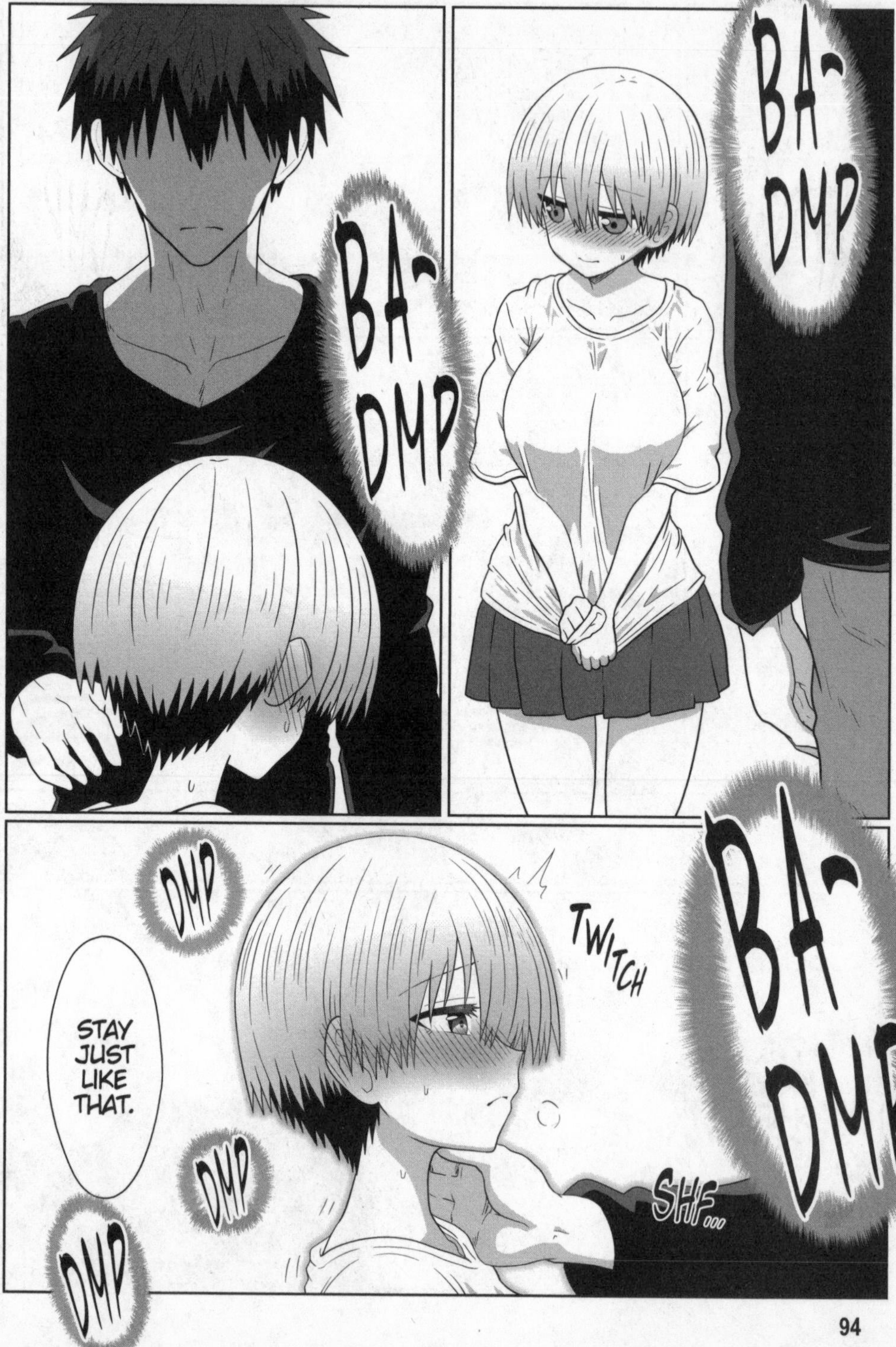
BA-DMP
BA-DMP
BA-DMP
TWITCH
SHF...
DMP
STAY JUST LIKE THAT.
DMP
DMP

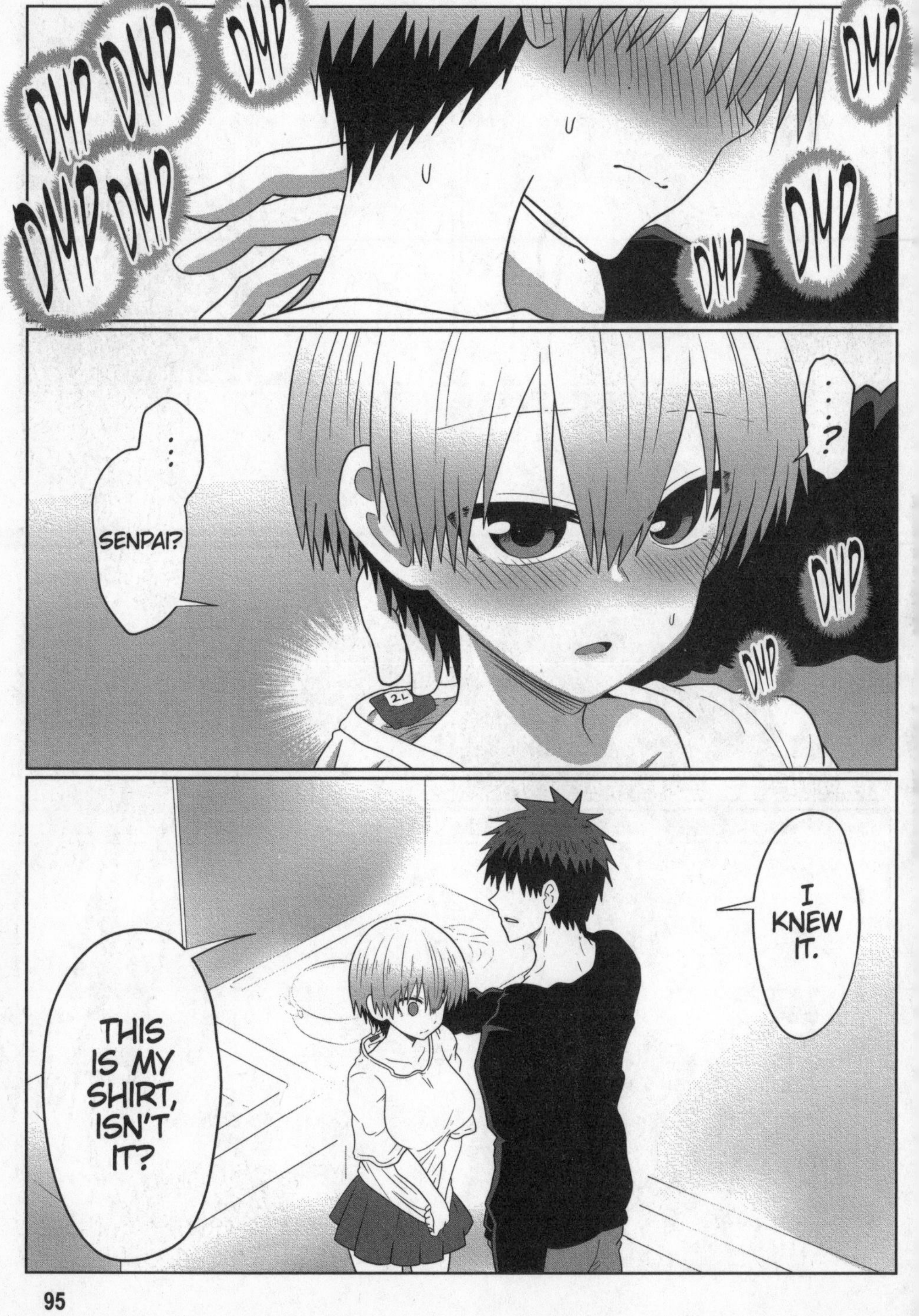
DMP
DMP
DMP
DMP
DMP DMP
DMP DMP
…?
DMP
DMP
…
SENPAI?
I KNEW IT.
THIS IS MY SHIRT, ISN'T IT?

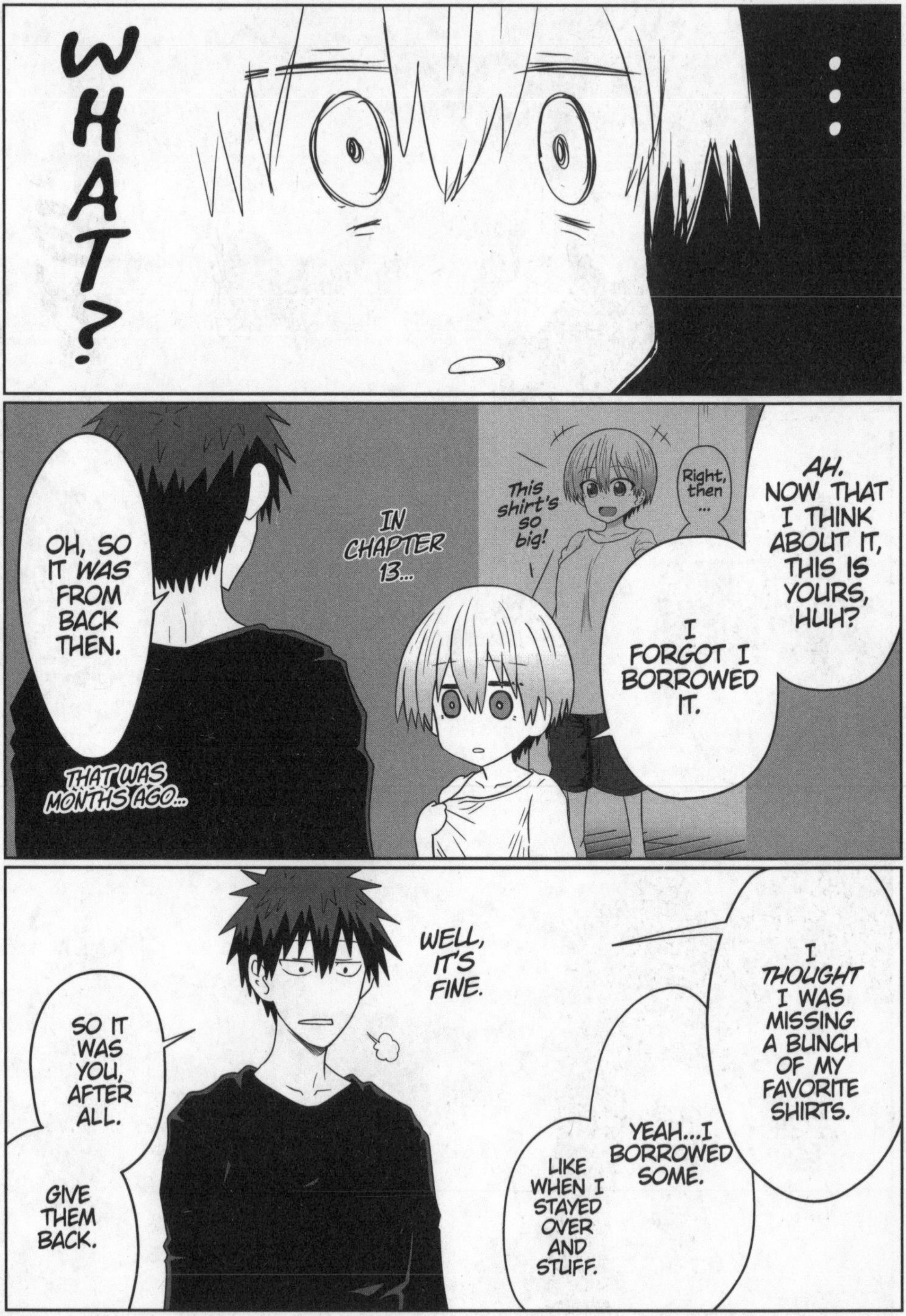
...
WHAT?
AH. NOW THAT I THINK ABOUT IT, THIS IS YOURS, HUH?
I FORGOT I BORROWED IT.
Right, then ...
This shirt's so big!
IN CHAPTER 13...
OH, SO IT WAS FROM BACK THEN.
THAT WAS MONTHS AGO...
I THOUGHT I WAS MISSING A BUNCH OF MY FAVORITE SHIRTS.
YEAH...I BORROWED SOME.
LIKE WHEN I STAYED OVER AND STUFF.
WELL, IT'S FINE.
SO IT WAS YOU, AFTER ALL.
GIVE THEM BACK.

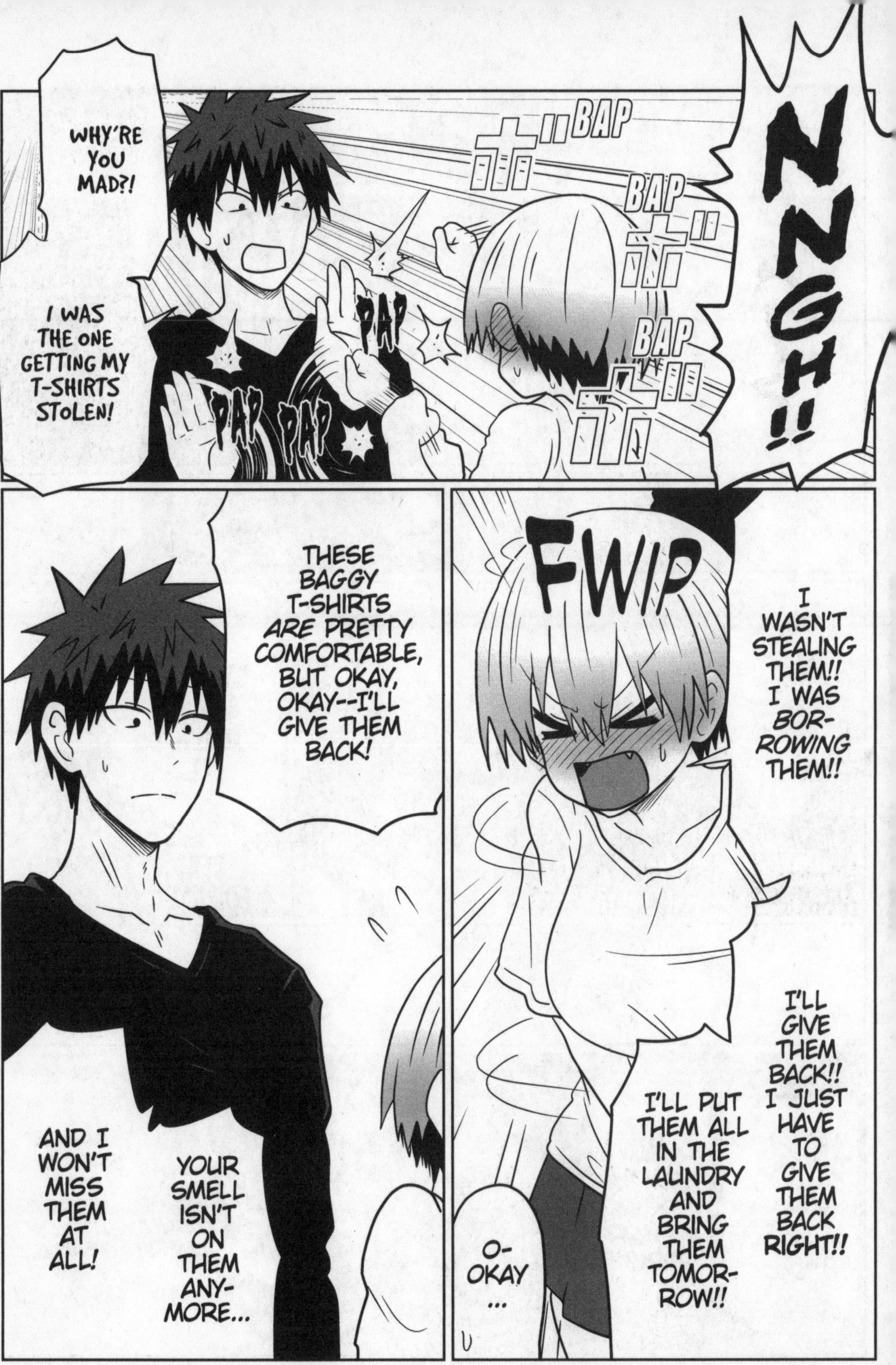
NNGH!!
BAP
BAP
BAP
PAP
PAP
PAP
WHY'RE YOU MAD?!
I WAS THE ONE GETTING MY T-SHIRTS STOLEN!
FWIP
I WASN'T STEALING THEM!! I WAS BOR-ROWING THEM!!
I'LL GIVE THEM BACK!! I JUST HAVE TO GIVE THEM BACK RIGHT!!
I'LL PUT THEM ALL IN THE LAUNDRY AND BRING THEM TOMOR-ROW!!
O-OKAY...
THESE BAGGY T-SHIRTS ARE PRETTY COMFORTABLE, BUT OKAY, OKAY--I'LL GIVE THEM BACK!
YOUR SMELL ISN'T ON THEM ANY-MORE...
AND I WON'T MISS THEM AT ALL!

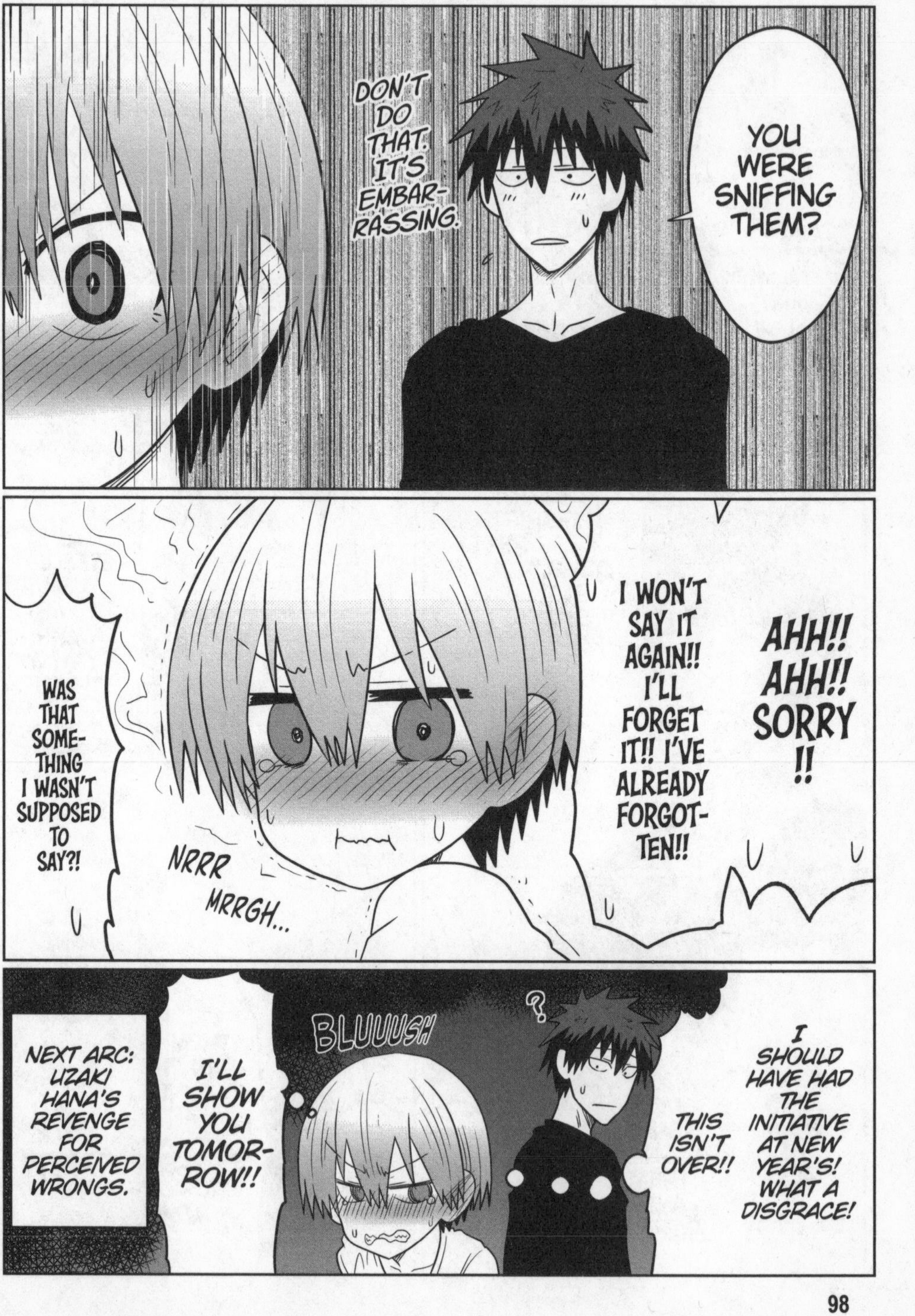
YOU WERE SNIFFING THEM?
DON'T DO THAT. IT'S EMBARRASSING.
AHH!! AHH!! SORRY!!
I WON'T SAY IT AGAIN!! I'LL FORGET IT!! I'VE ALREADY FORGOTTEN!!
NRRR MRRGH...
WAS THAT SOMETHING I WASN'T SUPPOSED TO SAY?!
I SHOULD HAVE HAD THE INITIATIVE AT NEW YEAR'S! WHAT A DISGRACE!
THIS ISN'T OVER!!
BLUUUSH
I'LL SHOW YOU TOMORROW!!
NEXT ARC: UZAKI HANA'S REVENGE FOR PERCEIVED WRONGS.

VOLUME 6
REJECTED COVER DRAFT

Uzaki-chan✫ Wants to Hang Out!

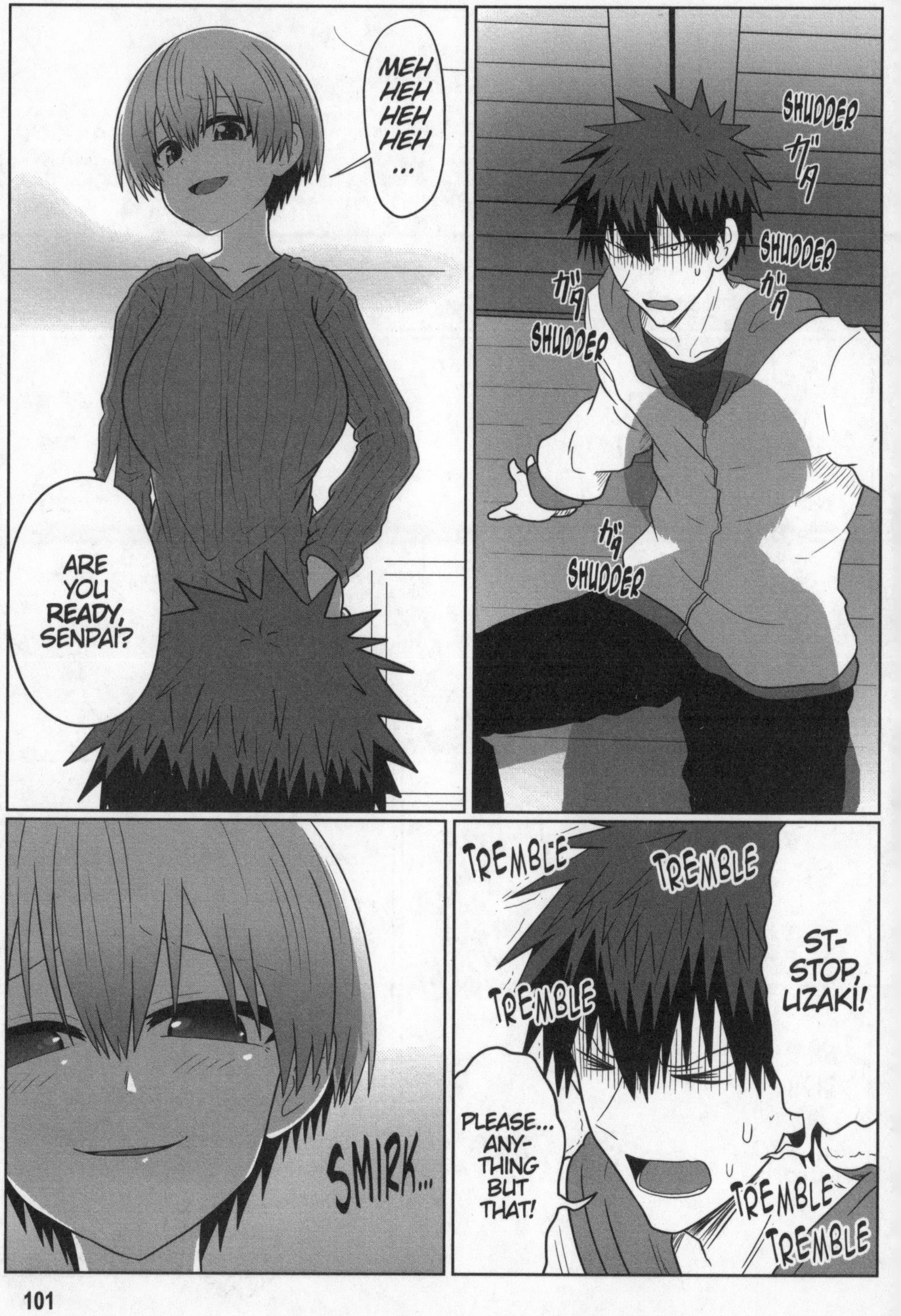
SHUDDER
ガタ
SHUDDER
ガタ
ガタ
SHUDDER
ガタ
SHUDDER
MEH HEH HEH HEH ...
ARE YOU READY, SENPAI?
TREMBLE
TREMBLE
TREMBLE
ST-STOP, UZAKI!
PLEASE... ANY-THING BUT THAT!
TREMBLE
TREMBLE
SMIRK...

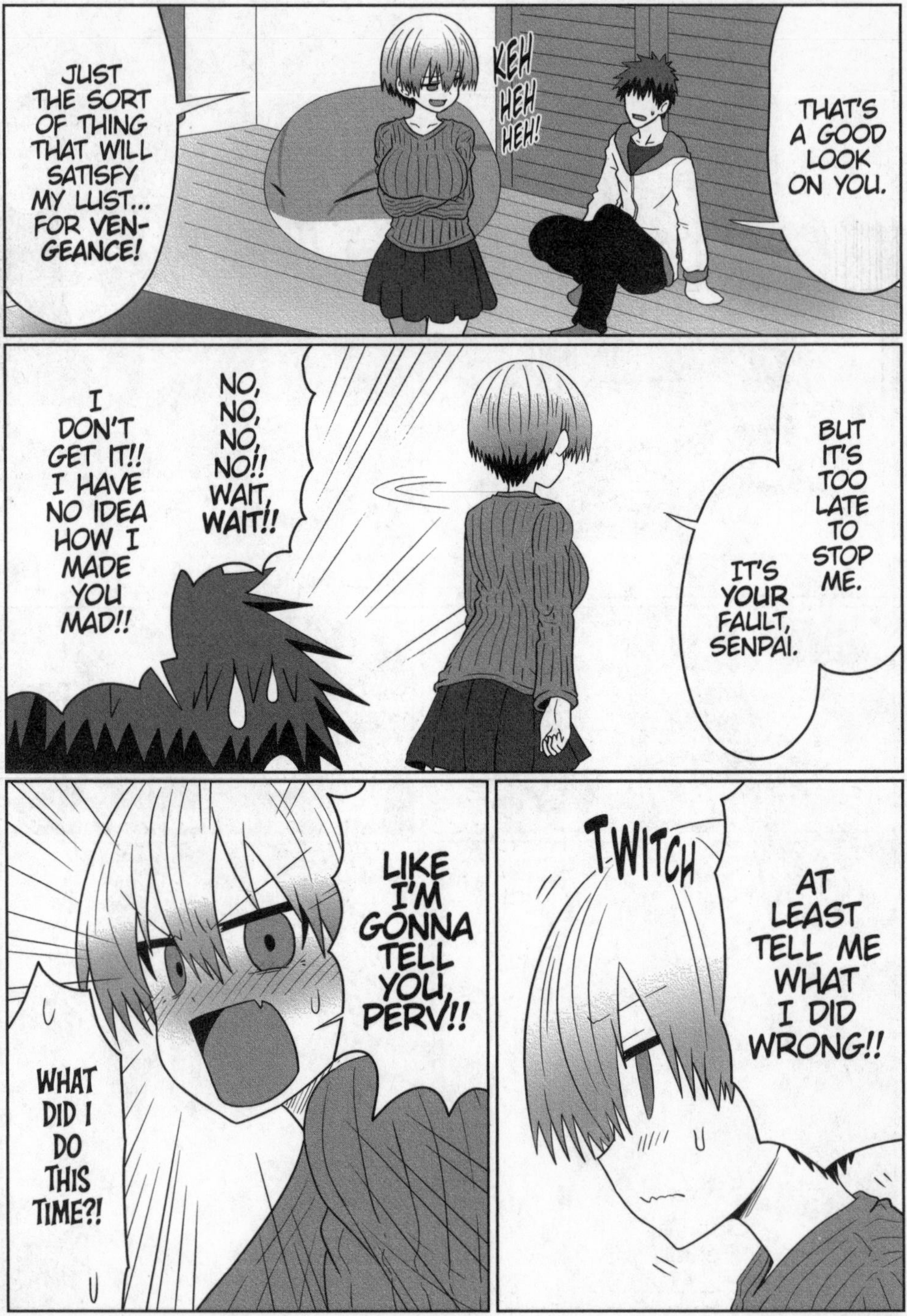
THAT'S A GOOD LOOK ON YOU.
KEH HEH HEH!
JUST THE SORT OF THING THAT WILL SATISFY MY LUST... FOR VEN-GEANCE!
BUT IT'S TOO LATE TO STOP ME.
IT'S YOUR FAULT, SENPAI.
NO, NO, NO, NO!! WAIT, WAIT!!
I DON'T GET IT!! I HAVE NO IDEA HOW I MADE YOU MAD!!
TWITCH
AT LEAST TELL ME WHAT I DID WRONG!!
LIKE I'M GONNA TELL YOU, PERV!!
WHAT DID I DO THIS TIME?!

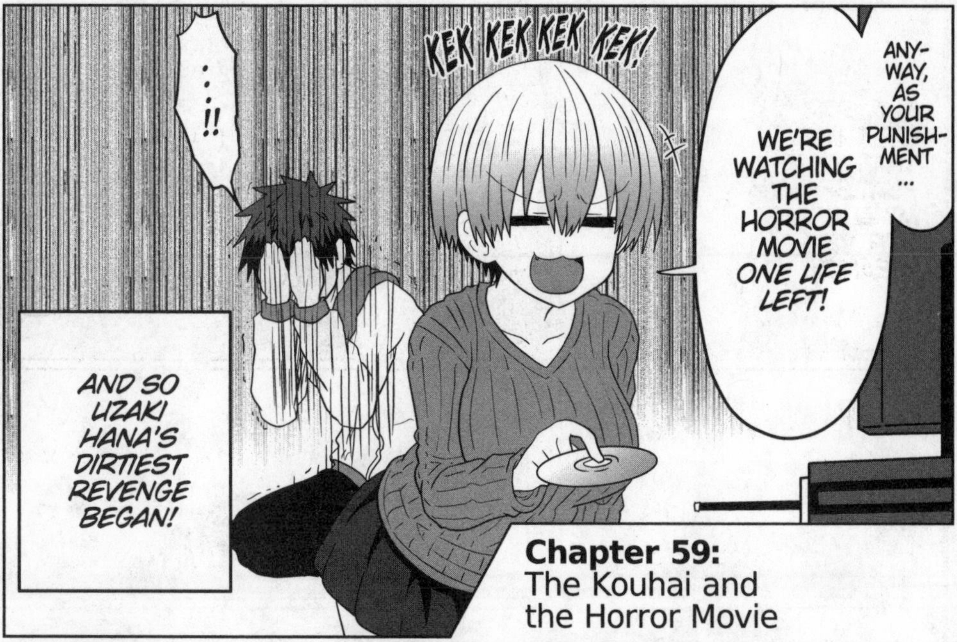
ANYWAY, AS YOUR PUNISHMENT...
WE'RE WATCHING THE HORROR MOVIE ONE LIFE LEFT!
KEK KEK KEK KEK!
...!!
AND SO UZAKI HANA'S DIRTIEST REVENGE BEGAN!

Chapter 59:
The Kouhai and the Horror Movie

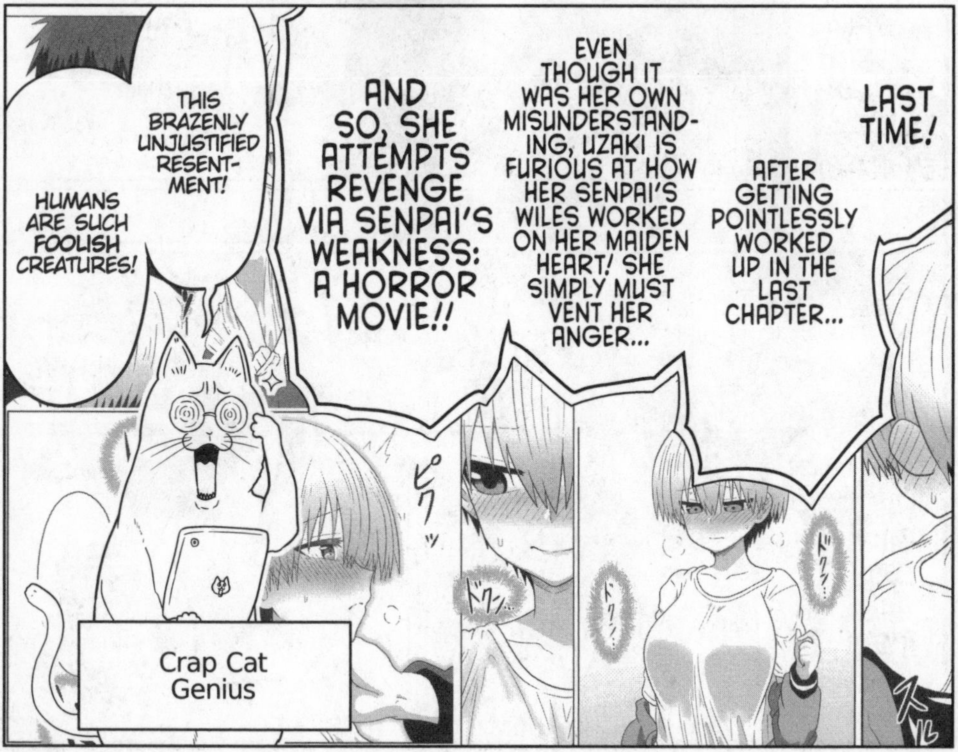
LAST TIME!
AFTER GETTING POINTLESSLY WORKED UP IN THE LAST CHAPTER...
EVEN THOUGH IT WAS HER OWN MISUNDERSTANDING, UZAKI IS FURIOUS AT HOW HER SENPAI'S WILES WORKED ON HER MAIDEN HEART! SHE SIMPLY MUST VENT HER ANGER...
AND SO, SHE ATTEMPTS REVENGE VIA SENPAI'S WEAKNESS: A HORROR MOVIE!!
THIS BRAZENLY UNJUSTIFIED RESENTMENT!
HUMANS ARE SUCH FOOLISH CREATURES!
Crap Cat Genius

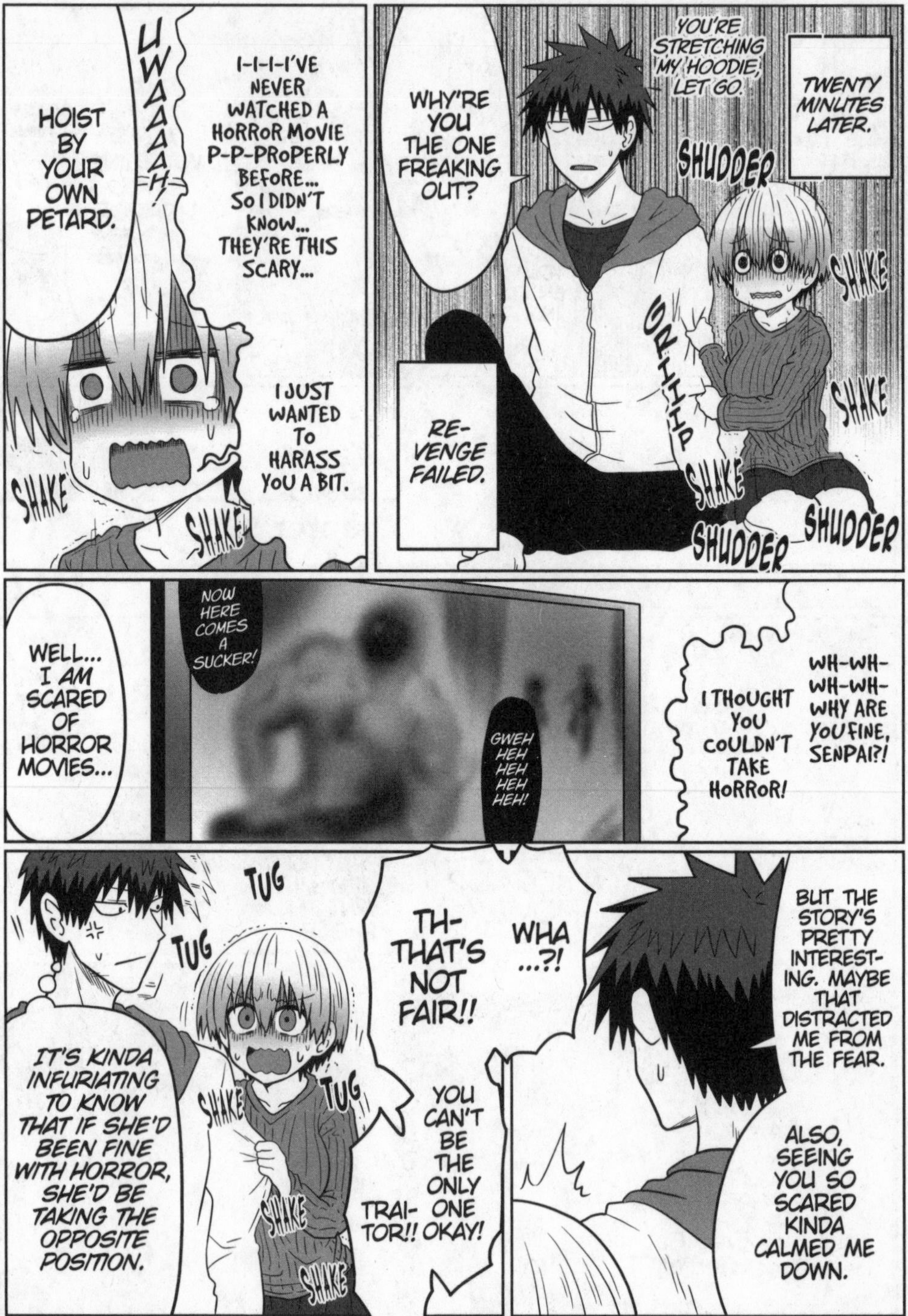
TWENTY MINUTES LATER.
YOU'RE STRETCHING MY HOODIE, LET GO.
SHUDDER
WHY'RE YOU THE ONE FREAKING OUT?
SHAKE
GRIIIP
SHAKE
REVENGE FAILED.
SHAKE
SHUDDER
SHUDDER
UWAAAAAH!
I-I-I-I'VE NEVER WATCHED A HORROR MOVIE P-P-PROPERLY BEFORE... SO I DIDN'T KNOW... THEY'RE THIS SCARY...
HOIST BY YOUR OWN PETARD.
I JUST WANTED TO HARASS YOU A BIT.
SHAKE
SHAKE
WH-WH-WH-WH-WHY ARE YOU FINE, SENPAI?!
I THOUGHT YOU COULDN'T TAKE HORROR!
NOW HERE COMES A SUCKER!
GWEH HEH HEH HEH HEH!
WELL... I AM SCARED OF HORROR MOVIES...
BUT THE STORY'S PRETTY INTERESTING. MAYBE THAT DISTRACTED ME FROM THE FEAR.
WHA...?!
ALSO, SEEING YOU SO SCARED KINDA CALMED ME DOWN.
TH-THAT'S NOT FAIR!!
YOU CAN'T BE THE ONLY ONE OKAY!
TRAITOR!!
TUG
TUG
TUG
SHAKE
SHAKE
SHAKE
IT'S KINDA INFURIATING TO KNOW THAT IF SHE'D BEEN FINE WITH HORROR, SHE'D BE TAKING THE OPPOSITE POSITION.

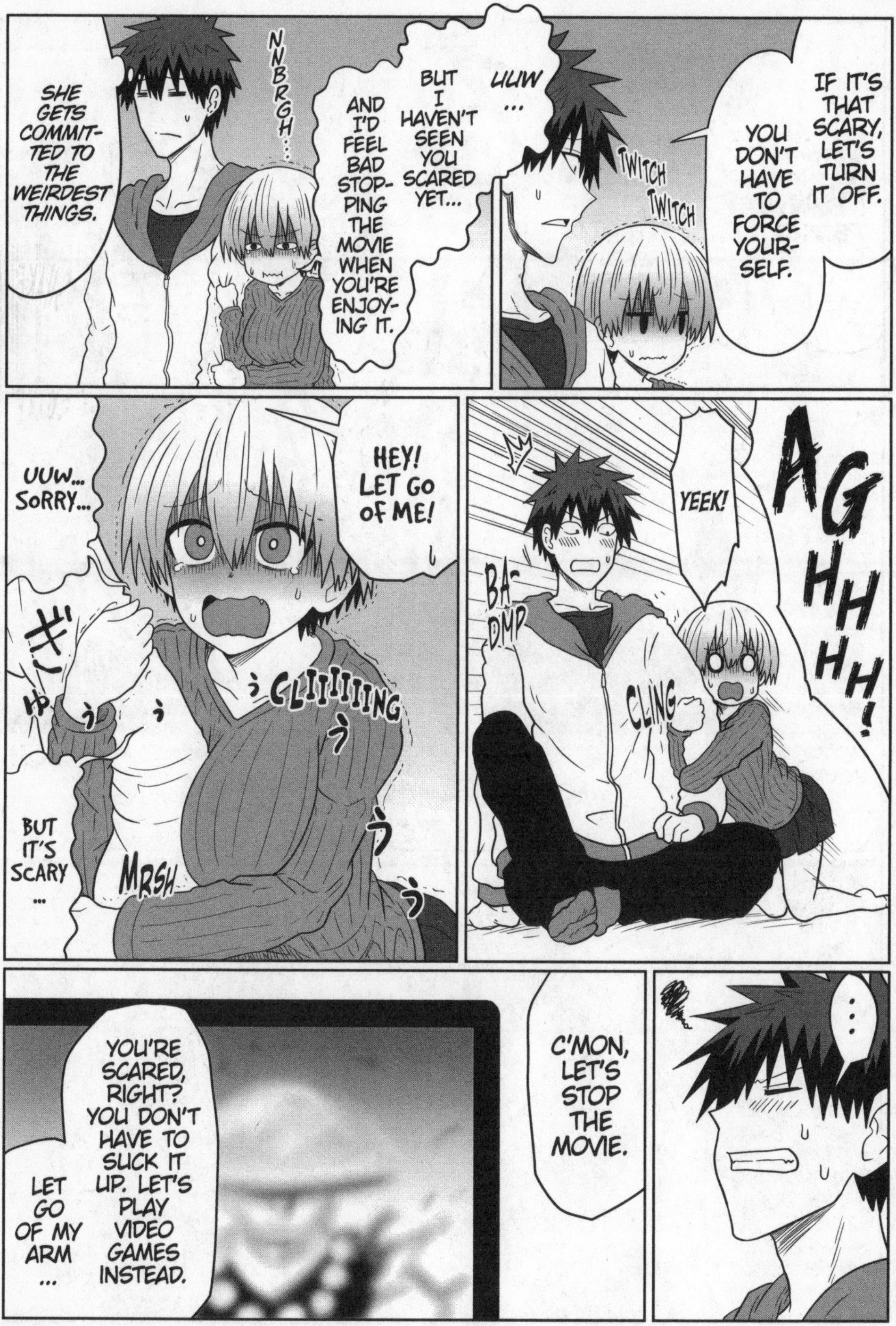
IF IT'S THAT SCARY, LET'S TURN IT OFF.
YOU DON'T HAVE TO FORCE YOURSELF.
TWITCH TWITCH
UUW...
BUT I HAVEN'T SEEN YOU SCARED YET...
AND I'D FEEL BAD STOPPING THE MOVIE WHEN YOU'RE ENJOYING IT.
NNBRGH...
SHE GETS COMMITTED TO THE WEIRDEST THINGS.
AGHHHHH!
YEEK!
BA-DMP
CLING
HEY! LET GO OF ME!
UUW... SORRY...
CLIIIIIING
ぎゅ
BUT IT'S SCARY...
MRSH
...
C'MON, LET'S STOP THE MOVIE.
YOU'RE SCARED, RIGHT? YOU DON'T HAVE TO SUCK IT UP. LET'S PLAY VIDEO GAMES INSTEAD.
LET GO OF MY ARM...

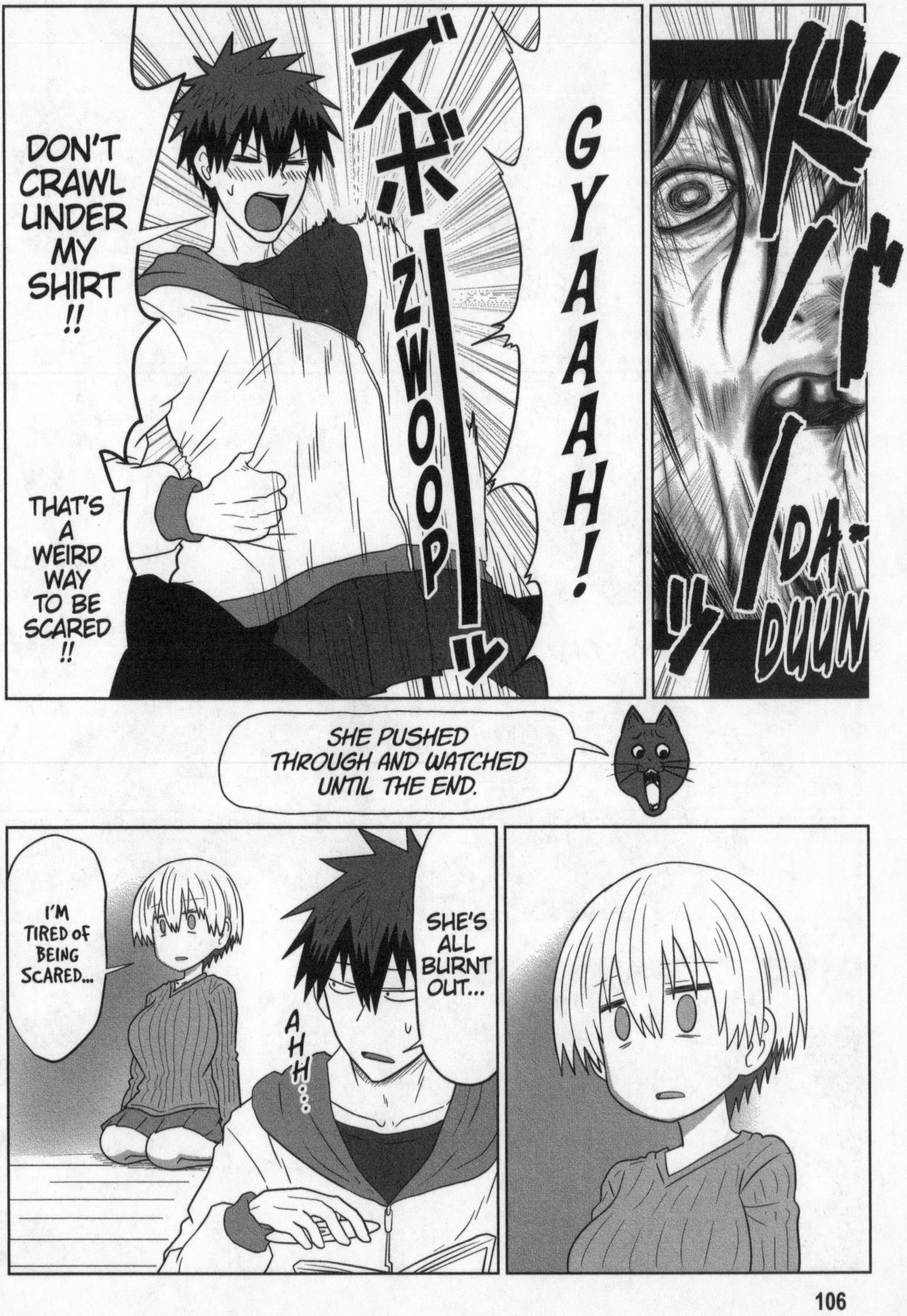
DA-DUUN
GYAAAH!
ZWOOP
DON'T CRAWL UNDER MY SHIRT!!
THAT'S A WEIRD WAY TO BE SCARED!!
SHE PUSHED THROUGH AND WATCHED UNTIL THE END.
SHE'S ALL BURNT OUT...
AHH...
I'M TIRED OF BEING SCARED...

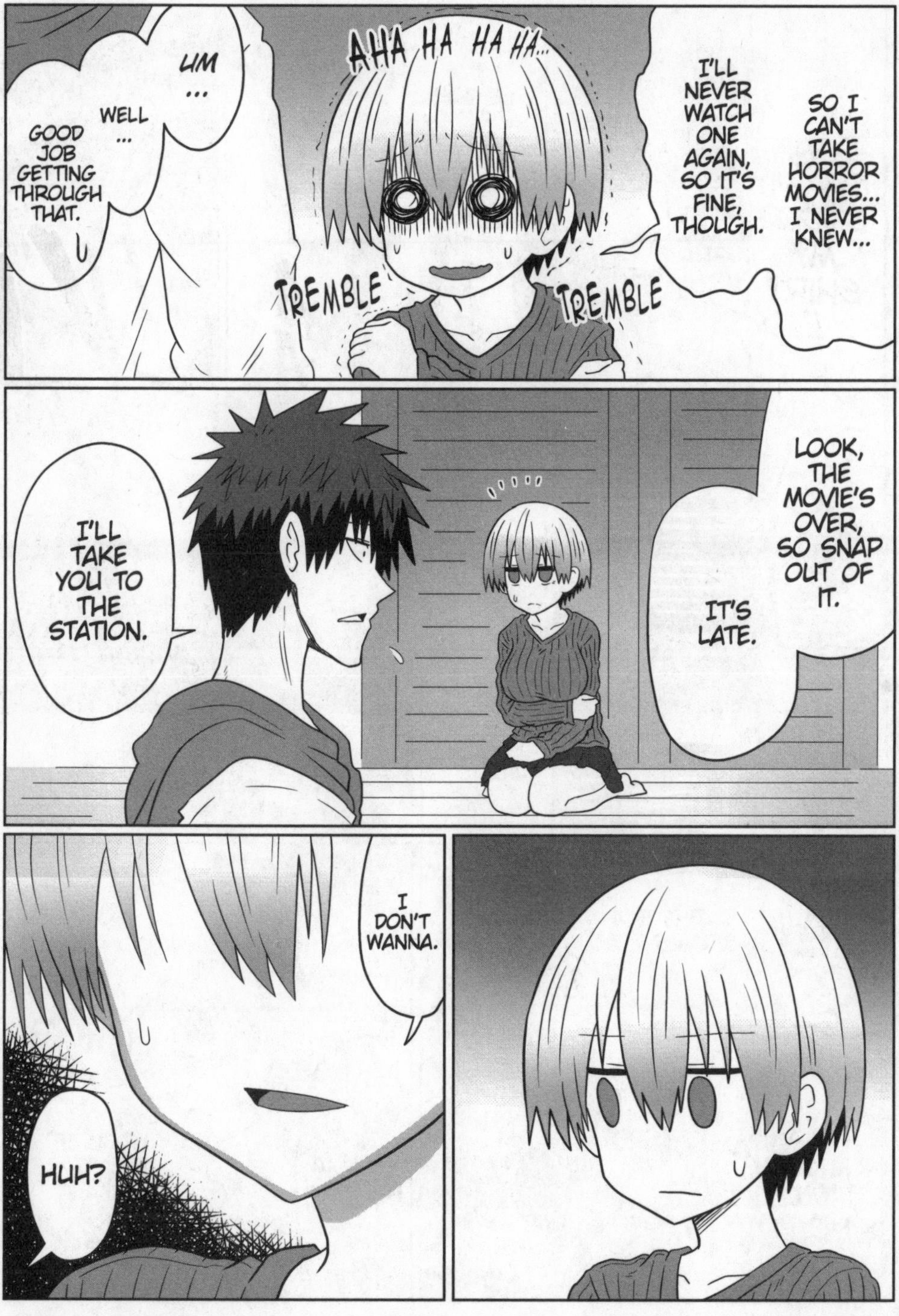
SO I CAN'T TAKE HORROR MOVIES... I NEVER KNEW...
I'LL NEVER WATCH ONE AGAIN, SO IT'S FINE, THOUGH.
AHA HA HA HA...
TREMBLE
TREMBLE
UM ...
WELL ...
GOOD JOB GETTING THROUGH THAT.
LOOK, THE MOVIE'S OVER, SO SNAP OUT OF IT.
IT'S LATE.
I'LL TAKE YOU TO THE STATION.
I DON'T WANNA.
HUH?

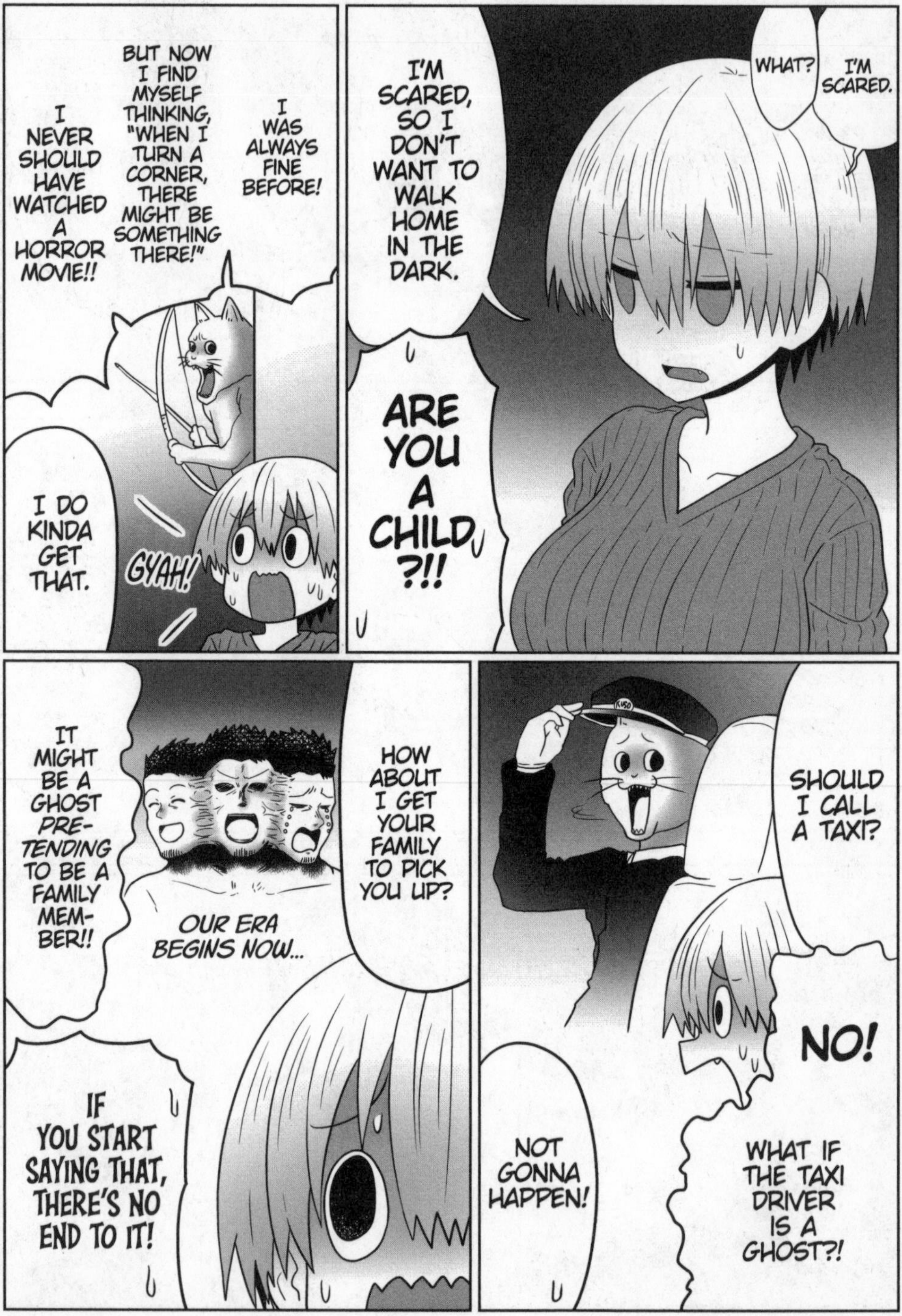
WHAT?
I'M SCARED.
I'M SCARED, SO I DON'T WANT TO WALK HOME IN THE DARK.
ARE YOU A CHILD?!!
I WAS ALWAYS FINE BEFORE!
BUT NOW I FIND MYSELF THINKING, "WHEN I TURN A CORNER, THERE MIGHT BE SOMETHING THERE!"
I NEVER SHOULD HAVE WATCHED A HORROR MOVIE!!
GYAH!
I DO KINDA GET THAT.
SHOULD I CALL A TAXI?
NO!
WHAT IF THE TAXI DRIVER IS A GHOST?!
NOT GONNA HAPPEN!
HOW ABOUT I GET YOUR FAMILY TO PICK YOU UP?
IT MIGHT BE A GHOST PRE-TENDING TO BE A FAMILY MEM-BER!!
OUR ERA BEGINS NOW...
IF YOU START SAYING THAT, THERE'S NO END TO IT!

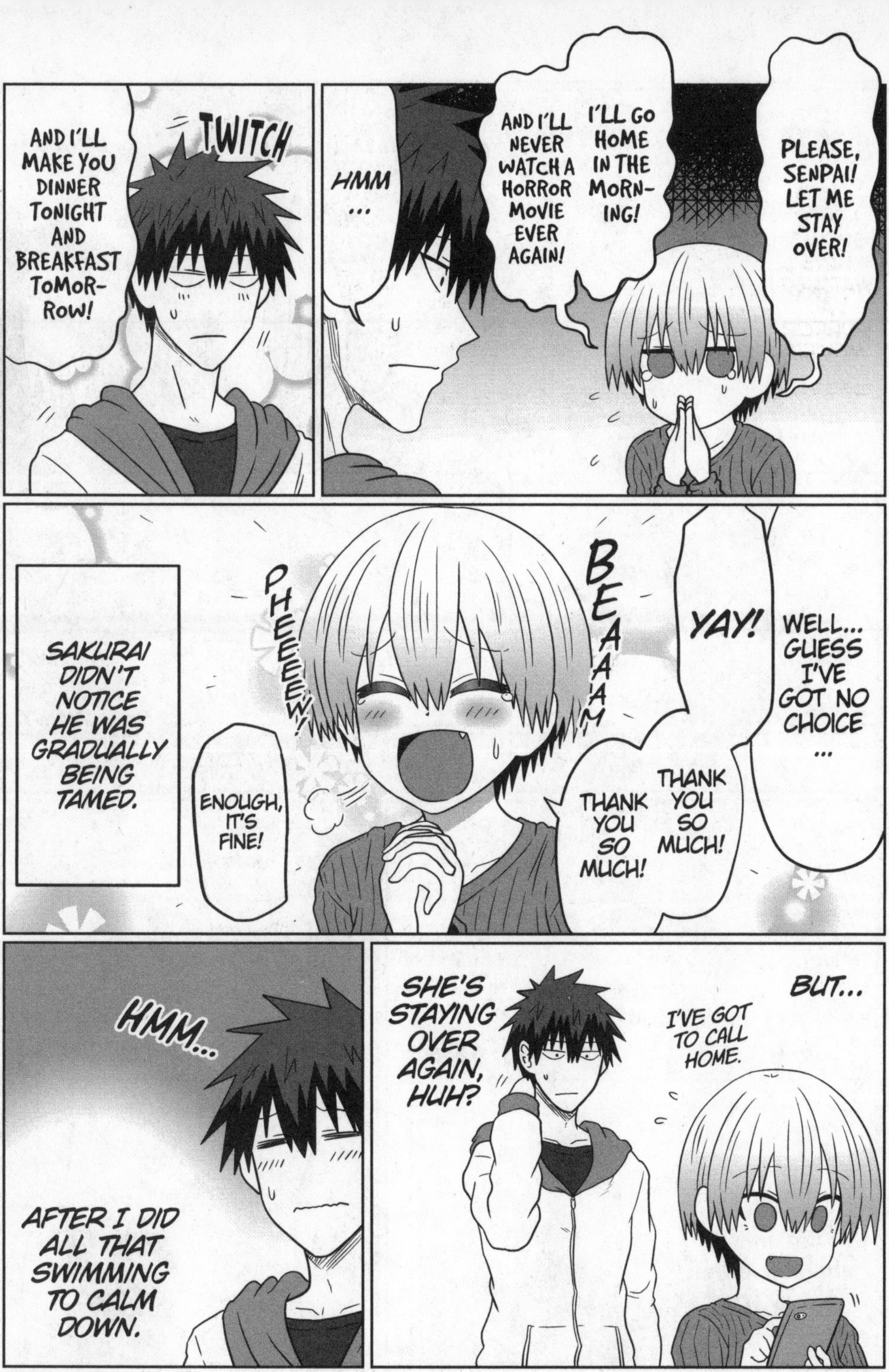
PLEASE, SENPAI! LET ME STAY OVER!
I'LL GO HOME IN THE MORNING!
AND I'LL NEVER WATCH A HORROR MOVIE EVER AGAIN!
HMM...
TWITCH
AND I'LL MAKE YOU DINNER TONIGHT AND BREAKFAST TOMORROW!
WELL... GUESS I'VE GOT NO CHOICE...
YAY!
BEAAAAM
THANK YOU SO MUCH!
THANK YOU SO MUCH!
PHEEEEEW!
ENOUGH, IT'S FINE!
SAKURAI DIDN'T NOTICE HE WAS GRADUALLY BEING TAMED.
BUT...
I'VE GOT TO CALL HOME.
SHE'S STAYING OVER AGAIN, HUH?
HMM...
AFTER I DID ALL THAT SWIMMING TO CALM DOWN.

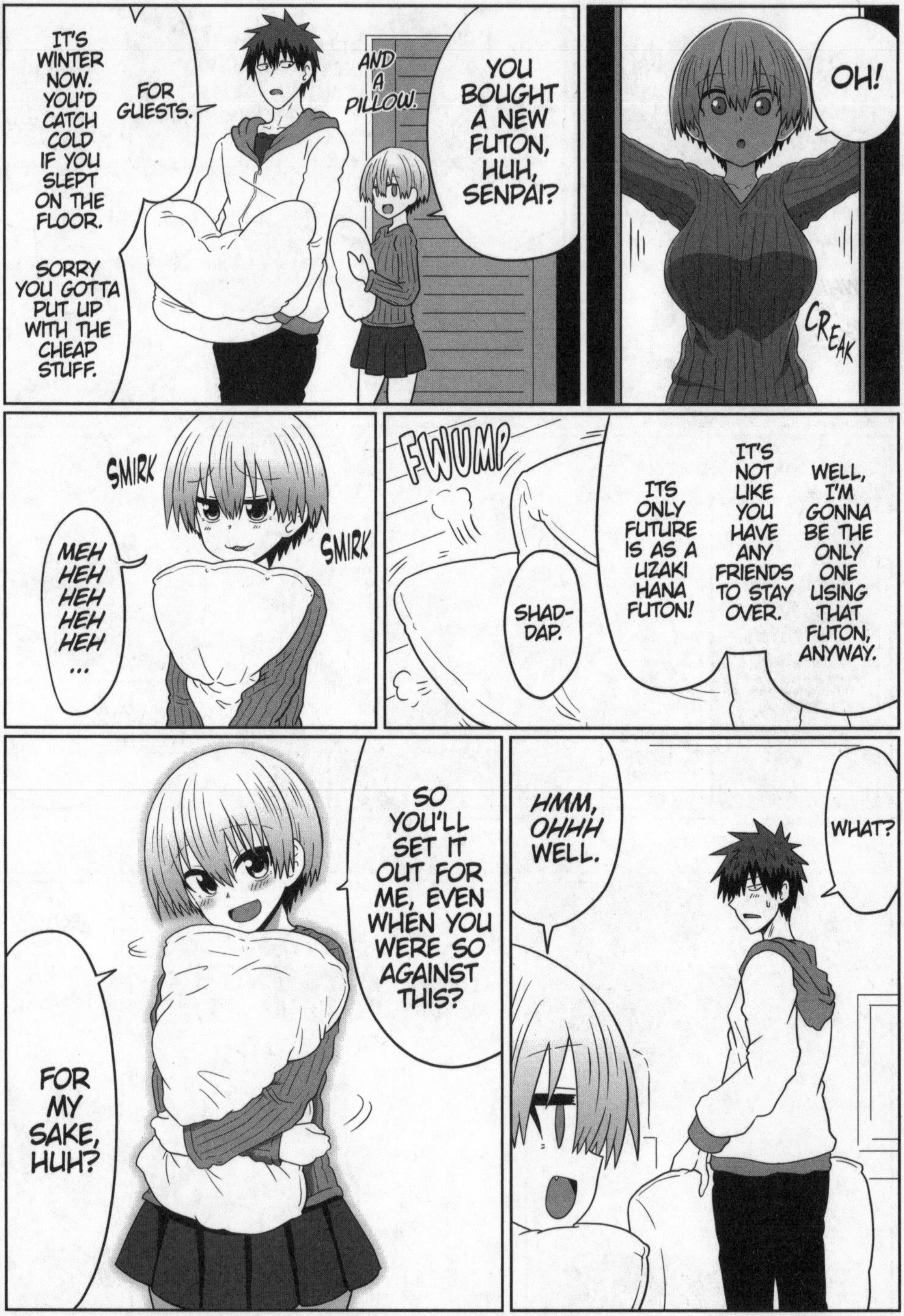

OH!
CREAK
YOU BOUGHT A NEW FUTON, HUH, SENPAI?
AND A PILLOW.
FOR GUESTS.
IT'S WINTER NOW. YOU'D CATCH COLD IF YOU SLEPT ON THE FLOOR.
SORRY YOU GOTTA PUT UP WITH THE CHEAP STUFF.
WELL, I'M GONNA BE THE ONLY ONE USING THAT FUTON, ANYWAY.
IT'S NOT LIKE YOU HAVE ANY FRIENDS TO STAY OVER.
ITS ONLY FUTURE IS AS A UZAKI HANA FUTON!
FWUMP
SHAD-DAP.
SMIRK
SMIRK
MEH HEH HEH HEH HEH ...
WHAT?
HMM, OHHH WELL.
SO YOU'LL SET IT OUT FOR ME, EVEN WHEN YOU WERE SO AGAINST THIS?
FOR MY SAKE, HUH?

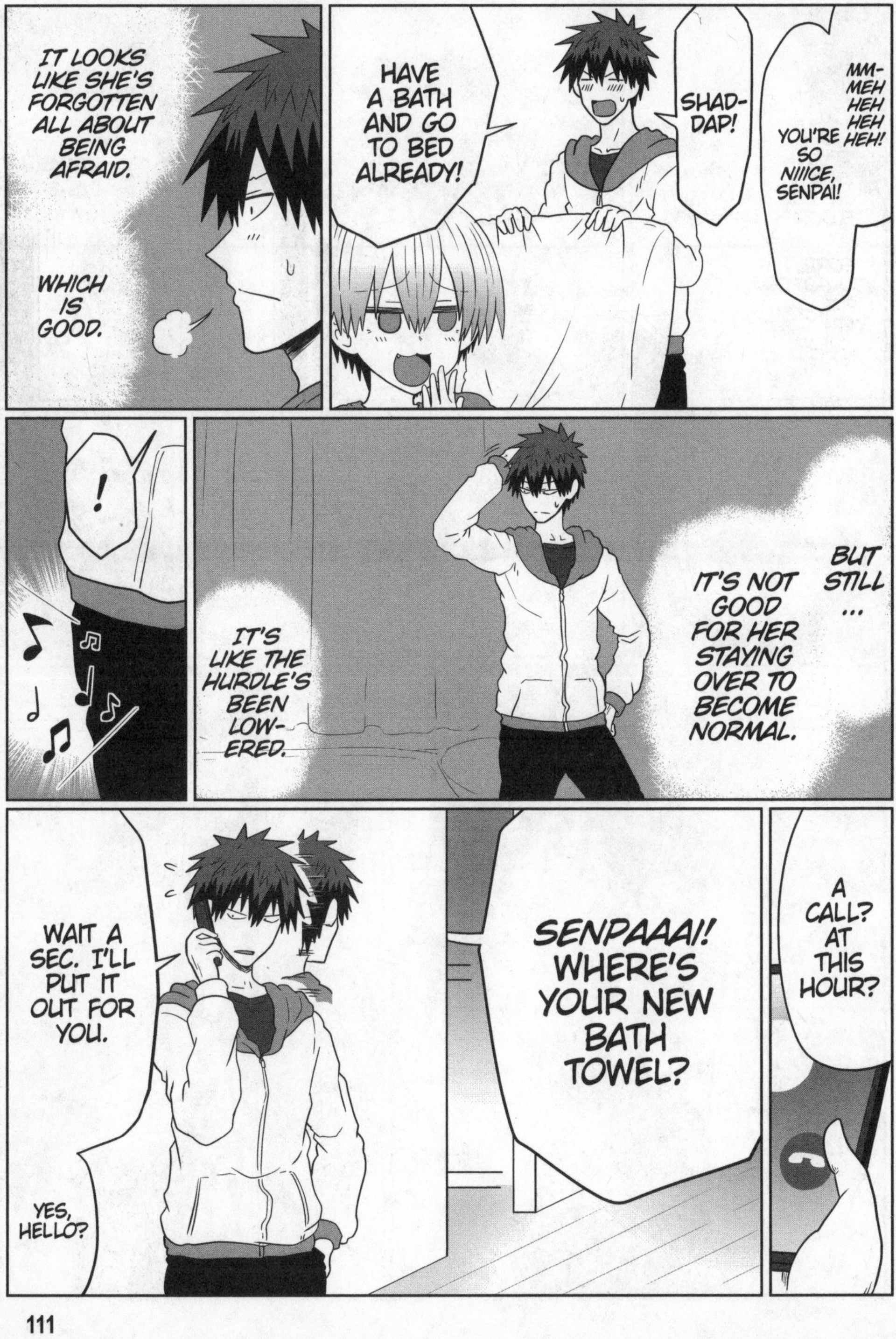
MM-MEH HEH HEH HEH!
YOU'RE SO NIIICE, SENPAI!
SHAD-DAP!
HAVE A BATH AND GO TO BED ALREADY!
IT LOOKS LIKE SHE'S FORGOTTEN ALL ABOUT BEING AFRAID.
WHICH IS GOOD.
BUT STILL ...
IT'S NOT GOOD FOR HER STAYING OVER TO BECOME NORMAL.
IT'S LIKE THE HURDLE'S BEEN LOW-ERED.
!
A CALL? AT THIS HOUR?
SENPAAAI! WHERE'S YOUR NEW BATH TOWEL?
WAIT A SEC. I'LL PUT IT OUT FOR YOU.
YES, HELLO?

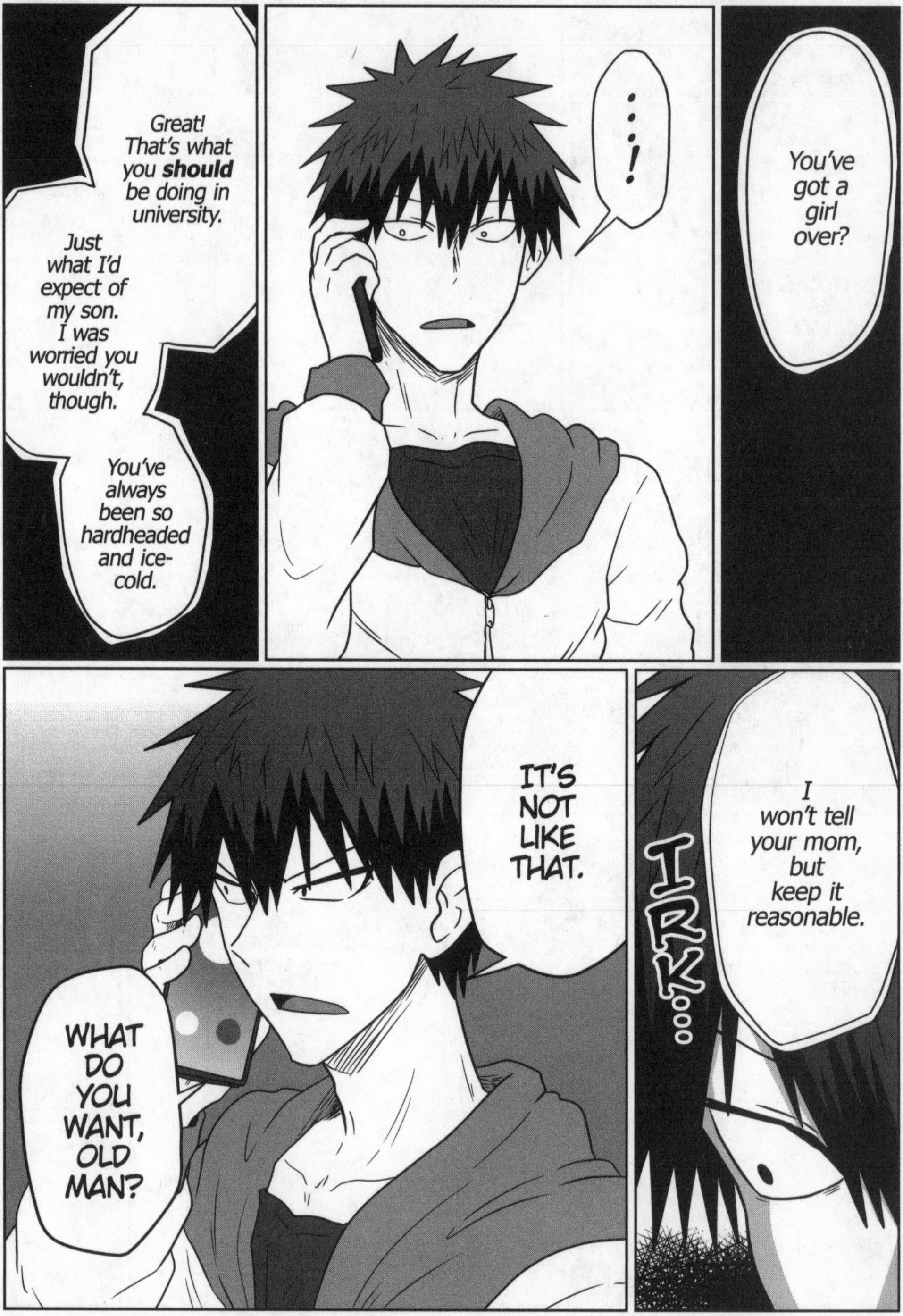
You've got a girl over?
...!
Great! That's what you **should** be doing in university.
Just what I'd expect of my son. I was worried you wouldn't, though.
You've always been so hardheaded and ice-cold.
I won't tell your mom, but keep it reasonable.
IRK...
IT'S NOT LIKE THAT.
WHAT DO YOU WANT, OLD MAN?

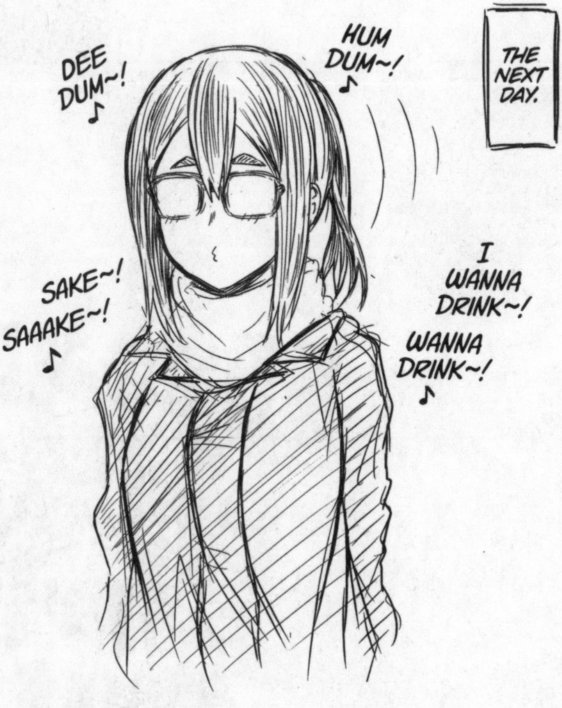
THE NEXT DAY.
HUM DUM~! ♪
DEE DUM~! ♪
I WANNA DRINK~!
WANNA DRINK~! ♪
SAKE~! SAAAKE~! ♪

Uzaki-chan ☆ Wants to Hang Out!

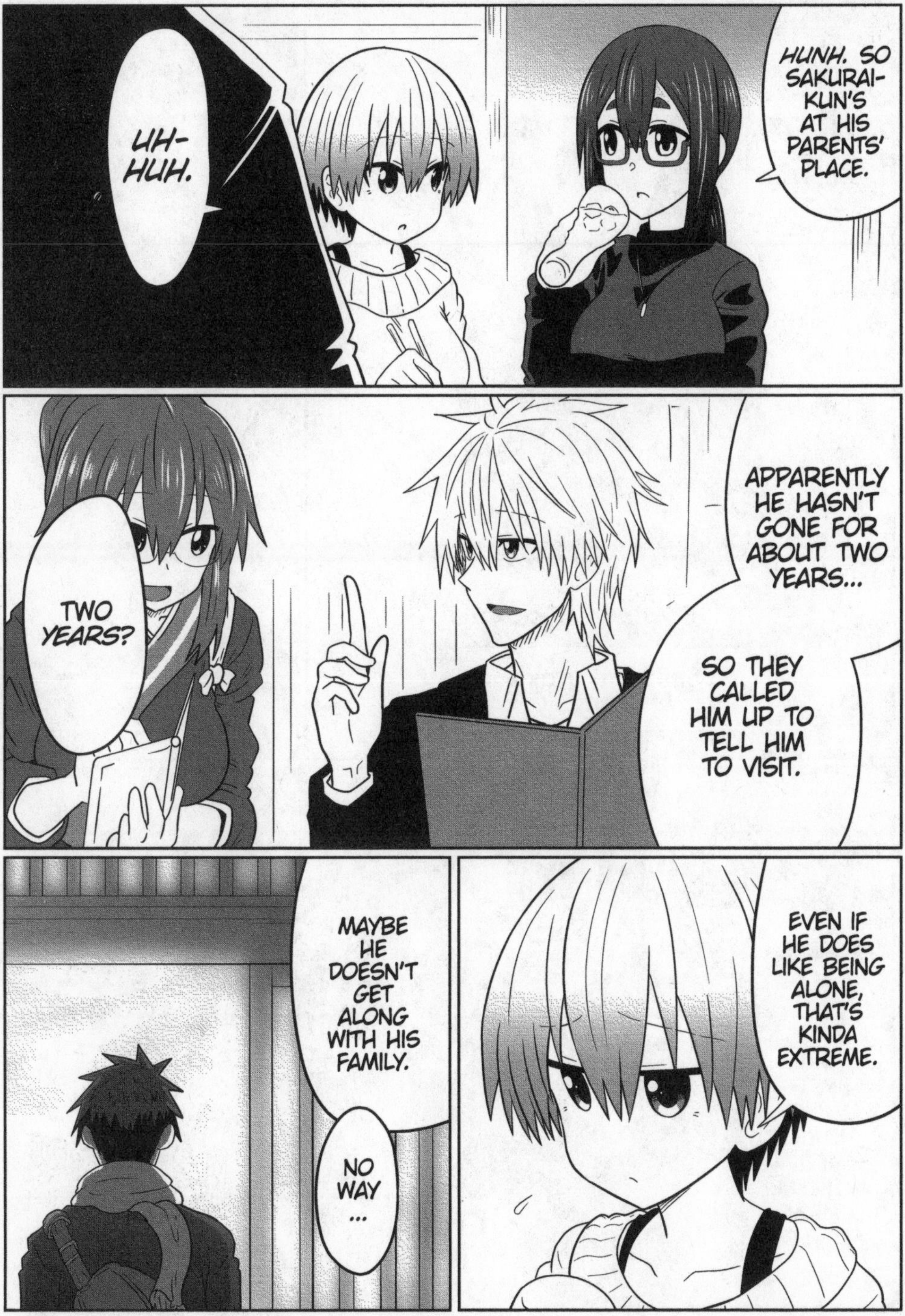
HUNH. SO SAKURAI-KUN'S AT HIS PARENTS' PLACE.
UH-HUH.
APPARENTLY HE HASN'T GONE FOR ABOUT TWO YEARS...
SO THEY CALLED HIM UP TO TELL HIM TO VISIT.
TWO YEARS?
EVEN IF HE DOES LIKE BEING ALONE, THAT'S KINDA EXTREME.
MAYBE HE DOESN'T GET ALONG WITH HIS FAMILY.
NO WAY ...

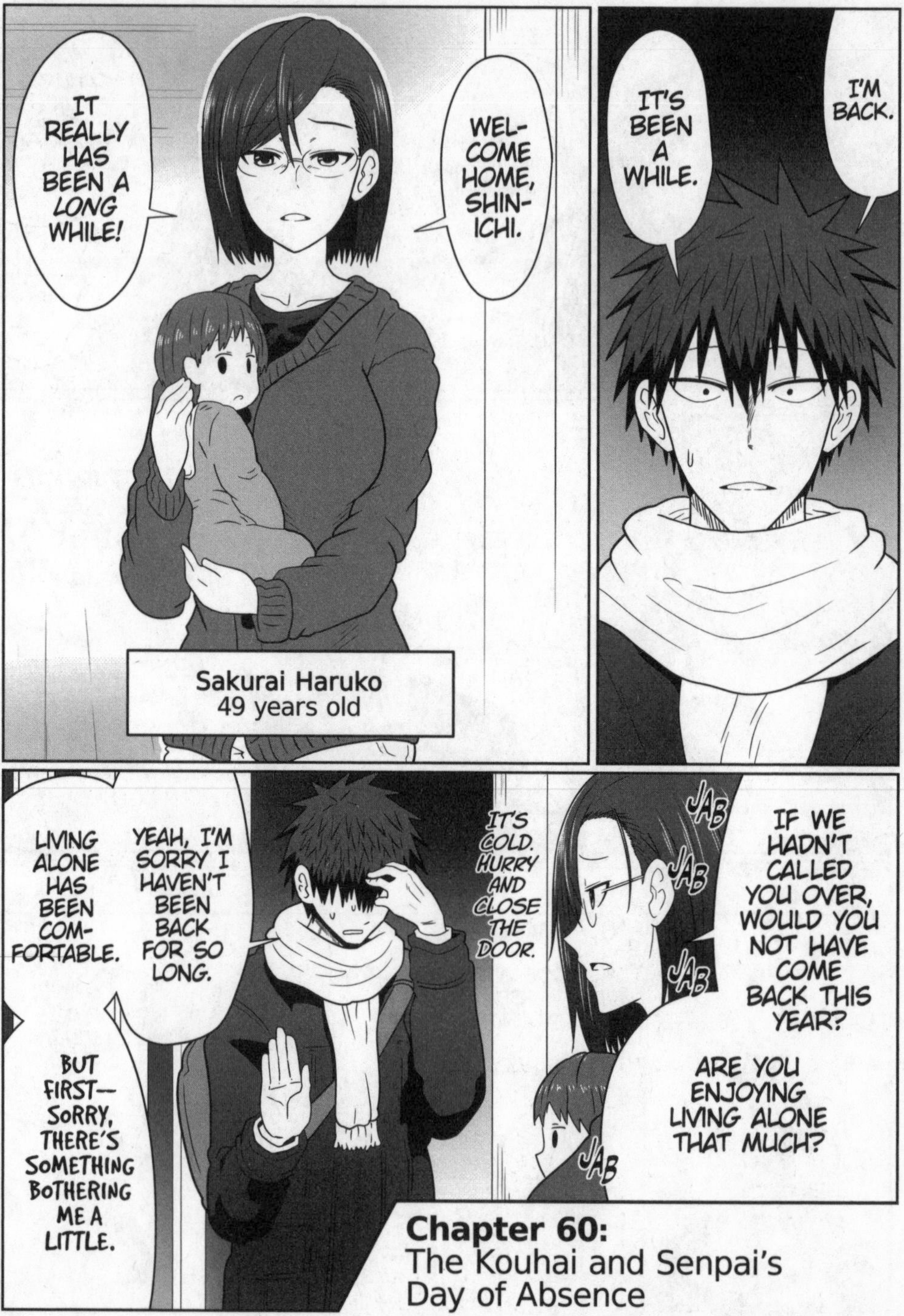
I'M BACK.
IT'S BEEN A WHILE.
WEL-COME HOME, SHIN-ICHI.
IT REALLY HAS BEEN A LONG WHILE!
Sakurai Haruko
49 years old
JAB
JAB
JAB
IF WE HADN'T CALLED YOU OVER, WOULD YOU NOT HAVE COME BACK THIS YEAR?
ARE YOU ENJOYING LIVING ALONE THAT MUCH?
JAB
IT'S COLD. HURRY AND CLOSE THE DOOR.
YEAH, I'M SORRY I HAVEN'T BEEN BACK FOR SO LONG.
LIVING ALONE HAS BEEN COM-FORTABLE.
BUT FIRST— SORRY, THERE'S SOMETHING BOTHERING ME A LITTLE.

Chapter 60:
The Kouhai and Senpai's Day of Absence

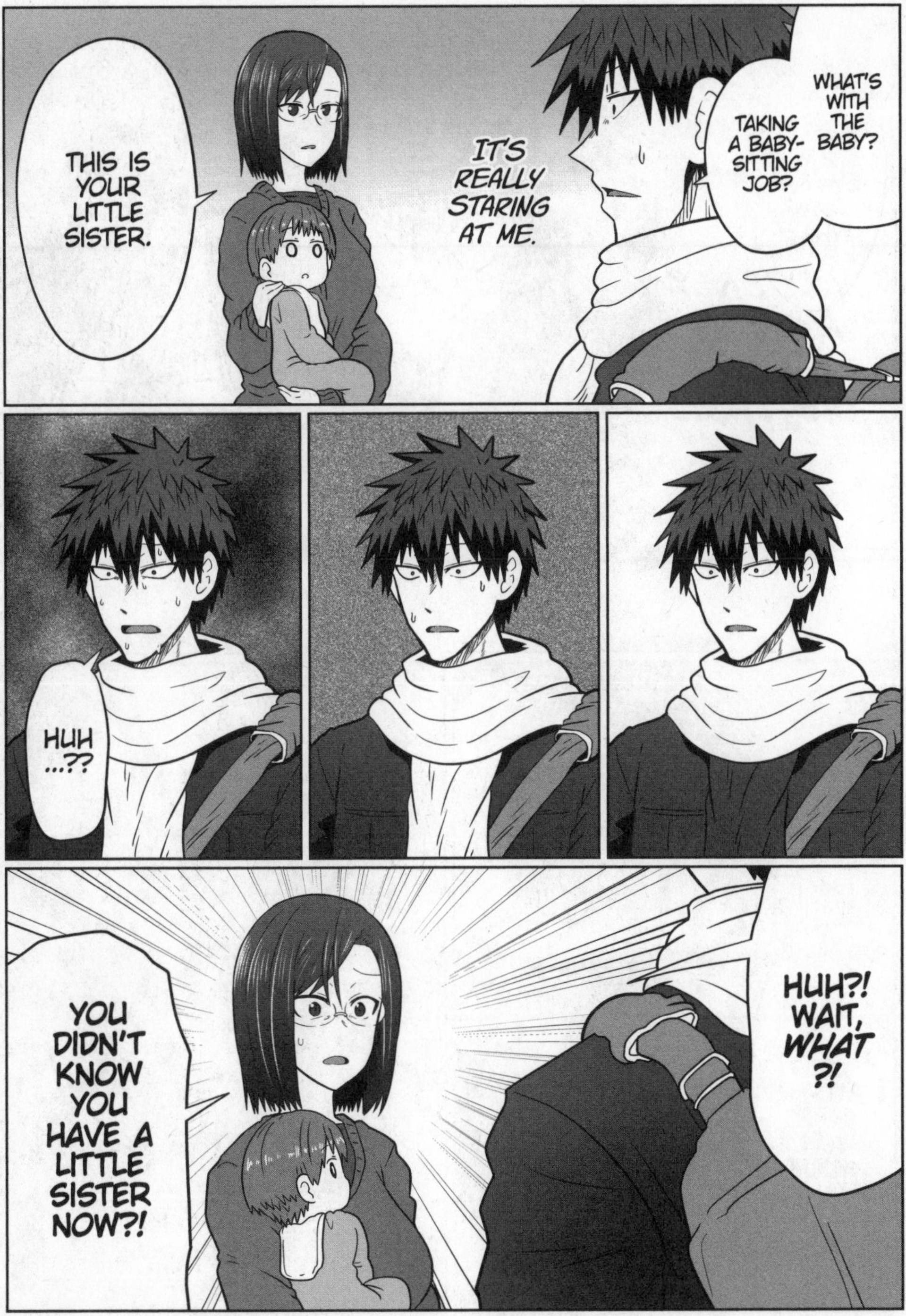
WHAT'S WITH THE BABY?
TAKING A BABY-SITTING JOB?
IT'S REALLY STARING AT ME.
THIS IS YOUR LITTLE SISTER.
HUH ...??
HUH?! WAIT, WHAT?!
YOU DIDN'T KNOW YOU HAVE A LITTLE SISTER NOW?!

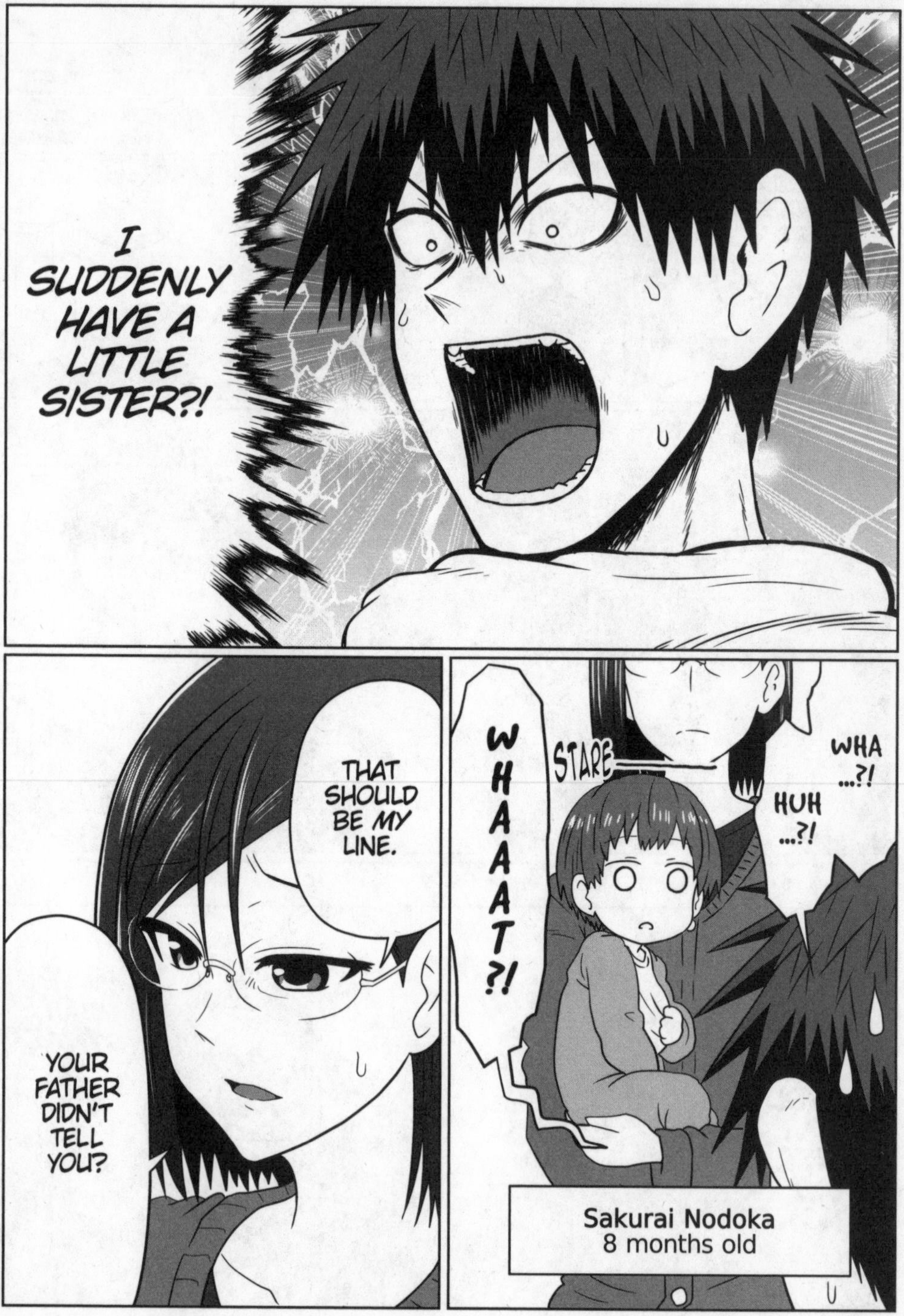
I SUDDENLY HAVE A LITTLE SISTER?!
WHA...?!
HUH...?!
STARE
WHAAAAT?!
Sakurai Nodoka
8 months old
THAT SHOULD BE MY LINE.
YOUR FATHER DIDN'T TELL YOU?

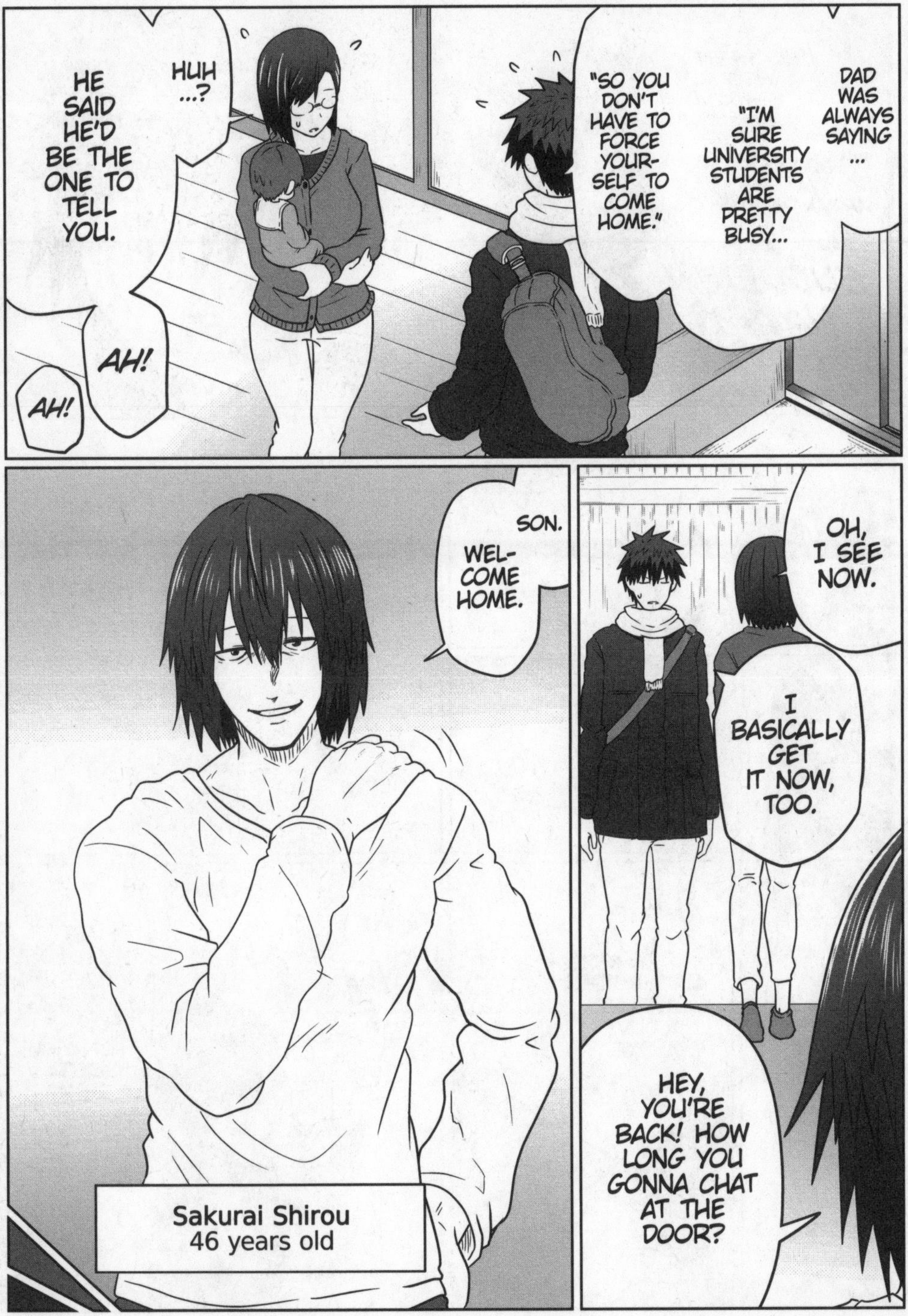
DAD WAS ALWAYS SAYING ...
"I'M SURE UNIVERSITY STUDENTS ARE PRETTY BUSY...
"SO YOU DON'T HAVE TO FORCE YOURSELF TO COME HOME."
HUH ...?
HE SAID HE'D BE THE ONE TO TELL YOU.
AH!
AH!
OH, I SEE NOW.
I BASICALLY GET IT NOW, TOO.
HEY, YOU'RE BACK! HOW LONG YOU GONNA CHAT AT THE DOOR?
SON.
WELCOME HOME.
Sakurai Shirou
46 years old

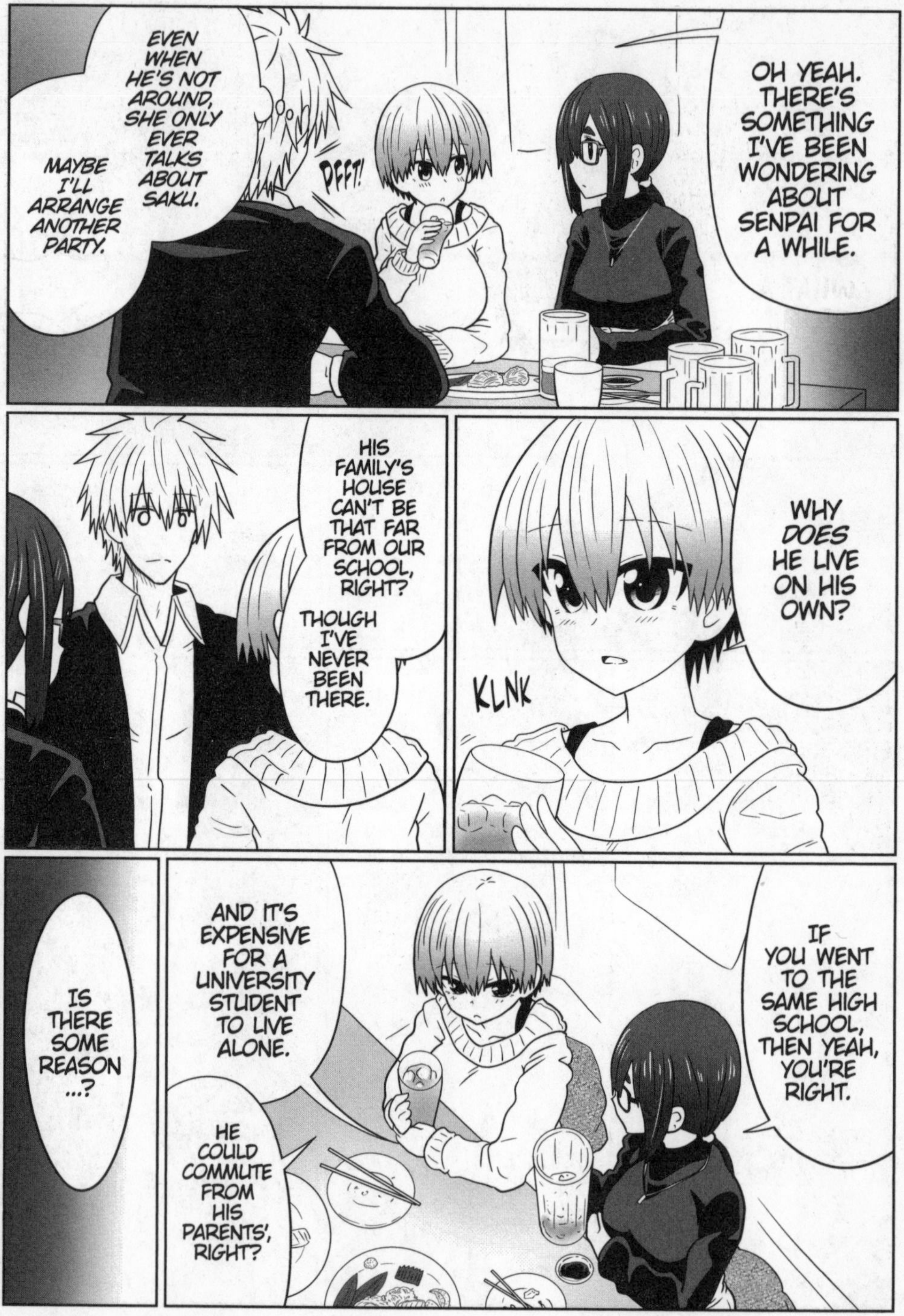
OH YEAH. THERE'S SOMETHING I'VE BEEN WONDERING ABOUT SENPAI FOR A WHILE.
PFFT!
EVEN WHEN HE'S NOT AROUND, SHE ONLY EVER TALKS ABOUT SAKU.
MAYBE I'LL ARRANGE ANOTHER PARTY.
WHY *DOES* HE LIVE ON HIS OWN?
KLNK
HIS FAMILY'S HOUSE CAN'T BE THAT FAR FROM OUR SCHOOL, RIGHT?
THOUGH I'VE NEVER BEEN THERE.
IF YOU WENT TO THE SAME HIGH SCHOOL, THEN YEAH, YOU'RE RIGHT.
AND IT'S EXPENSIVE FOR A UNIVERSITY STUDENT TO LIVE ALONE.
HE COULD COMMUTE FROM HIS PARENTS', RIGHT?
IS THERE SOME REASON ...?

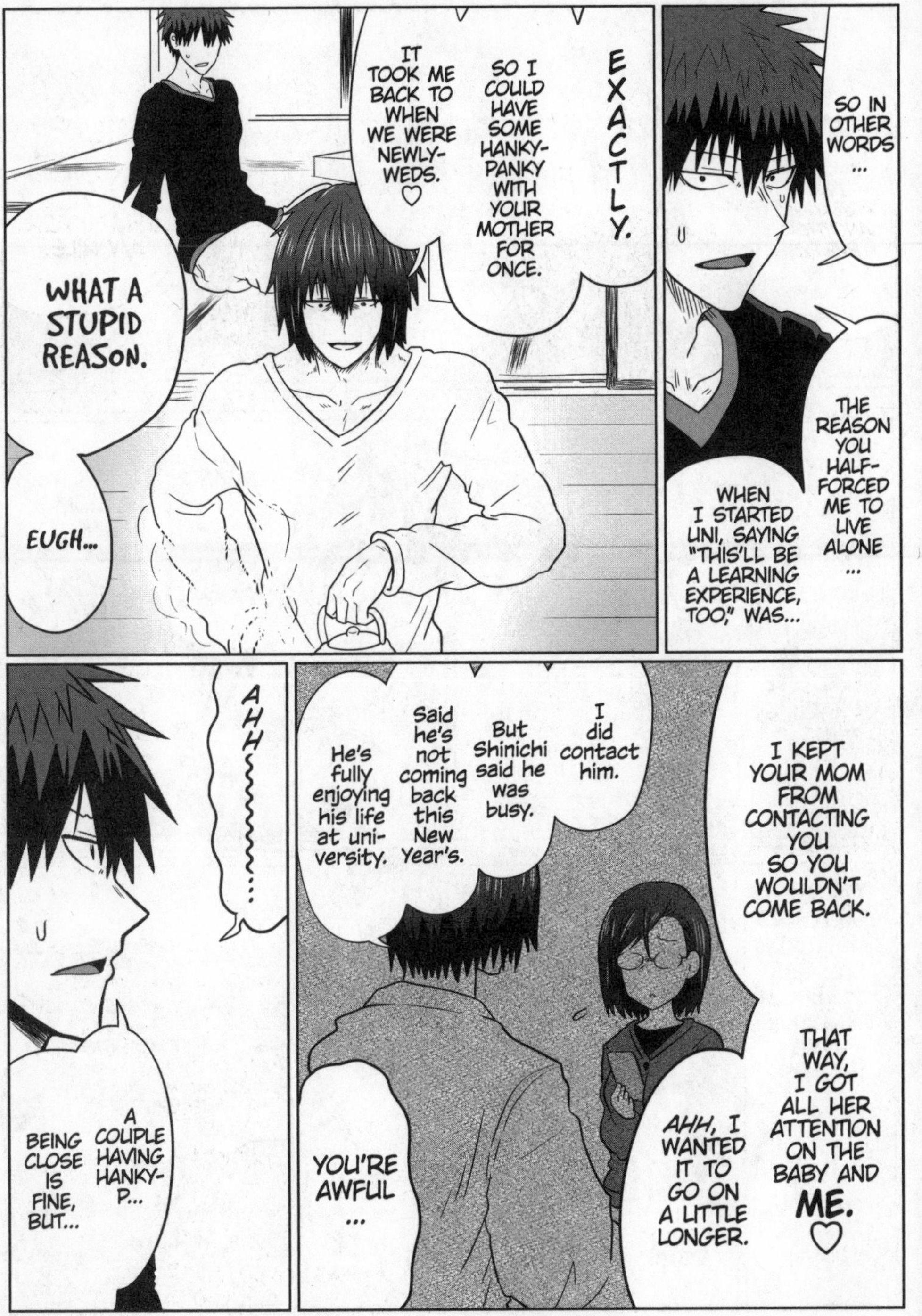
SO IN OTHER WORDS ...
THE REASON YOU HALF-FORCED ME TO LIVE ALONE ...
WHEN I STARTED UNI, SAYING "THIS'LL BE A LEARNING EXPERIENCE, TOO," WAS...
EXACTLY.
SO I COULD HAVE SOME HANKY-PANKY WITH YOUR MOTHER FOR ONCE.
IT TOOK ME BACK TO WHEN WE WERE NEWLY-WEDS. ♡
WHAT A STUPID REASON.
EUGH...
I KEPT YOUR MOM FROM CONTACTING YOU SO YOU WOULDN'T COME BACK.
I did contact him.
But Shinichi said he was busy.
Said he's not coming back this New Year's.
He's fully enjoying his life at university.
THAT WAY, I GOT ALL HER ATTENTION ON THE BABY AND ME. ♡
AHH, I WANTED IT TO GO ON A LITTLE LONGER.
YOU'RE AWFUL ...
AHH~~~...
A COUPLE HAVING HANKY-P...
BEING CLOSE IS FINE, BUT...

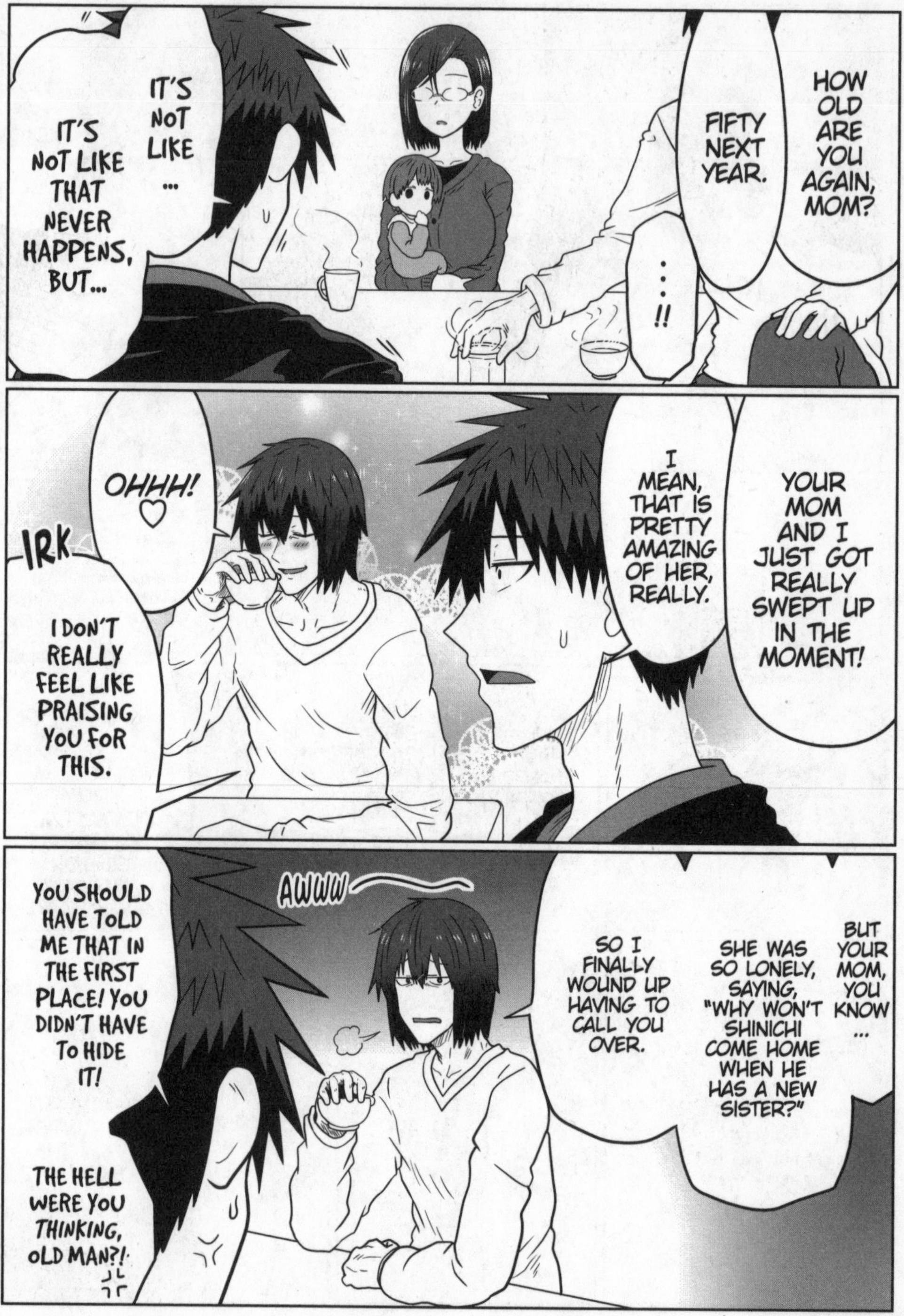
HOW OLD ARE YOU AGAIN, MOM?
FIFTY NEXT YEAR.
...!!
IT'S NOT LIKE...
IT'S NOT LIKE THAT NEVER HAPPENS, BUT...
YOUR MOM AND I JUST GOT REALLY SWEPT UP IN THE MOMENT!
I MEAN, THAT IS PRETTY AMAZING OF HER, REALLY.
OHHH! ♡
IRK
I DON'T REALLY FEEL LIKE PRAISING YOU FOR THIS.
BUT YOUR MOM, YOU KNOW...
SHE WAS SO LONELY, SAYING, "WHY WON'T SHINICHI COME HOME WHEN HE HAS A NEW SISTER?"
SO I FINALLY WOUND UP HAVING TO CALL YOU OVER.
AWWW
YOU SHOULD HAVE TOLD ME THAT IN THE FIRST PLACE! YOU DIDN'T HAVE TO HIDE IT!
THE HELL WERE YOU THINKING, OLD MAN?!

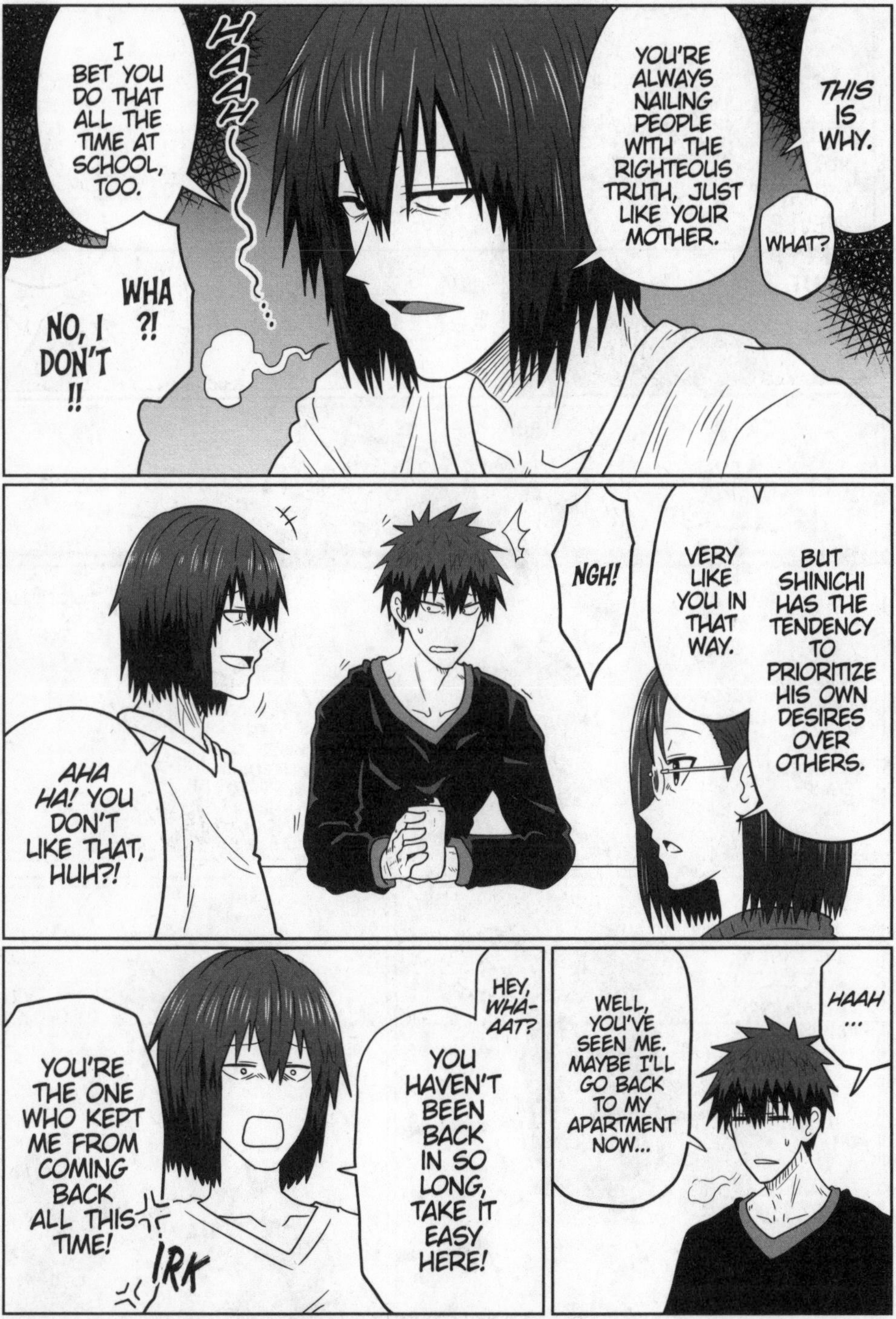
THIS IS WHY.
YOU'RE ALWAYS NAILING PEOPLE WITH THE RIGHTEOUS TRUTH, JUST LIKE YOUR MOTHER.
WHAT?
HAAAH~...
I BET YOU DO THAT ALL THE TIME AT SCHOOL, TOO.
WHA ?!
NO, I DON'T !!
BUT SHINICHI HAS THE TENDENCY TO PRIORITIZE HIS OWN DESIRES OVER OTHERS.
VERY LIKE YOU IN THAT WAY.
NGH!
AHA HA! YOU DON'T LIKE THAT, HUH?!
HAAH ...
WELL, YOU'VE SEEN ME. MAYBE I'LL GO BACK TO MY APARTMENT NOW...
HEY, WHA-AAT?
YOU HAVEN'T BEEN BACK IN SO LONG, TAKE IT EASY HERE!
YOU'RE THE ONE WHO KEPT ME FROM COMING BACK ALL THIS TIME!
IRK

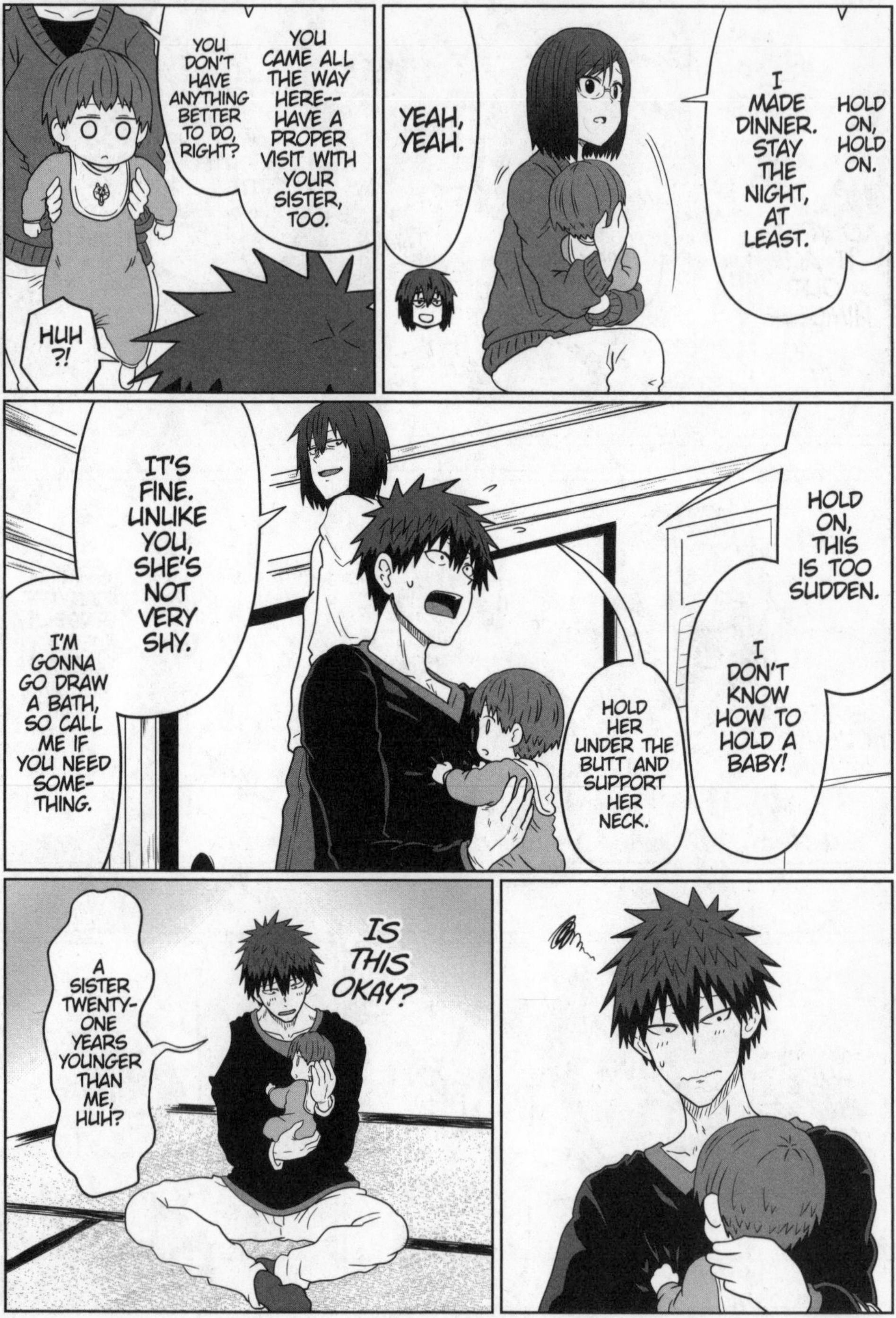
HOLD ON, HOLD ON.
I MADE DINNER. STAY THE NIGHT, AT LEAST.
YEAH, YEAH.
YOU CAME ALL THE WAY HERE-- HAVE A PROPER VISIT WITH YOUR SISTER, TOO.
YOU DON'T HAVE ANYTHING BETTER TO DO, RIGHT?
HUH ?!
HOLD ON, THIS IS TOO SUDDEN.
I DON'T KNOW HOW TO HOLD A BABY!
HOLD HER UNDER THE BUTT AND SUPPORT HER NECK.
IT'S FINE. UNLIKE YOU, SHE'S NOT VERY SHY.
I'M GONNA GO DRAW A BATH, SO CALL ME IF YOU NEED SOME-THING.
IS THIS OKAY?
A SISTER TWENTY-ONE YEARS YOUNGER THAN ME, HUH?

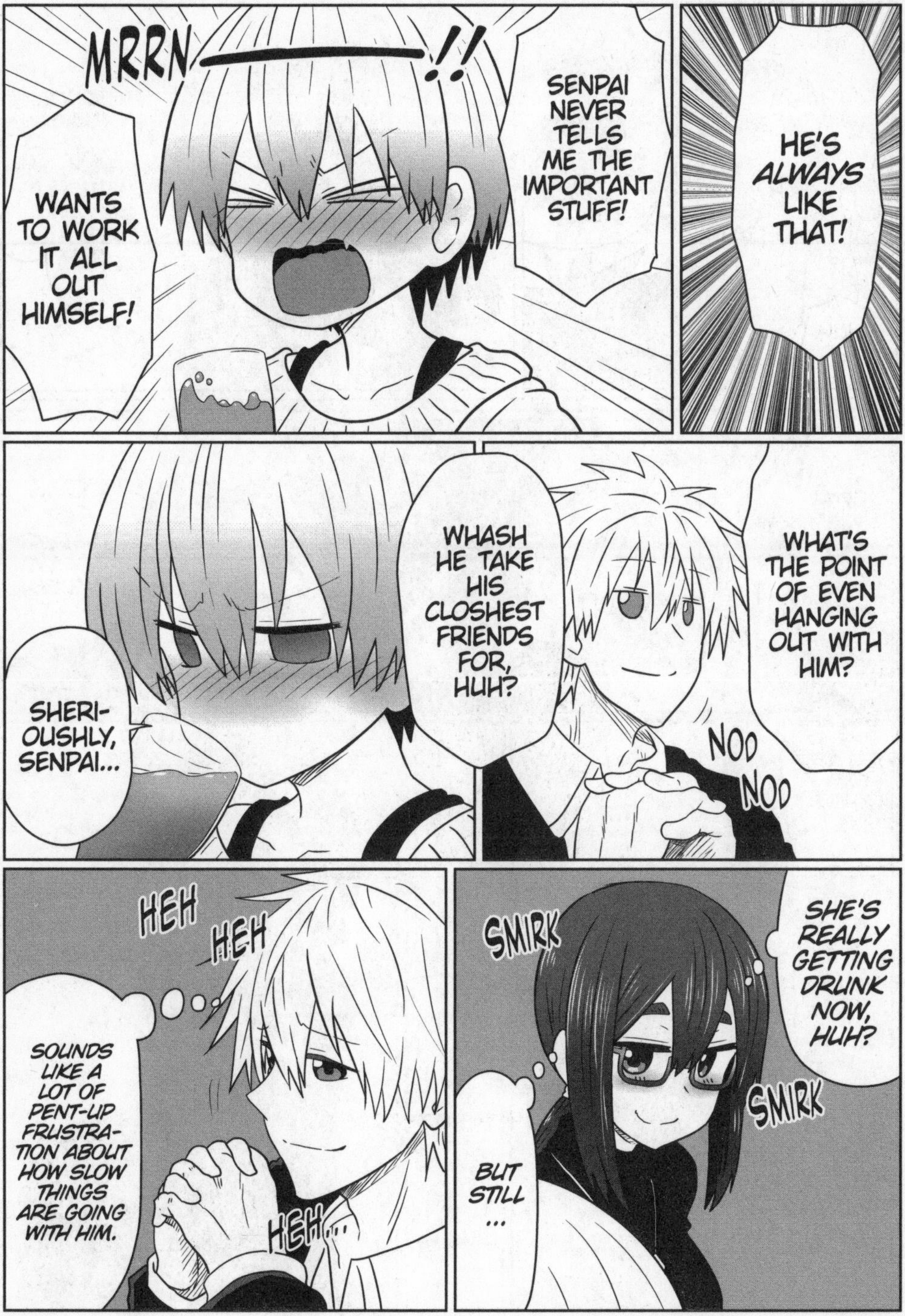
HE'S ALWAYS LIKE THAT!
SENPAI NEVER TELLS ME THE IMPORTANT STUFF!
MRRN—!!
WANTS TO WORK IT ALL OUT HIMSELF!
WHAT'S THE POINT OF EVEN HANGING OUT WITH HIM?
NOD NOD
WHASH HE TAKE HIS CLOSHEST FRIENDS FOR, HUH?
SHERI-OUSHLY, SENPAI...
SHE'S REALLY GETTING DRUNK NOW, HUH?
SMIRK
SMIRK
BUT STILL ...
HEH HEH
SOUNDS LIKE A LOT OF PENT-UP FRUSTRA-TION ABOUT HOW SLOW THINGS ARE GOING WITH HIM.
HEH...

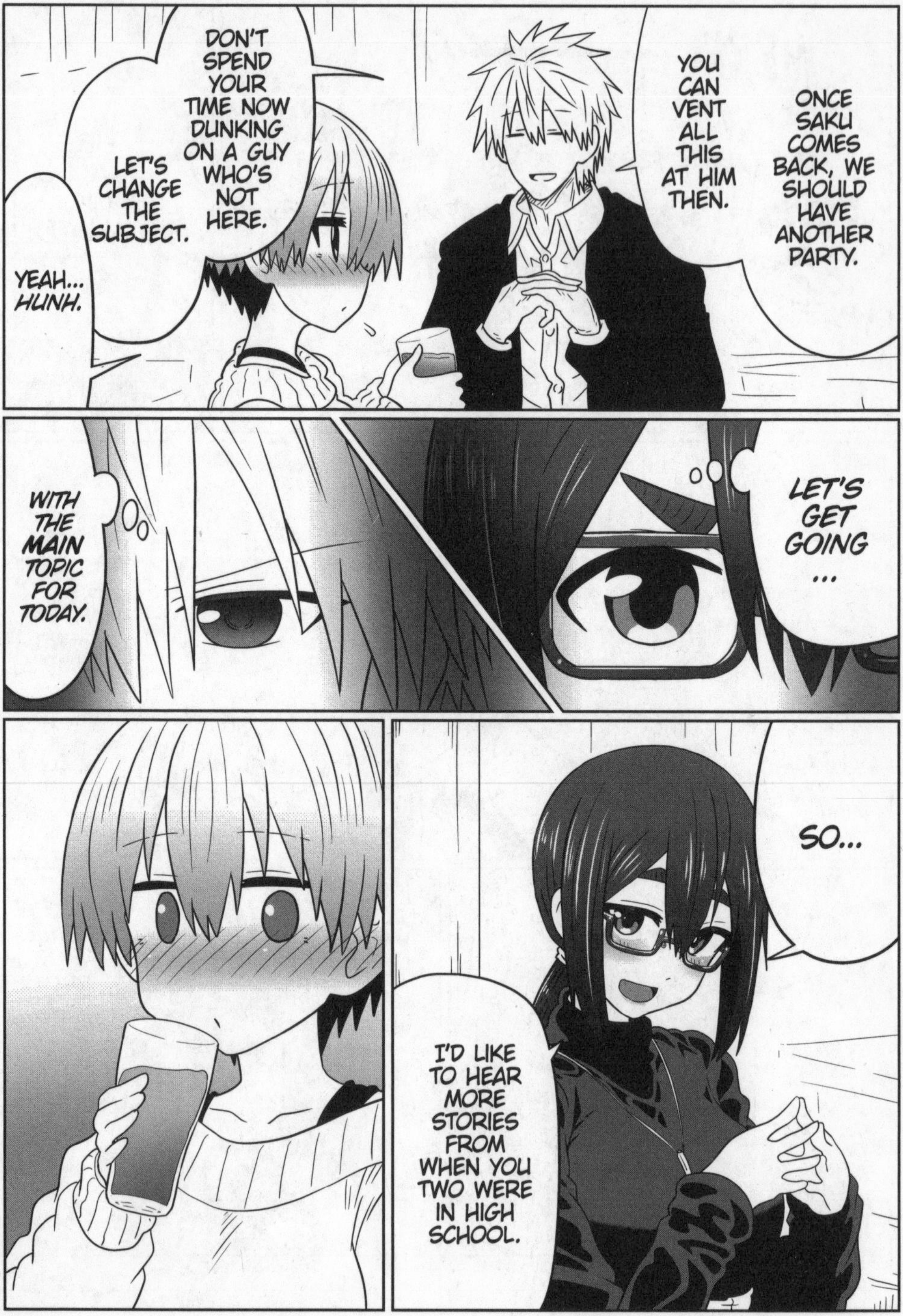
ONCE SAKU COMES BACK, WE SHOULD HAVE ANOTHER PARTY.
YOU CAN VENT ALL THIS AT HIM THEN.
DON'T SPEND YOUR TIME NOW DUNKING ON A GUY WHO'S NOT HERE.
LET'S CHANGE THE SUBJECT.
YEAH... HUNH.
LET'S GET GOING ...
WITH THE MAIN TOPIC FOR TODAY.
SO...
I'D LIKE TO HEAR MORE STORIES FROM WHEN YOU TWO WERE IN HIGH SCHOOL.

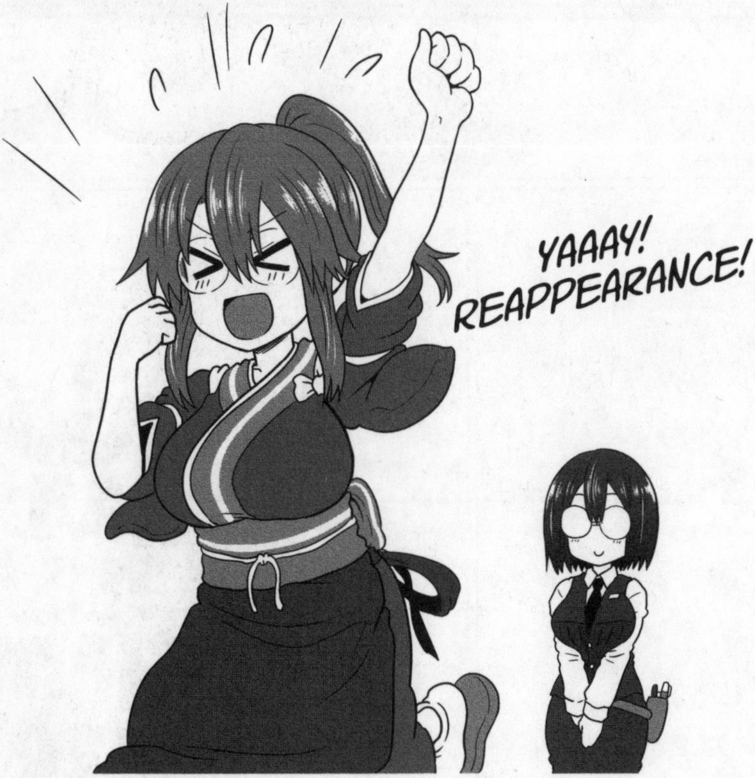
YAAAY! REAPPEARANCE!

Uzaki-chan ☆ Wants to Hang Out!

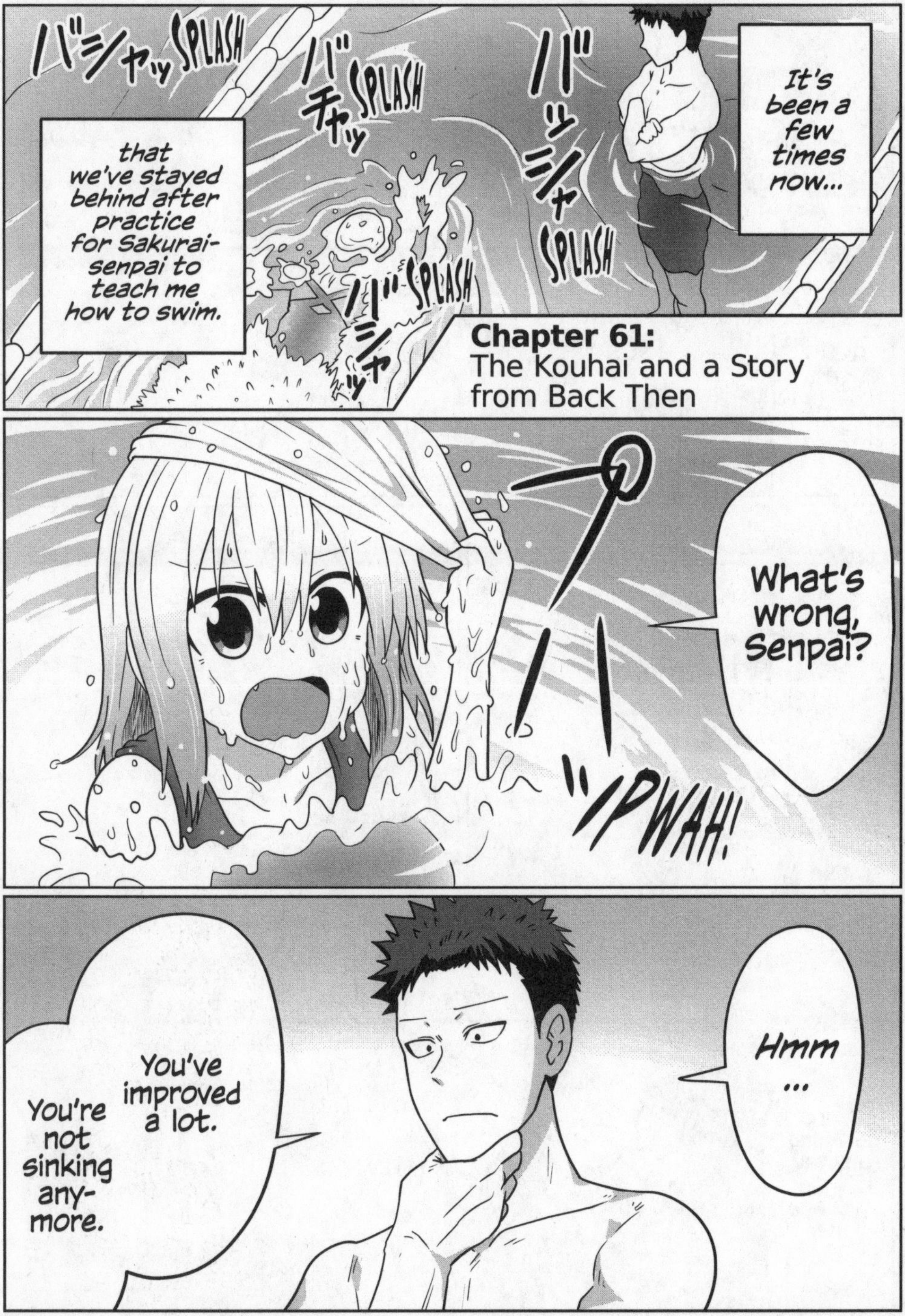
It's been a few times now...
バッシャ SPLASH
バチャッ SPLASH
バシャッ SPLASH
that we've stayed behind after practice for Sakurai-senpai to teach me how to swim.
バシャッ SPLASH
Chapter 61:
The Kouhai and a Story from Back Then
What's wrong, Senpai?
PWAH!
Hmm ...
You've improved a lot.
You're not sinking any-more.

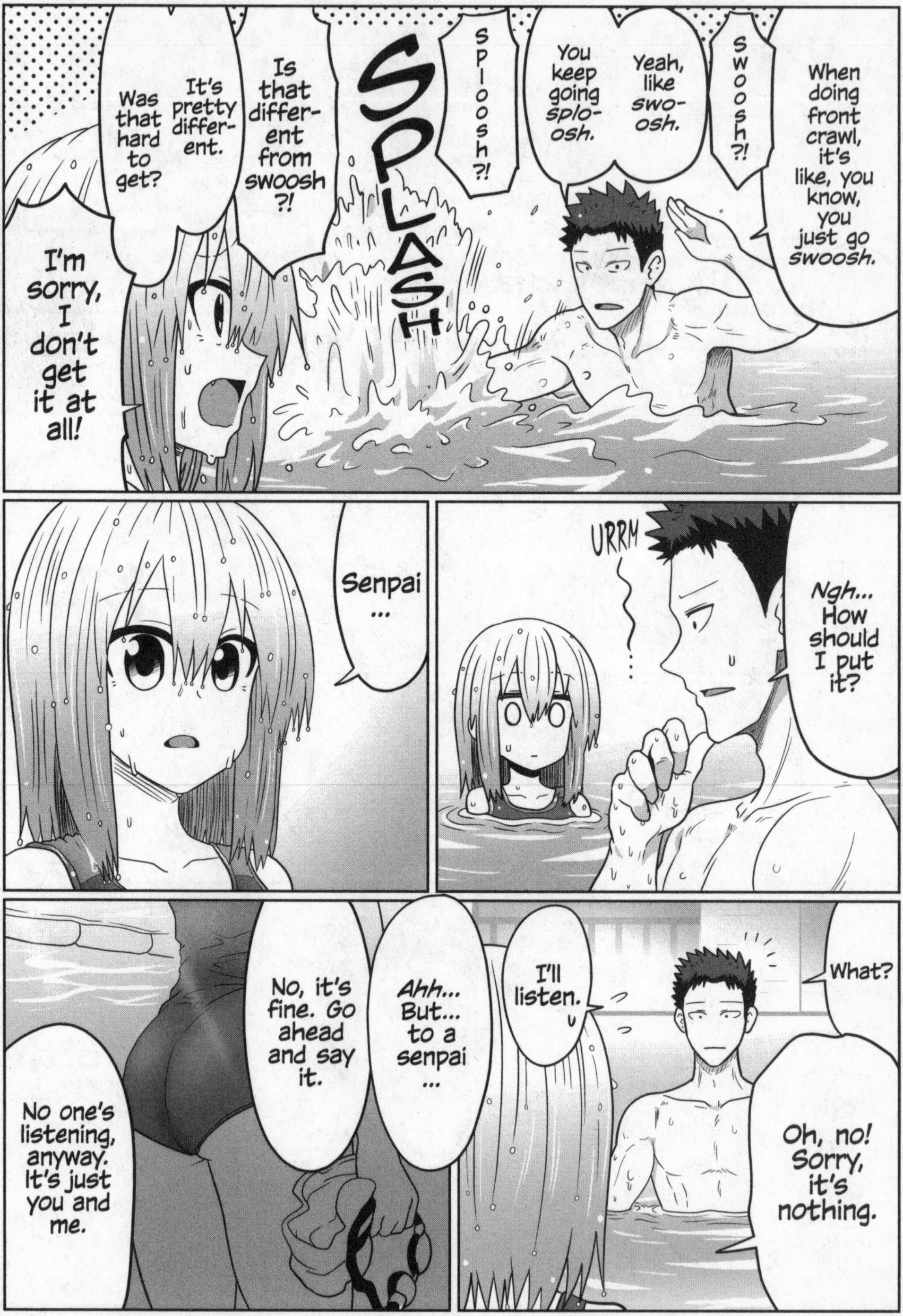
When doing front crawl, it's like, you know, you just go *swoosh.*
Swoosh?!
Yeah, like *swo-osh.*
You keep going *splo-osh.*
Sploosh?!
SPLASH
Is that different from swoosh?!
It's pretty different.
Was that hard to get?
I'm sorry, I don't get it at all!
URRM
Ngh... How should I put it?
Senpai...
What?
Oh, no! Sorry, it's nothing.
I'll listen.
Ahh... But... to a senpai...
No, it's fine. Go ahead and say it.
No one's listening, anyway. It's just you and me.

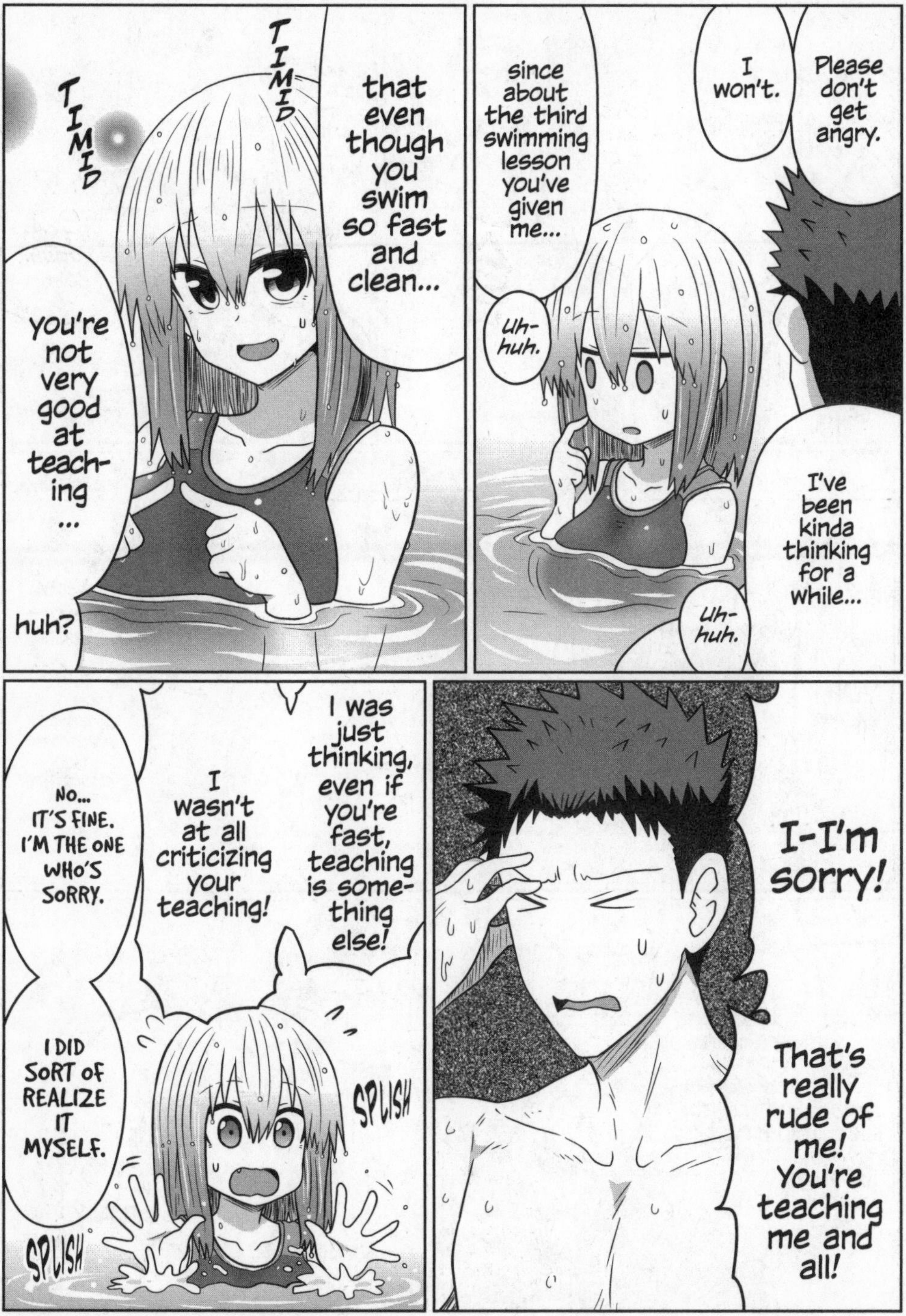
Please don't get angry.
I won't.
I've been kinda thinking for a while...
Uh-huh.
since about the third swimming lesson you've given me...
Uh-huh.
TIMID TIMID
that even though you swim so fast and clean...
you're not very good at teaching...
huh?
I-I'm sorry!
That's really rude of me! You're teaching me and all!
I was just thinking, even if you're fast, teaching is something else!
I wasn't at all criticizing your teaching!
SPLISH
SPLISH
No... IT'S FINE. I'M THE ONE WHO'S SORRY.
I DID SORT OF REALIZE IT MYSELF.

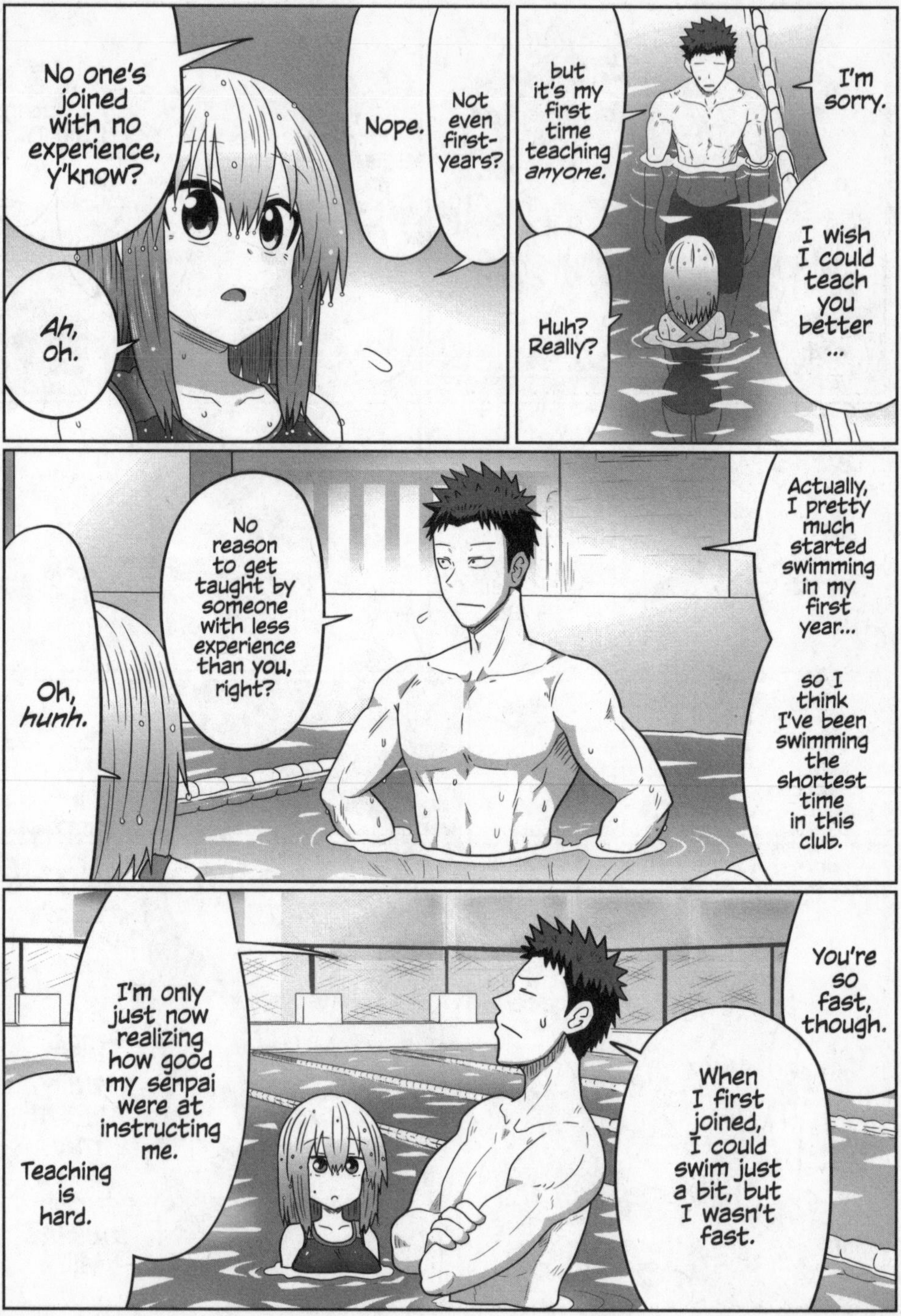
I'm sorry.
I wish I could teach you better...
but it's my first time teaching *anyone.*
Huh? Really?
Not even first-years?
Nope.
No one's joined with no experience, y'know?
Ah, oh.
Actually, I pretty much started swimming in my first year...
so I think I've been swimming the shortest time in this club.
No reason to get taught by someone with less experience than you, right?
Oh, *hunh.*
You're so fast, though.
When I first joined, I could swim just a bit, but I wasn't fast.
I'm only just now realizing how good my senpai were at instructing me.
Teaching is hard.

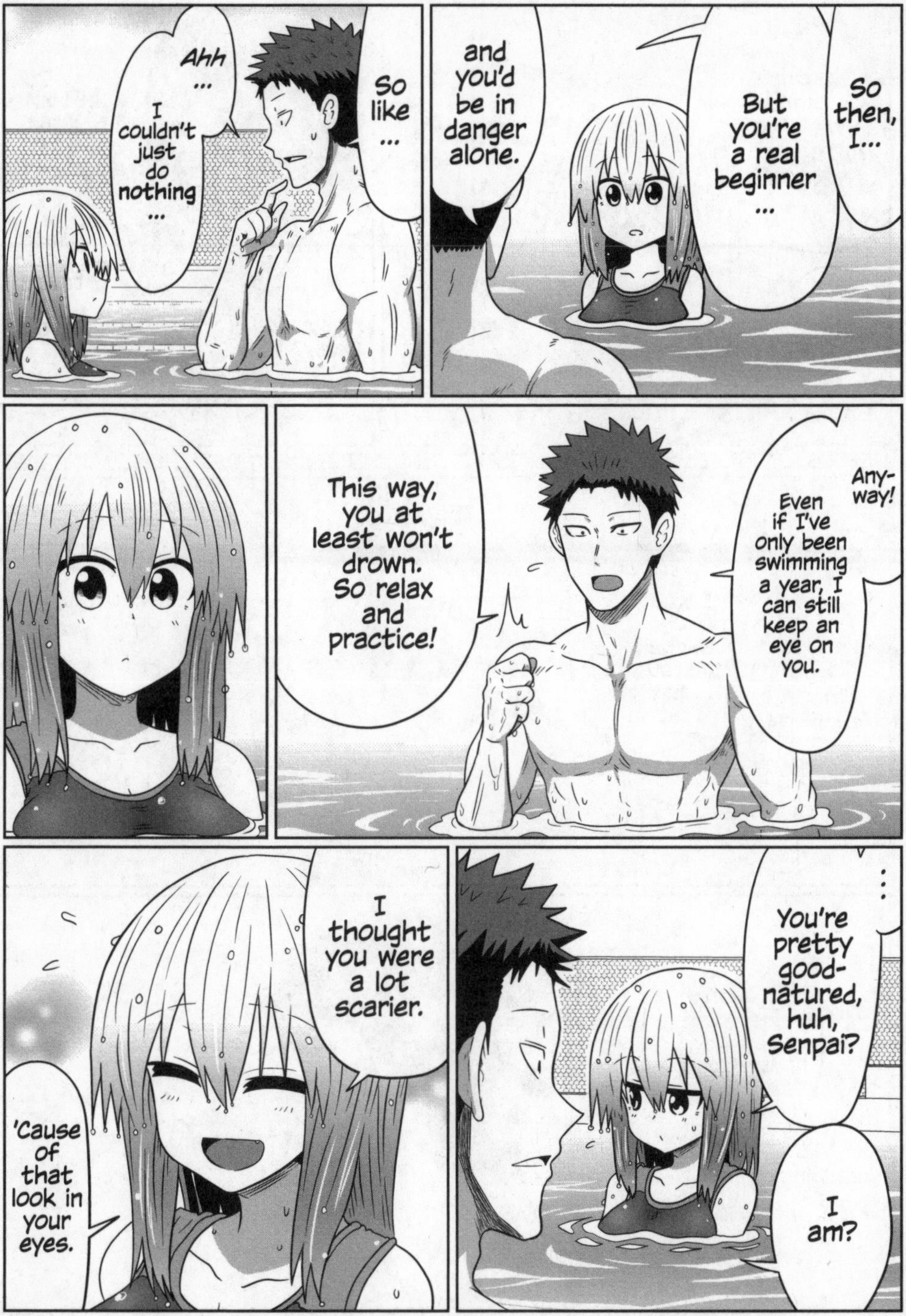
So then, I...
But you're a real beginner ...
and you'd be in danger alone.
So like ...
Ahh ... I couldn't just do nothing ...
Any-way!
Even if I've only been swimming a year, I can still keep an eye on you.
This way, you at least won't drown. So relax and practice!
...
You're pretty good-natured, huh, Senpai?
I am?
I thought you were a lot scarier.
'Cause of that look in your eyes.

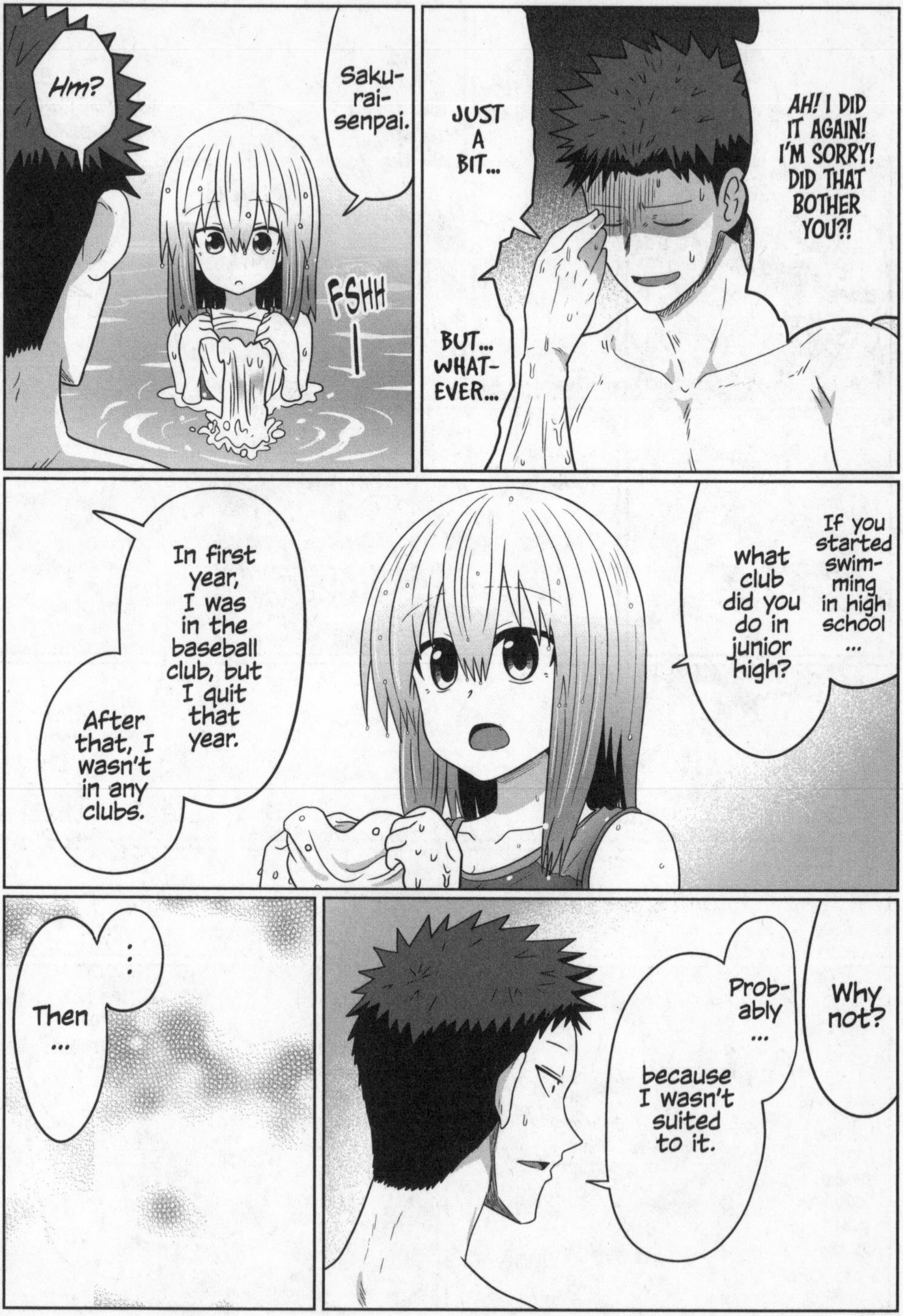
AH! I DID IT AGAIN! I'M SORRY! DID THAT BOTHER YOU?!
JUST A BIT...
BUT... WHAT-EVER...
Saku-rai-senpai.
FSHH
Hm?
If you started swim-ming in high school ...
what club did you do in junior high?
In first year, I was in the baseball club, but I quit that year.
After that, I wasn't in any clubs.
Why not?
Prob-ably ...
because I wasn't suited to it.
...
Then ...

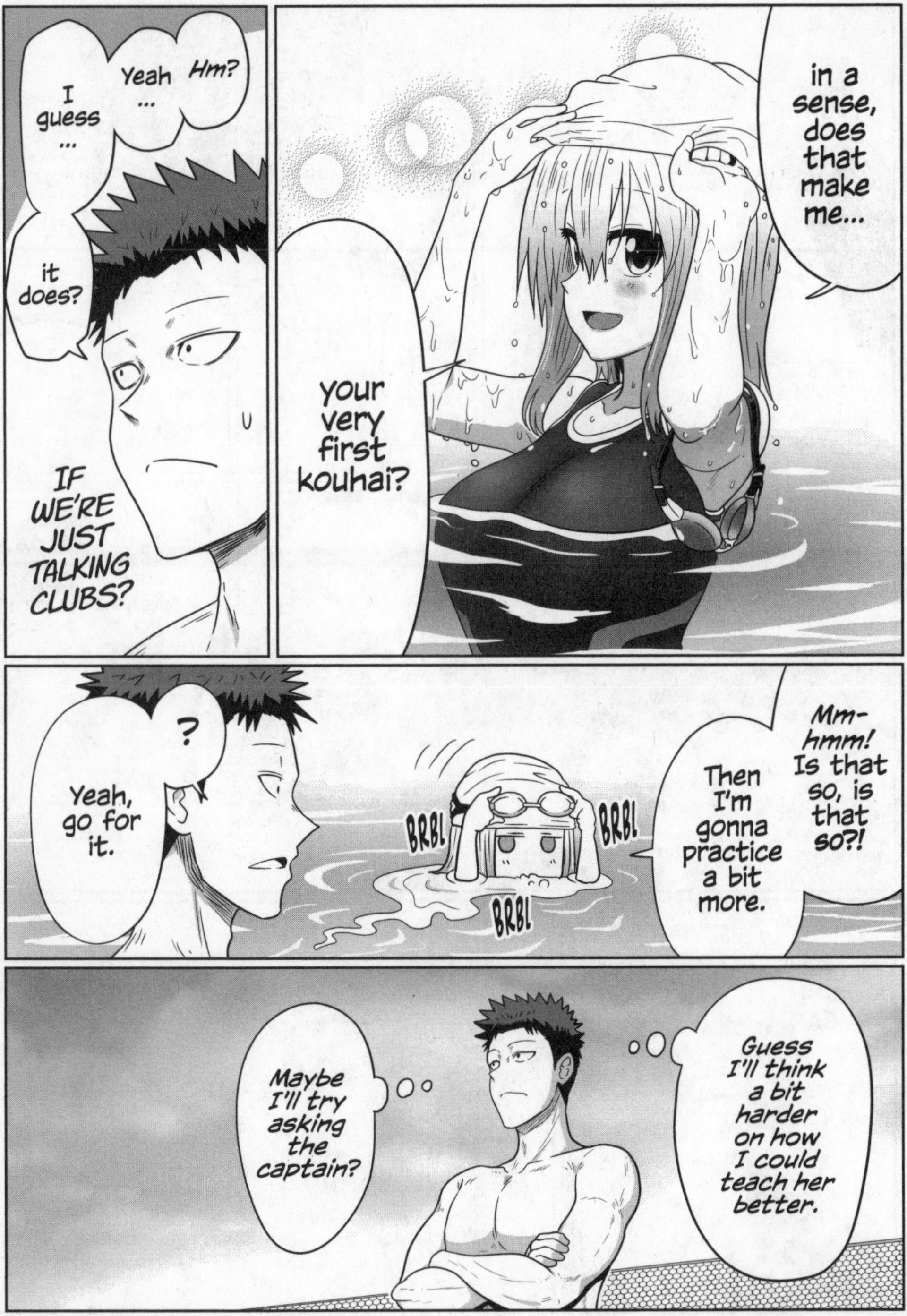
in a sense, does that make me...
your very first kouhai?
Hm?
Yeah... I guess...
it does?
IF WE'RE JUST TALKING CLUBS?
Mm-hmm! Is that so, is that so?!
Then I'm gonna practice a bit more.
BRBL
BRBL
BRBL
?
Yeah, go for it.
Guess I'll think a bit harder on how I could teach her better.
Maybe I'll try asking the captain?

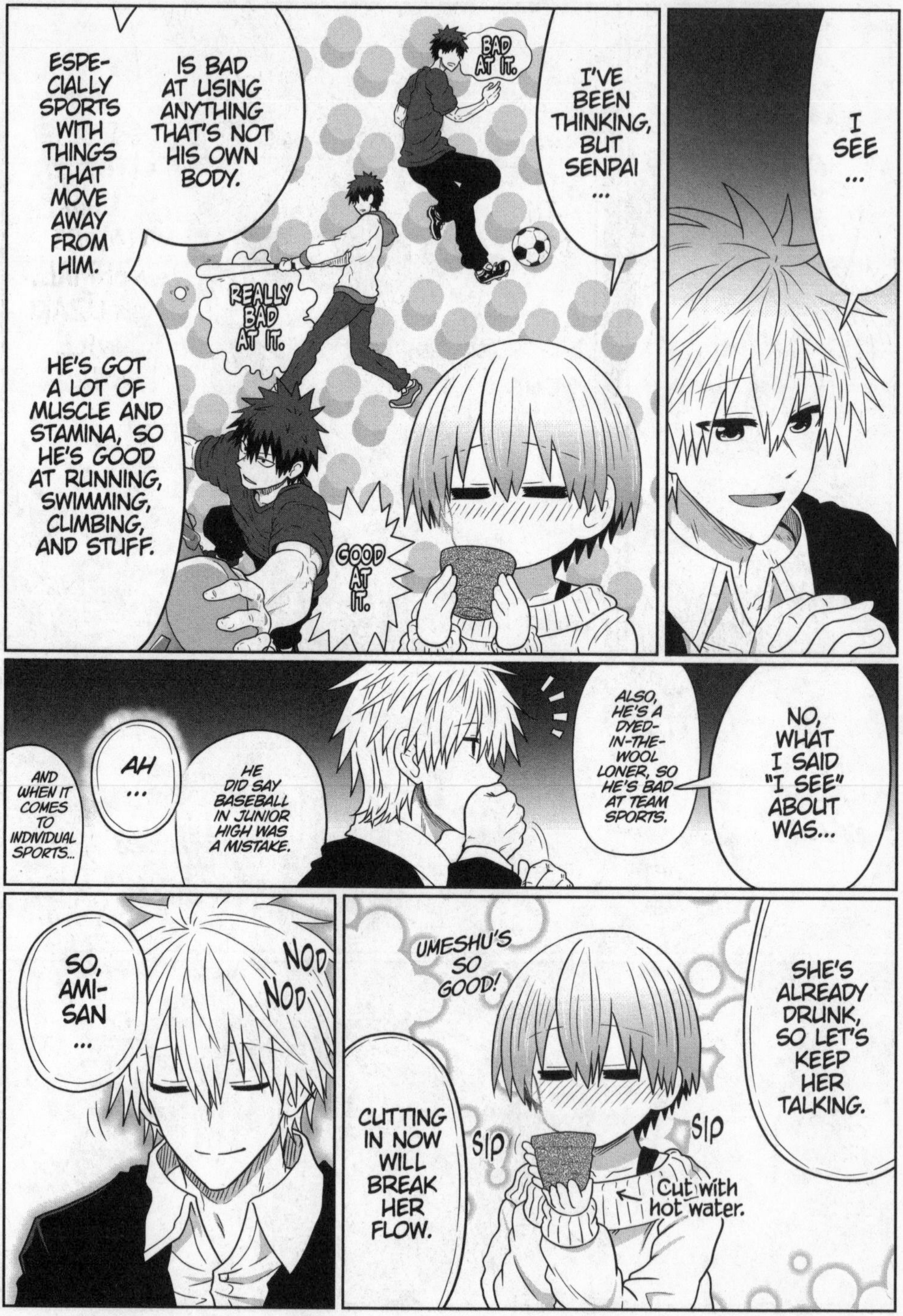
I SEE ...
I'VE BEEN THINKING, BUT SENPAI ...
BAD AT IT.
IS BAD AT USING ANYTHING THAT'S NOT HIS OWN BODY.
ESPE-CIALLY SPORTS WITH THINGS THAT MOVE AWAY FROM HIM.
REALLY BAD AT IT.
GOOD AT IT.
HE'S GOT A LOT OF MUSCLE AND STAMINA, SO HE'S GOOD AT RUNNING, SWIMMING, CLIMBING, AND STUFF.
NO, WHAT I SAID "I SEE" ABOUT WAS...
ALSO, HE'S A DYED-IN-THE-WOOL LONER, SO HE'S BAD AT TEAM SPORTS.
HE DID SAY BASEBALL IN JUNIOR HIGH WAS A MISTAKE.
AH ...
AND WHEN IT COMES TO INDIVIDUAL SPORTS...
SHE'S ALREADY DRUNK, SO LET'S KEEP HER TALKING.
UMESHU'S SO GOOD!
SIP
SIP
CUTTING IN NOW WILL BREAK HER FLOW.
Cut with hot water.
NOD
NOD
SO, AMI-SAN ...

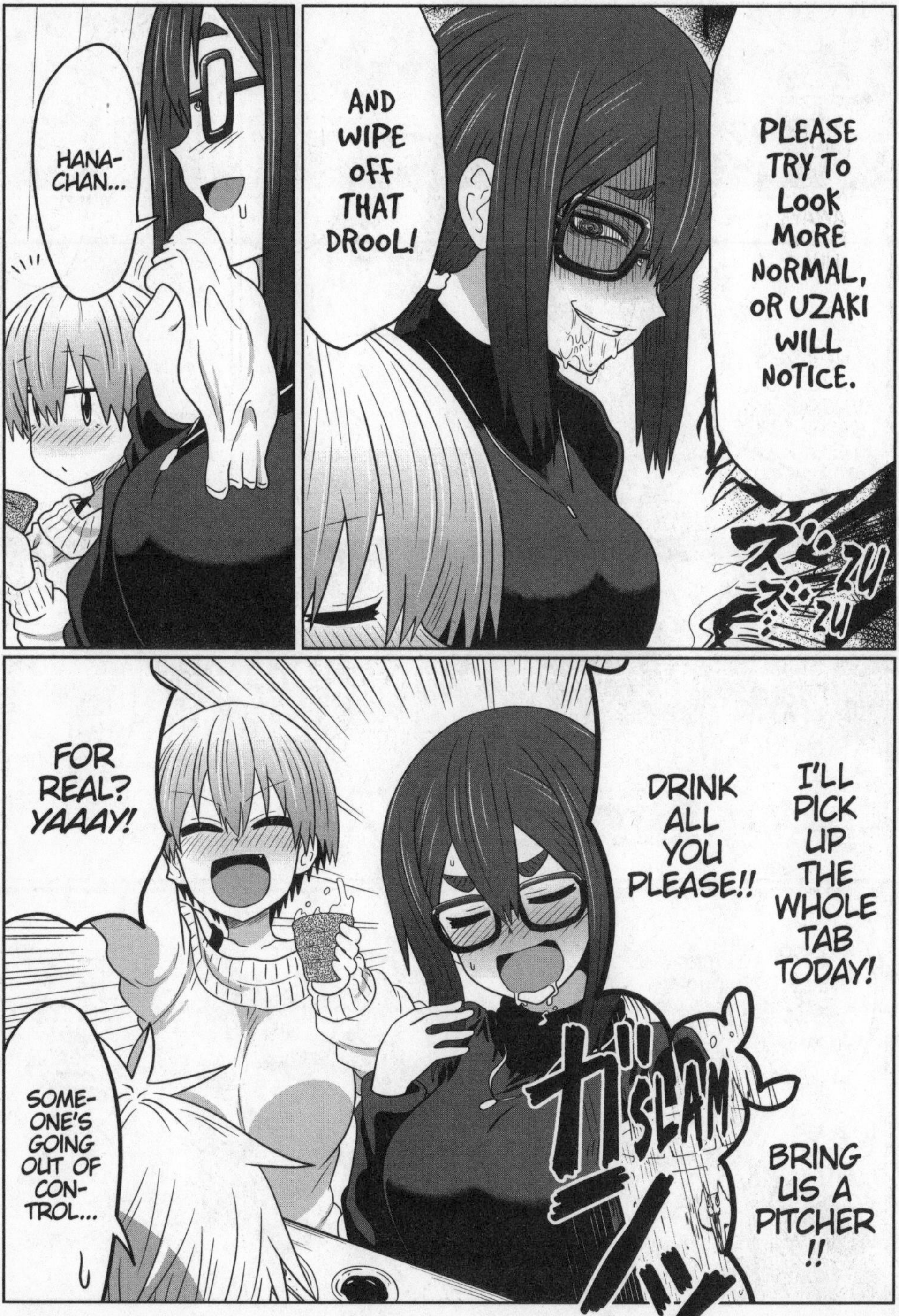
PLEASE TRY TO LOOK MORE NORMAL, OR UZAKI WILL NOTICE.
AND WIPE OFF THAT DROOL!
ZU ZU
HANA-CHAN...
I'LL PICK UP THE WHOLE TAB TODAY!
DRINK ALL YOU PLEASE!!
BRING US A PITCHER!!
SLAM
FOR REAL? YAAAY!
SOME-ONE'S GOING OUT OF CON-TROL...

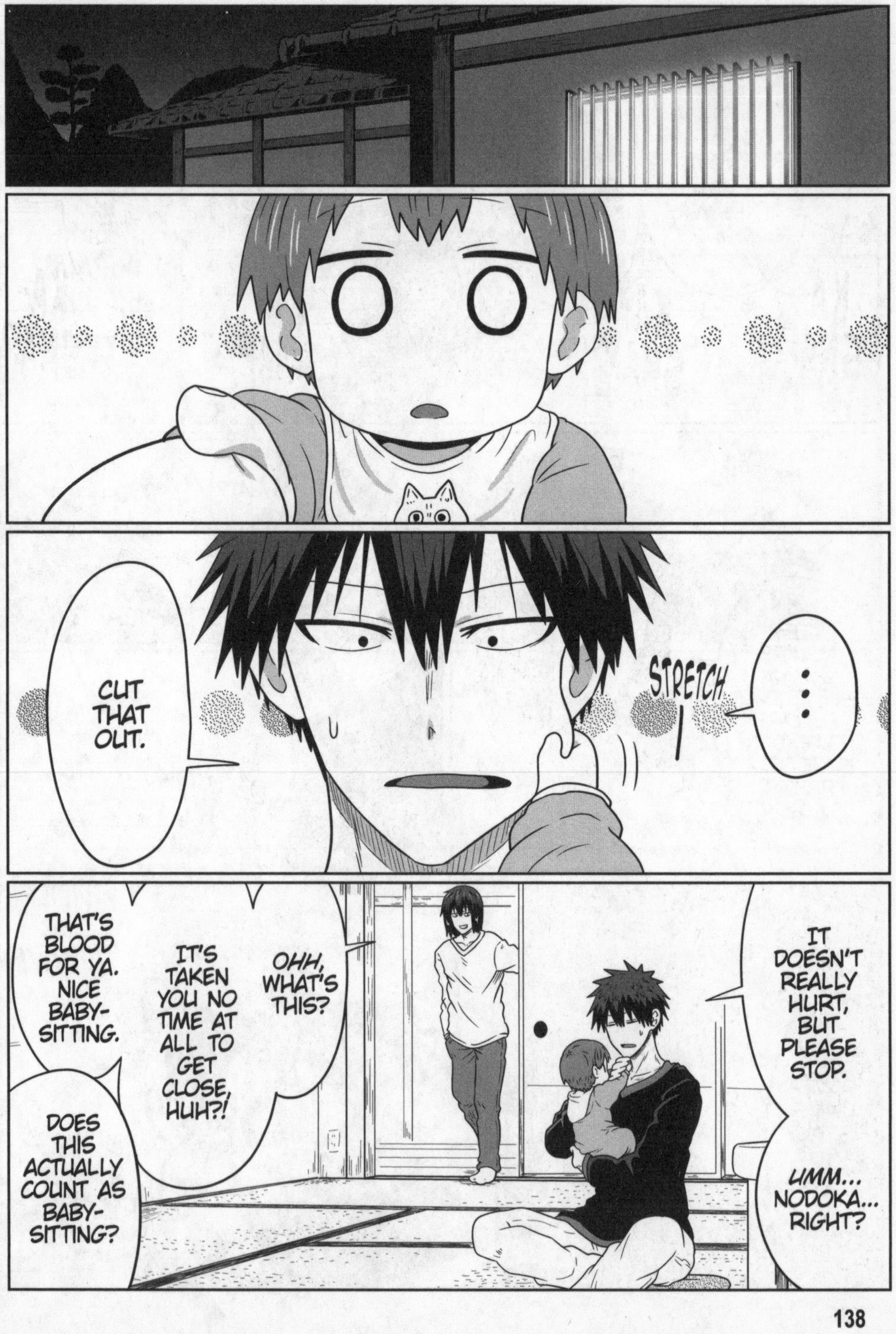
...
STRETCH
CUT THAT OUT.
IT DOESN'T REALLY HURT, BUT PLEASE STOP.
UMM... NODOKA... RIGHT?
OHH, WHAT'S THIS?
IT'S TAKEN YOU NO TIME AT ALL TO GET CLOSE, HUH?!
THAT'S BLOOD FOR YA. NICE BABY-SITTING.
DOES THIS ACTUALLY COUNT AS BABY-SITTING?

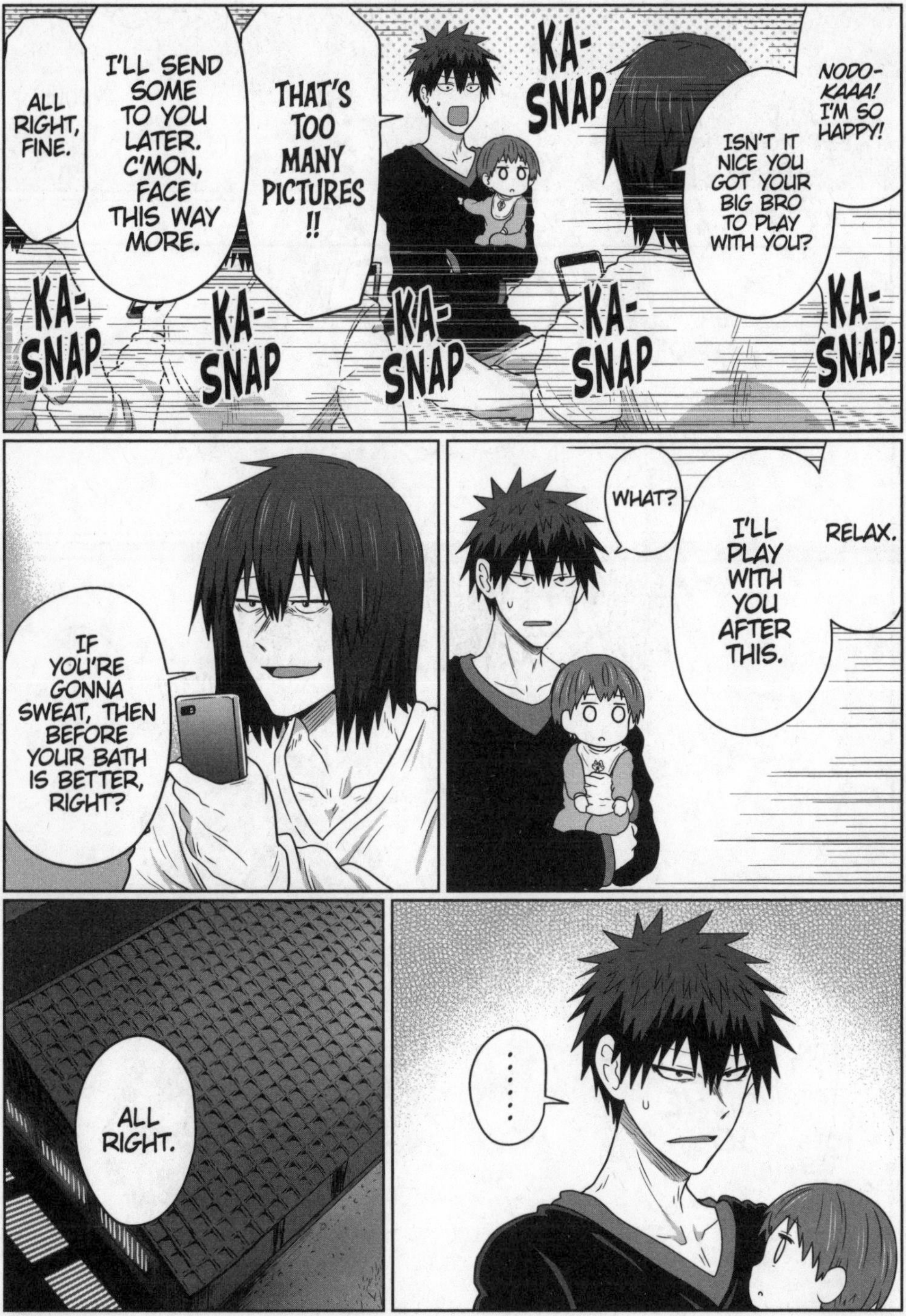
NODO-KAAA! I'M SO HAPPY!
ISN'T IT NICE YOU GOT YOUR BIG BRO TO PLAY WITH YOU?
KA-SNAP
KA-SNAP
THAT'S TOO MANY PICTURES!!
I'LL SEND SOME TO YOU LATER. C'MON, FACE THIS WAY MORE.
ALL RIGHT, FINE.
KA-SNAP
KA-SNAP
KA-SNAP
KA-SNAP
RELAX.
I'LL PLAY WITH YOU AFTER THIS.
WHAT?
IF YOU'RE GONNA SWEAT, THEN BEFORE YOUR BATH IS BETTER, RIGHT?
......
ALL RIGHT.

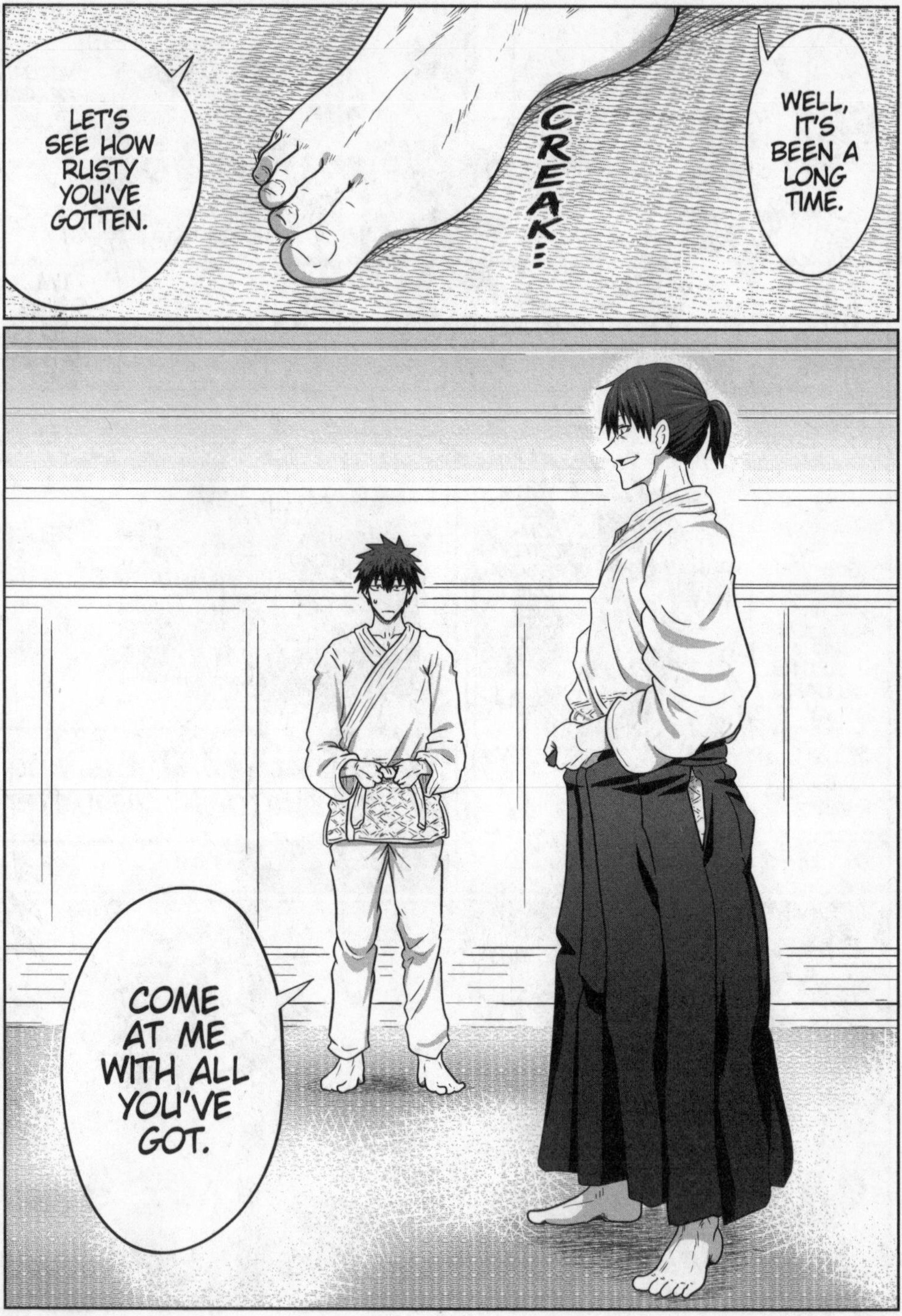
WELL, IT'S BEEN A LONG TIME.
CREAK...
LET'S SEE HOW RUSTY YOU'VE GOTTEN.
COME AT ME WITH ALL YOU'VE GOT.

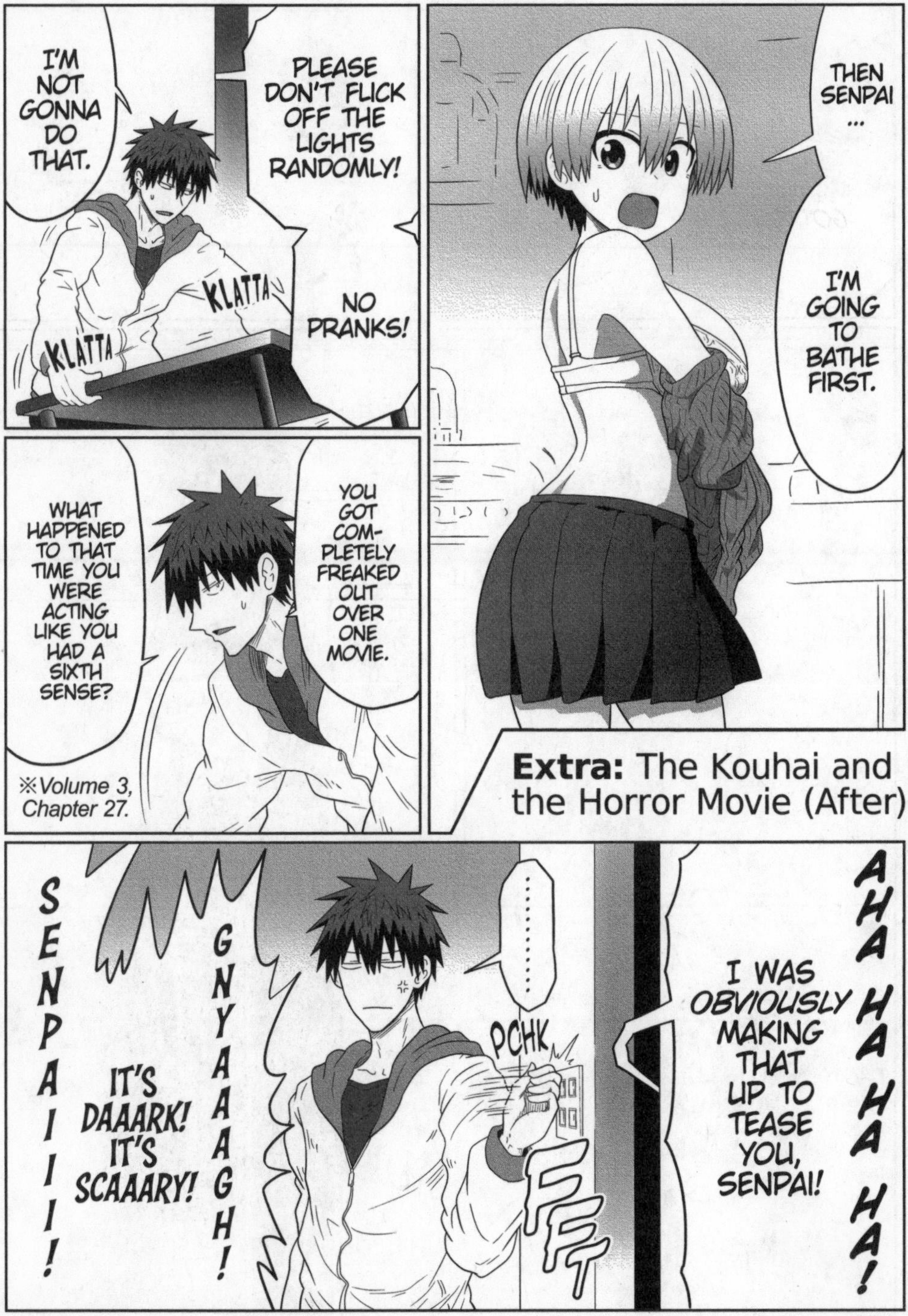
THEN SENPAI ...
I'M GOING TO BATHE FIRST.
Extra: The Kouhai and the Horror Movie (After)
PLEASE DON'T FLICK OFF THE LIGHTS RANDOMLY!
NO PRANKS!
I'M NOT GONNA DO THAT.
KLATTA
KLATTA
YOU GOT COMPLETELY FREAKED OUT OVER ONE MOVIE.
WHAT HAPPENED TO THAT TIME YOU WERE ACTING LIKE YOU HAD A SIXTH SENSE?
※Volume 3, Chapter 27.
AHAHAHAHAHA!
I WAS OBVIOUSLY MAKING THAT UP TO TEASE YOU, SENPAI!
......
PCHK
FFT
GNYAAAAGH!
IT'S DAAARK! IT'S SCAAARY!
SENPAIII!

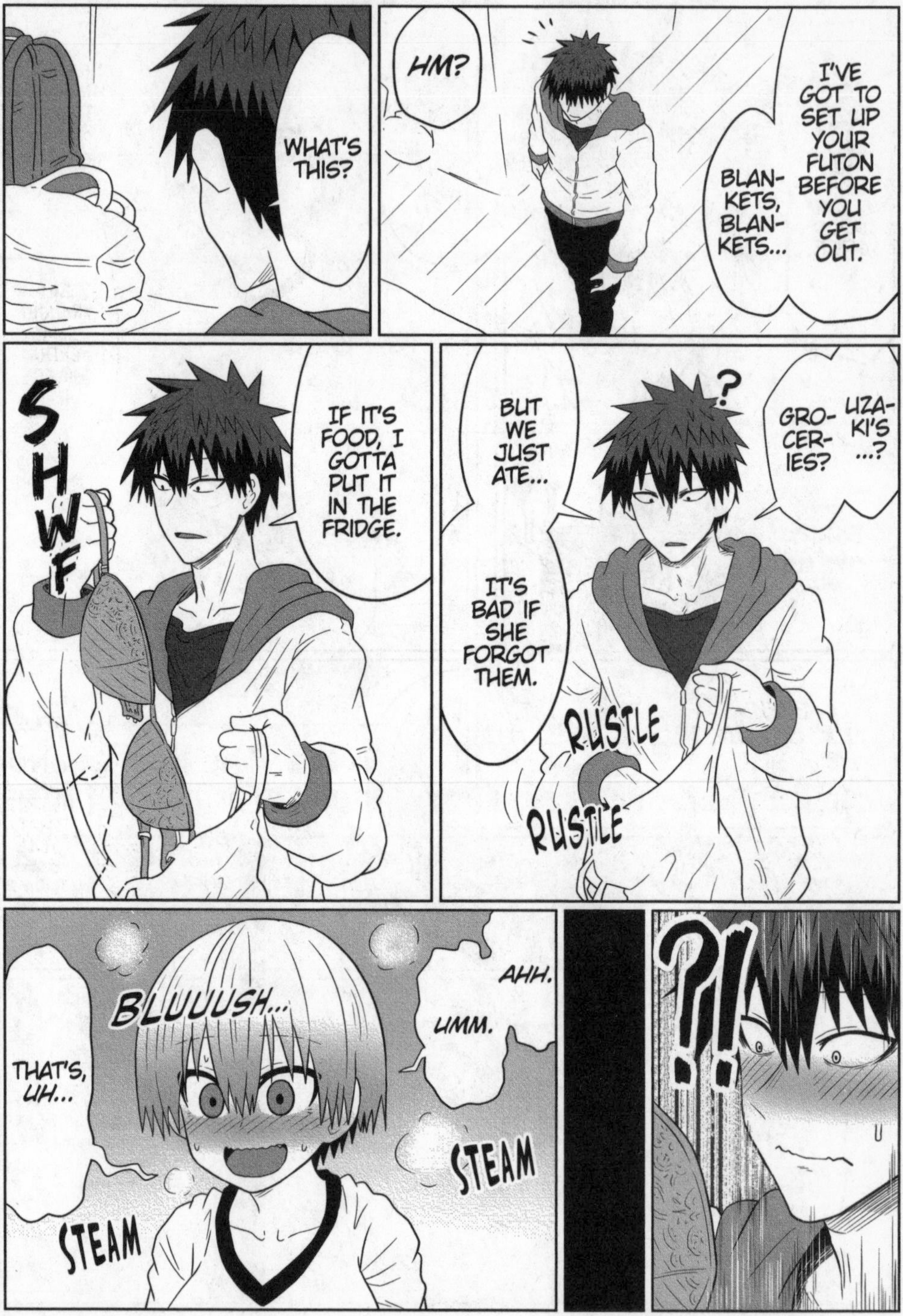
I'VE GOT TO SET UP YOUR FUTON BEFORE YOU GET OUT.
BLAN-KETS, BLAN-KETS...
HM?
WHAT'S THIS?
UZA-KI'S ...?
GRO-CER-IES?
?
BUT WE JUST ATE...
IT'S BAD IF SHE FORGOT THEM.
RUSTLE
RUSTLE
IF IT'S FOOD, I GOTTA PUT IT IN THE FRIDGE.
SHWF
?!
AHH.
UMM.
BLUUUSH...
THAT'S, UH...
STEAM
STEAM

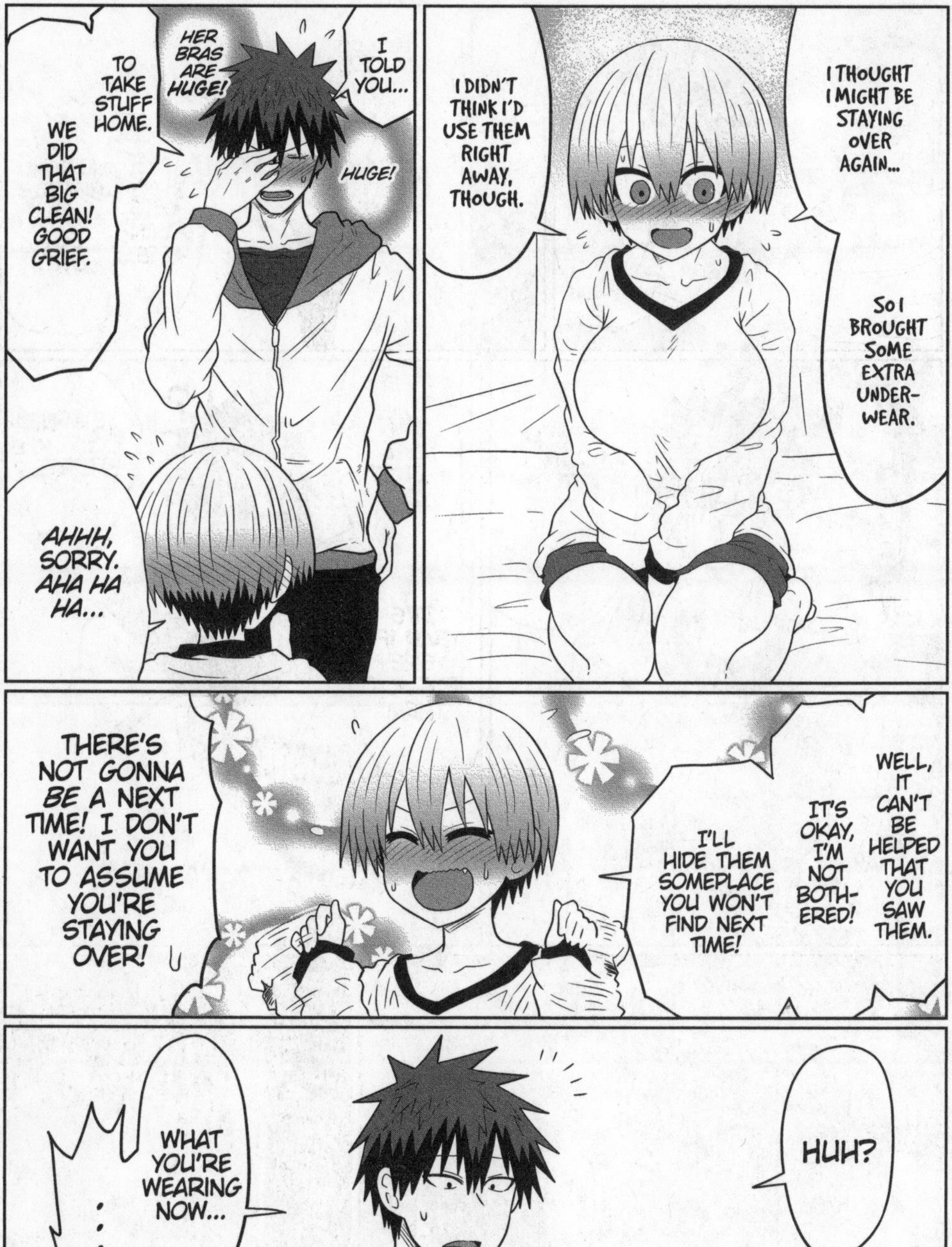

I THOUGHT I MIGHT BE STAYING OVER AGAIN...
SO I BROUGHT SOME EXTRA UNDER-WEAR.
I DIDN'T THINK I'D USE THEM RIGHT AWAY, THOUGH.
I TOLD YOU...
HER BRAS ARE HUGE!
HUGE!
TO TAKE STUFF HOME.
WE DID THAT BIG CLEAN! GOOD GRIEF.
AHHH, SORRY. AHA HA HA...
WELL, IT CAN'T BE HELPED THAT YOU SAW THEM.
IT'S OKAY, I'M NOT BOTH-ERED!
I'LL HIDE THEM SOMEPLACE YOU WON'T FIND NEXT TIME!
THERE'S NOT GONNA BE A NEXT TIME! I DON'T WANT YOU TO ASSUME YOU'RE STAYING OVER!
HUH?
WHAT YOU'RE WEARING NOW...
...!!

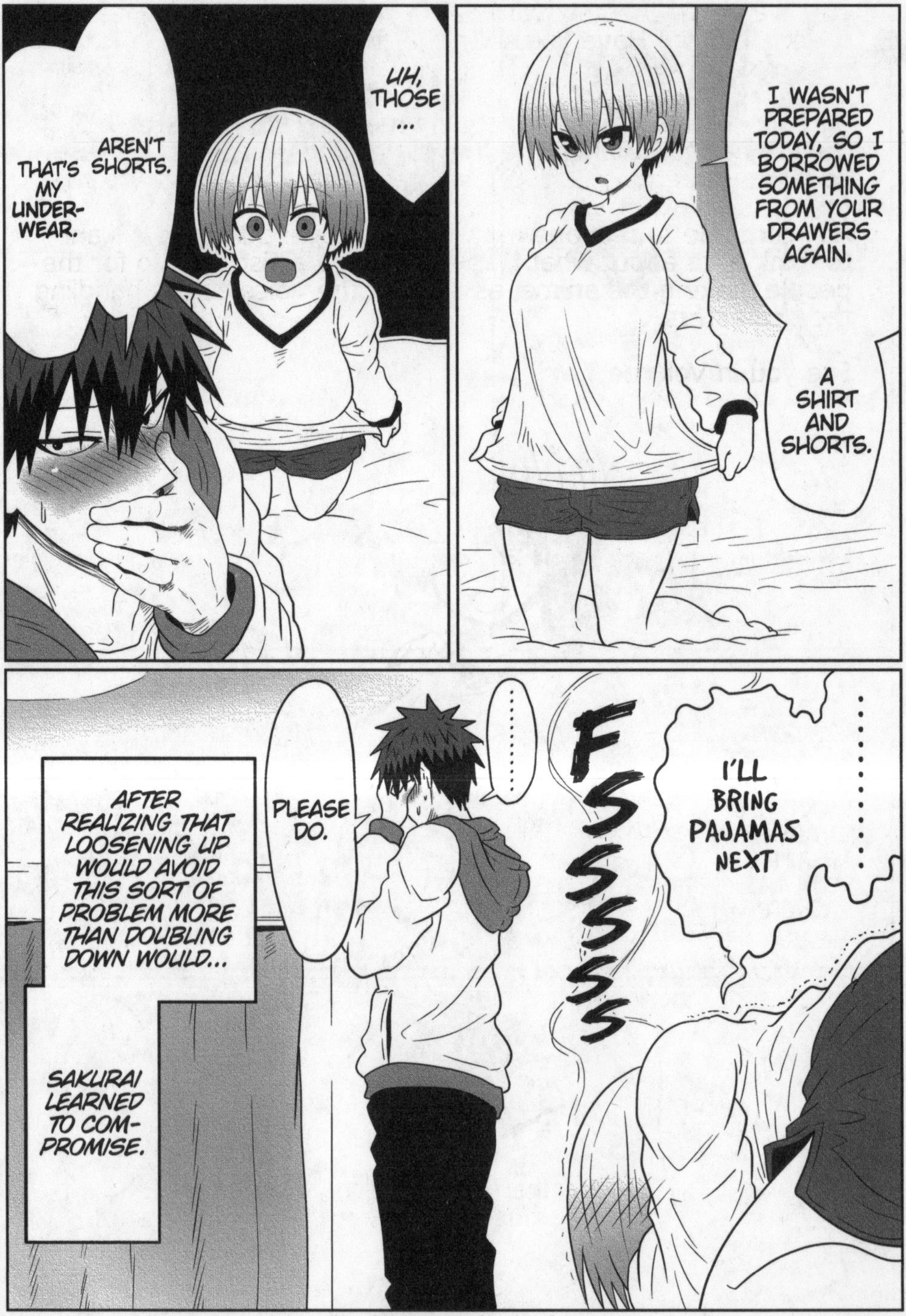
I WASN'T PREPARED TODAY, SO I BORROWED SOMETHING FROM YOUR DRAWERS AGAIN.
A SHIRT AND SHORTS.
UH, THOSE ...
AREN'T SHORTS. THAT'S MY UNDERWEAR.
......
I'LL BRING PAJAMAS NEXT
FSSSSSS
......
PLEASE DO.
AFTER REALIZING THAT LOOSENING UP WOULD AVOID THIS SORT OF PROBLEM MORE THAN DOUBLING DOWN WOULD...
SAKURAI LEARNED TO COMPROMISE.

To be continued...

Thank you to everyone who bought Volume 6. Because of you, we've reached six volumes of *Uzaki* in our fourth year of serialization! Have you seen the anime that began in summer 2020?

When it ended, I thought I could breathe a sigh of relief, but then my editor notified me they'd decided on a second season. So I'll be struggling through hell yet again... I'm gonna **do** this!

As I continue to manage my work and level things up, I want to think a lot about what I, as the manga artist, can do for the people making the anime, as well for the voice actors handling the characters.

See you in Volume 7.

TAKE

Ikari Manatsu-san, thank you very much for working as my assistant!

SEVEN SEAS ENTERTAINMENT PRESENTS

Uzaki-chan Wants to Hang Out!
VOLUME 6
story and art by TAKE

TRANSLATION
Jennifer Ward

ADAPTATION
T Campbell

LETTERING
Ludwig Sacramento

COVER DESIGN
Hanase Qi

PROOFREADER
Kurestin Armada
Dawn Davis

EDITOR
Jenn Grunigen

PREPRESS TECHNICIAN
Rhiannon Rasmussen-Silverstein

PRODUCTION MANAGER
Lissa Pattillo

MANAGING EDITOR
Julie Davis

ASSOCIATE PUBLISHER
Adam Arnold

PUBLISHER
Jason DeAngelis

UZAKI CHAN WA ASOBITAI! VOL.6
© Take 2021
First published in Japan in 2021 by KADOKAWA CORPORATION, Tokyo.
English translation rights arranged with KADOKAWA CORPORATION, Tokyo.

Seven Seas press and purchase enquiries can be sent to Marketing Manager Lianne Sentar at press@gomanga.com. Information regarding the distribution and purchase of digital editions is available from Digital Manager CK Russell at digital@gomanga.com.

Seven Seas and the Seven Seas logo are trademarks of Seven Seas Entertainment. All rights reserved.

ISBN: 978-1-64827-389-6

Printed in Canada

First Printing: December 2021

10 9 8 7 6 5 4 3 2 1

FOLLOW US ONLINE: www.sevenseasentertainment.com

READING DIRECTIONS

This book reads from *right to left*, Japanese style. If this is your first time reading manga, you start reading from the top right panel on each page and take it from there. If you get lost, just follow the numbered diagram here. It may seem backwards at first, but you'll get the hang of it! Have fun!!

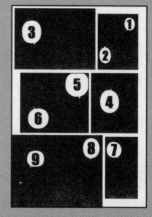